From Smart Cities to the Metaverse

This book delivers a comprehensive exploration of the rapidly evolving intersection between immersive technologies and the gaming industry, providing a detailed analysis of current innovations, diverse applications, and the transformative landscape of virtual experiences. It meticulously examines the core technologies driving this evolution, including augmented reality (AR), virtual reality (VR), and artificial intelligence (AI), offering readers a clear and insightful understanding of their impact across various sectors, with a particular emphasis on the dynamic realm of gaming.

The book's key highlights encompass in-depth chapters dedicated to the fundamental technological principles underpinning immersive experiences, practical game design methodologies tailored for these innovative environments, and a critical evaluation of the ethical, social, and environmental considerations associated with the widespread adoption of these technologies. It underscores the profound importance and significant impact of these technologies in enhancing user engagement, fostering groundbreaking innovation, and shaping the future of interactive experiences. By incorporating real-world examples and adopting a forward-looking perspective, it empowers readers with knowledge that transcends the boundaries of gaming, extending its applicability to diverse fields such as urban planning and sustainability initiatives.

This valuable resource is primarily tailored for professionals and students actively engaged in the fields of game development, immersive technology, and digital media. It caters to individuals at upper undergraduate and professional levels who seek a deeper comprehension of immersive technologies and their practical applications.

Noradila Nordin was awarded the prestigious King's Scholarship by the Government of Malaysia to pursue her PhD at University College London. She is currently a lecturer at the School of Games & Creative Technology, University for the Creative Arts (UCA) in the United Kingdom.

Norliza Katuk is an associate professor of Cybersecurity at the School of Computing, Universiti Utara Malaysia (UUM). Her research interests include information security and privacy, and cybersecurity awareness, and she has published widely in international journals and serves as a reviewer for several esteemed publications.

Adib Habbal is an associate professor of Computer Engineering and the founding head of the Innovative Networked Systems (INETs) Research Group at the Faculty of Engineering, Karabük University, Türkiye.

From Smart Cities to the Metaverse

Games, Immersive Experiences, and the Future of Digital Interaction

Edited by
Noradila Nordin, Norliza Katuk,
and Adib Habbal

CRC Press
Taylor & Francis Group
Boca Raton London New York

CRC Press is an imprint of the
Taylor & Francis Group, an **informa** business

Designed cover image: Shutterstock

First edition published 2026
by CRC Press
2385 NW Executive Center Drive, Suite 320, Boca Raton FL 33431

and by CRC Press
4 Park Square, Milton Park, Abingdon, Oxon, OX14 4RN

CRC Press is an imprint of Taylor & Francis Group, LLC

ISBN: 9781041119678 (hbk)
ISBN: 9781041119654 (pbk)
ISBN: 9781003662433 (ebk)

DOI: 10.1201/9781003662433

Typeset in Palatino
by codeMantra

Contents

Section III Building Immersive and Game-Driven Digital Worlds

Section IV Society and the Human Experience in Immersive Worlds

Preface

The convergence of technology, society, and human imagination defines the 21st century. The rise of smart cities, the emergence of the metaverse, and the proliferation of immersive technologies have fundamentally reshaped the way we live, learn, work, and interact. This book, *From Smart Cities to the Metaverse: Games, Immersive Experiences, and the Future of Digital Interaction*, is a reflection of this transformative era—an era in which the boundaries between the physical and digital worlds are rapidly dissolving, and where games and immersive experiences are no longer confined to entertainment but are central to education, social innovation, sustainability, and human well-being.

The chapters in this book illustrate a remarkable diversity of inquiry and innovation. They move seamlessly across domains—urban planning, education, healthcare, sustainability, social welfare, identity, and spirituality—demonstrating the far-reaching potential of immersive technologies. Collectively, they present a vision of digital interaction not as a novelty, but as a profound shift in how societies imagine futures, create meaning, and build inclusive communities.

In **Section I**, the foundations are laid. Readers are introduced to the technological, cultural, and conceptual underpinnings of immersive technologies and their integration into smart city ecosystems. The discussion extends from the architecture of game engines and artificial intelligence to the ways metaverse platforms redefine tourism, governance, and citizen engagement.

Section II brings the discourse into action, presenting case studies of immersive applications across varied contexts. Here, augmented reality and virtual reality become tools for cultural preservation, environmental innovation, and social empowerment. Whether reliving the Kedah–Siam War through augmented reality storytelling, exploring disaster preparedness in Japan's smart cities, or designing digital donation platforms to support marginalised communities, these chapters demonstrate how immersive technologies can inspire new forms of participation and shared responsibility.

Section III explores the role of games and game-based interventions in shaping sustainable and inclusive futures. Games are examined not only as entertainment but also as engines of learning, awareness, and behavioural change. From waste sorting education for children to eco-awareness in schools and interventions for dyslexic learners, the studies highlight how play and interactivity can foster resilience, accessibility, and empowerment across society.

Finally, **Section IV** confronts the social and human dimensions of these digital transformations. Here, readers encounter the pressing questions of privacy, security, and social boundaries in the metaverse, as well as the emergence of avatars as vehicles of self-expression, social identity, and participation in virtual economies. These chapters remind us that technology must always remain anchored in human values, ensuring that immersive futures are not only innovative but also equitable and compassionate.

This book is not simply a collection of academic studies. It is a tapestry of insights, experiments, and visions that underscore the transformative capacity of immersive technologies. It reflects the commitment of scholars and practitioners from across disciplines to interrogate, design, and reimagine how digital interaction can shape better futures.

We hope this book will serve as both an inspiration and a resource for researchers seeking new directions, educators exploring innovative pedagogies, policymakers envisioning smarter, more inclusive societies, and anyone curious about how games, immersive experiences, and digital interaction are redefining the human experience.

As editors, we are deeply grateful to the contributors whose work fills these pages with rigour and imagination. Their scholarship exemplifies the courage to explore new frontiers, the responsibility to address societal needs, and the creativity to turn possibility into practice.

It is our conviction that the ideas presented here will spark further inquiry, collaboration, and innovation—moving us ever closer to a future where technology is not only advanced but also profoundly human.

Noradila Nordin, Norliza Katuk, and Adib Habbal
Editors

Acknowledgements

The editors would like to extend their deepest appreciation to all contributors, whose expertise and commitment have significantly shaped this book. Each chapter reflects a shared vision of how games, immersive technologies, and digital interaction can transform societies and create inclusive futures.

We are especially grateful to the authors whose chapters originated from the tenth International Conference on Computing and Informatics (ICOCI 2025), held in Medan, Indonesia, on 25–26 June 2025. The conference was organised by the School of Computing, Universiti Utara Malaysia, in collaboration with Universitas Islam Negeri Sumatera Utara (UINSU), Universitas Islam Negeri Sunan Gunung Djati Bandung, and the University of Technology and Applied Sciences, Oman. Their valuable contributions, first shared in that forum, now form a significant part of this book and ensure that the insights presented at ICOCI 2025 will reach an even wider audience.

Finally, we would like to thank our colleagues, reviewers, and institutional partners for their unwavering support, encouragement, and collaboration in bringing this project to fruition.

Contributors

Mohd Adib Abd Muin
Islamic Business School
Universiti Utara Malaysia
Sintok, Kedah Darul Aman, Malaysia

Nur Azzah Abu Bakar
School of Computing
Universiti Utara Malaysia
Sintok, Kedah Darul Aman, Malaysia

Rehab Albeladi
Department of Computer Science
Taibah University
Tayba, Madinah, Saudi Arabia

Armansyah
Department of Computer Science
Universitas Islam Negeri Sumatera Utara
Kabupaten Deli Serdang, Sumatera Utara, Indonesia

Azizi Ab Aziz
School of Computing
Universiti Utara Malaysia
Sintok, Kedah Darul Aman, Malaysia

Fakhrul Anuar Aziz
School of Multimedia Technologies and Communication
Universiti Utara Malaysia
Sintok, Kedah Darul Aman, Malaysia

Sophie Azlan
School of Computing and Creative Media
University of Wollongong
Wollongong, NSW, Malaysia

Azizah Che Omar
School of Technology Multimedia and Communication
Universiti Utara Malaysia
Sintok, Kedah Darul Aman, Malaysia

Noraziah ChePa
School of Computing
Universiti Utara Malaysia
Sintok, Kedah Darul Aman, Malaysia

Amzari Ghazali
Faculty of Data Science and Computing
Universiti Malaysia Kelantan
Kota Bharu, Kelantan, Malaysia

Adib Habbal
Faculty of Engineering, Computer Engineering Department
Karabük University
Merkez/Karabük, Türkiye

Muhammad Siddik Hasibuan
Department of Computer Science
Universitas Islam Negeri Sumatera Utara
Kabupaten Deli Serdang, Sumatera Utara, Indonesia

John Hii Ing Kieng
Vortex XR Lab
Taylor's University
Subang Jaya, Selangor, Malaysia

Juha Huhtakallio
Edugametion Oy
Helsinki, Finland

Husniza Husni
School of Computing
Universiti Utara Malaysia
Sintok, Kedah Darul Aman, Malaysia

Azham Hussain
School of Computing
Universiti Utara Malaysia
Sintok, Kedah Darul Aman, Malaysia

Tan Chin Ike
School of Computing
Asia Pacific University of Technology & Innovation
Kuala Lumpur, Malaysia

Muhammad Ikhsan
Department of Computer Science
Universitas Islam Negeri Sumatera Utara
Kabupaten Deli Serdang, Sumatera Utara, Indonesia

Norliza Katuk
School of Computing
Universiti Utara Malaysia
Sintok, Kedah Darul Aman, Malaysia

Kai Lun Lee
School of Economics, Finance and Banking
Universiti Utara Malaysia
Sintok, Kedah Darul Aman, Malaysia

Laura Lim Sie-Yi
School of Computing
Universiti Utara Malaysia
Sintok, Kedah Darul Aman, Malaysia

Aidil Halim Lubis
Department of Computer Science
Universitas Islam Negeri Sumatera Utara
Kabupaten Deli Serdang, Sumatera Utara, Indonesia

Hafizan Mat Som
Faculty of Science, Management and Computing
Universiti Teknologi PETRONAS
Seri Iskandar, Perak, Malaysia

Hanhan Maulana
Faculty of Engineering and Computer Science
Universitas Komputer Indonesia
Kota Bandung, Jawa Barat, Indonesia

Ahmad Hanis Mohd Shabli
School of Computing
Universiti Utara Malaysia
Sintok, Kedah Darul Aman, Malaysia

Siti Azreena Mubin
School of Computing
Asia Pacific University of Technology & Innovation
Kuala Lumpur, Malaysia

Yusuf Ramadhan Nasution
Department of Computer Science
Universitas Islam Negeri Sumatera Utara
Kabupaten Deli Serdang, Sumatera Utara, Indonesia

Muhammad Nur Affendy Nor'a
School of Computing
Asia Pacific University of Technology & Innovation (APU)
Kuala Lumpur, Malaysia

Noradila Nordin
School of Games and Creative Technology
University for the Creative Arts
Farnham, Surrey, United Kingdom

Zubaida Nila
Ammobox Studios Sdn. Bhd.
Subang Jaya, Selangor, Malaysia

Mohd Adan Omar
School of Computing
Universiti Utara Malaysia
Sintok, Kedah Darul Aman, Malaysia

Herman Surdianto Soegoto
Faculty of Engineering and Computer Science
Universitas Komputer Indonesia
Kota Bandung, Jawa Barat, Indonesia

Jacob Sow Tian You
School of Computing
Asia Pacific University of Technology & Innovation
Kuala Lumpur, Malaysia

Sriani
Department of Computer Science
Universitas Islam Negeri Sumatera Utara
Kabupaten Deli Serdang, Sumatera Utara, Indonesia

Irfan Dwiguna Sumitra
Faculty of Engineering and Computer Science
Universitas Komputer Indonesia
Kota Bandung, Jawa Barat, Indonesia

Wan Hussain Wan Ishak
School of Computing
Universiti Utara Malaysia
Sintok, Kedah Darul Aman, Malaysia

Juncheng Wang
School of Games & Creative Technology
University for the Creative Arts
Farnham, Surrey, United Kingdom

Yong Jie Wong
Department of Bioenvironmental Design
Kyoto University of Advanced Science
Kyoto, Japan

Norhana Yusof
School of Technology Multimedia and Communication
Universiti Utara Malaysia
Sintok, Kedah Darul Aman, Malaysia

Rifki Aqila Zaidan
Faculty of Engineering and Computer Science
Universitas Komputer Indonesia
Kota Bandung, Jawa Barat, Indonesia

Section I

Foundations of Games and Immersive Technologies

1

Immersive Metaverse Applications: From Games to Reality

Noradila Nordin, Norliza Katuk, and Adib Habbal

1.1 Foundations of Immersive Experiences in the Metaverse

In the metaverse, extended reality (XR) is a core technology for delivering immersive experiences. XR provides rich and interactive digital spaces that allow users to create and engage with dynamic environments. Within this broad umbrella, XR consists of virtual reality (VR), which immerses users in simulated environments, augmented reality (AR), which overlays digital content onto the physical world, and mixed reality (MR), which integrates AR and VR, enabling real-time interaction between virtual and physical objects. These technologies, AR, VR, MR, and XR, serve as the foundational interface for users to perceive and interact with the metaverse (Buhalis & Karatay, 2022; Kim, 2024).

Five fundamental elements define the seamless and immersive nature of the metaverse, which are immersion and realism, user interaction and socialisation, scalability and interoperability, continuity and economy, and ubiquity with physical–virtual integration (Nordin et al., 2026). In supporting the fundamental elements of the metaverse, avatars serve as the social and cultural representation of users within XR environments. Avatars can be animated in real time through motion tracking and action recognition, which reflects users' natural movements in virtual environments. These movements are facilitated by headsets, controllers, and full-body trackers for accuracy. In addition, sensory technologies such as accelerometers, gyroscopes, magnetometers, depth sensors, infrared and ambient light sensors, haptic devices, eye tracking, voice recognition, and biosensors further enhance the realism and interactivity of users in the metaverse (Bhattacharya et al., 2023). These sensory technologies enable users to fully immerse themselves in the environment and move and respond intuitively through avatars.

Additionally, these interactions must be underpinned by robust networking and computational infrastructure. High-speed 5G and emerging 6G networks, combined with edge and cloud computing, enable low-latency,

DOI: 10.1201/9781003662433-2

high-bandwidth communication, allowing motion data, haptic feedback, and visual rendering to operate seamlessly across multiple users and devices. Internet of Things (IoT) and the Internet of Everything (IoE) extend connectivity by linking people, processes, and data within an integrated ecosystem, while networking innovations such as the Tactile Internet enhance real-time responsiveness (Buhalis et al., 2023; Zawish et al., 2024). Without such infrastructure, the immersive experience of XR and avatars would be severely constrained.

Complementing these systems, enabler technologies such as artificial intelligence (AI) and blockchain provide intelligence, persistence, and security within the metaverse. AI supports adaptive environments, real-time user interaction, movement prediction, non-player character behaviour, and avatar and scene generation. Blockchain underpins decentralised, transparent, and secure transactions, enabling the management of digital assets and non-fungible tokens while facilitating economic activity within virtual worlds (Nendya et al., 2025; Kaitane et al., 2024; Ramezani et al., 2024). These technologies integrate with XR and sensory systems to create interactive, socially connected, and persistent environments.

These environments are the digital twins, mirror worlds, and virtual worlds. A digital twin provides interactive replicas of physical environments. It dynamically enables users to explore tourism destinations and heritage sites. Mirror worlds replicate large-scale physical environments, while virtual worlds are entirely computer-generated and can incorporate both digital twins and mirror worlds. In metaverse tourism, digital twins allow visitors to engage with historical objects, navigate destinations, and experience personalised, narrative-driven content. It reduces physical limitations through VRs, enhancing visitors' accessibility, engagement, and pre-travel decision-making (Buhalis & Karatay, 2022; Go & Kang, 2023; Murti et al., 2023; Shamim et al., 2025).

Therefore, in establishing an immersive metaverse experience, these elements, technologies, infrastructures, and supported environments must be integrated to ensure dynamic, interactive, and secure environments where users can socialise, collaborate, learn, and participate, not just within the games and tourism domains, but also in other areas.

1.2 Metaverse Applications in Gaming and Entertainment

Gaming has been a primary driver of the metaverse, providing immersive environments where users interact, create, and explore persistent virtual worlds. Within the metaverse, games extend beyond entertainment, serving as platforms for social interaction, digital economies, and experiential learning. Core immersive technologies such as AR, VR, MR, XR, and haptic feedback enable players to engage with virtual spaces in ways that mirror or extend real-world experiences. Popular platforms, including Roblox, Sandbox, and Decentraland, exemplify how gaming integrates user-generated content, collaborative activities, and virtual economies, illustrating the potential of the metaverse to transform digital interaction (Bandyopadhyay et al., 2023; Ramezani et al., 2024).

Gaming has long been recognised as one of the first domains to apply concepts associated with the metaverse (Oliveira & Cruz, 2023). Merging video games, VR, and social networks enables users to transcend physical limitations and engage socially, economically, and culturally through avatars. Games within the metaverse, unlike traditional video games, emphasise real-time social interaction, engagement with expansive environments, and user-driven content generation (Nendya et al., 2025). In doing so, gaming not only advances interactive entertainment but also contributes to new modes of digital communication and well-being.

The metaverse is associated with AR and VR. Game engines such as Unreal and Unity are platforms that offer ready-made solutions and technical infrastructure for AR and VR applications (Jungherr & Schlarb, 2022). These game engines offer solutions for rendering, simulation, and translating physical movements into digital experiences. Recent innovations have extended these game engines beyond conventional AR and VR. It places them at the centre of XR development within immersive metaverse game environments (Bhattacharya et al., 2023; Kaitane et al., 2024).

A defining element of gaming within the metaverse is interactivity. Games that support customisation, decision-making, and diverse player activities foster stronger engagement, while collaborative multiplayer systems promote teamwork and community-building (Bhattacharya et al., 2023). These qualities align with the growing demand for personalised and socially connected experiences. Furthermore, games are one of the key components within metaverse ecosystems. It offers competitive and collaborative opportunities that enrich gameplay and provide insights into player behaviour (Nendya et al., 2025).

Commercial and social gaming provide some of the earliest and most visible examples of applications within the metaverse. Fortnite is an example of a gaming environment that facilitates rudimentary interactions across multiple brand and story worlds while establishing a sense of place and narrative continuity. Although these features remain distant from the vision of a fully integrated platform, Fortnite demonstrates the potential of gamification to structure user objectives and engagement (Jungherr & Schlarb, 2022). Player interactions often involve consumption, such as purchasing branded outfits or engaging in non-verbal emotive gestures during communal events. It simultaneously enables social expression and interaction. By functioning as a nexus of franchised story worlds, Fortnite allows players to perform brand allegiances, infusing their gameplay with meaning and highlighting the operational logic of a game-engine-based metaverse.

Similarly, Decentraland is a platform where gaming and social interaction are deeply intertwined (Guidi & Michienzi, 2022). Players navigate a three-dimensional (3D) world with avatars, interacting with objects and constructions created by other players. Functioning as a social virtual world, Decentraland enables user-generated content and social experiences within a decentralised framework. Players can build structures, engage with others, and participate in communal activities, demonstrating how the metaverse can integrate gaming with social and creative expression.

Extending beyond entertainment, metaverse games can be implemented within the tourism domain. By combining game mechanics with metaverse tourism, users can have immersive experiences that are both informative and engaging, as these require active participation rather than passivity. For example, cultural and heritage sites can be transformed into interactive, informative, and educational, as well as virtually accessible locations. Visitors are encouraged to explore the sites virtually before or alongside their physical visits (Buhalis & Karatay, 2022). It allows them to plan their visit more effectively. In metaverse tourism, gamification facilitates scenario development and activities to optimise user experience and engagement. It shows high potential for reshaping visitors' cultural experiences, as these experiences in the metaverse may not be replicable in person at the sites due to historical constraints. The versatility of the metaverse across domains, such as tourism in this example, enables meaningful experiences that extend beyond conventional gaming. Depending on the content generated, the metaverse can offer not just information, but also social interaction opportunities.

1.3 Transforming Tourism and Cultural Heritage through Metaverse Experiences

Tourism has long embraced digital innovations. It has evolved from providing online booking platforms to enabling virtual tours within the last few years. The metaverse represents the next stage in this evolution. It offers immersive and interactive environments that expand how destinations, attractions, and cultural experiences are designed and developed.

The term metaverse refers to a space where technologies such as AR, VR, and MR are integrated with MRs, both physical and virtual environments. Virtual tourism typically refers to digital-only simulations. Metaverse tourism, on the other hand, combines physical infrastructures, such as attractions and facilities, with virtual ecosystems generated from user-generated content, AI, and digital economies. Therefore, metaverse tourism can be defined as tourism that provides experiences through collective spatial environments enhanced by multisensory information processing across both physical and virtual domains (Go & Kang, 2023).

The metaverse enables immersive cultural experiences, interactive storytelling, and the exploration of landmarks. It offers visitors alternative ways to experience destinations without physical travel, thereby expanding accessibility and creating new opportunities for the tourism industry to deliver products and services (Buhalis & Karatay, 2022; Murti et al., 2023). A significant attraction of metaverse tourism lies in its ability to virtually pre-visit destinations. It allows visitors to explore attractions, compare facilities, and customise itineraries before committing to any physical visit. These practices enrich preparation and on-site experiences. As a result, consumer behaviour, tourism marketing, and destination management are expected to be transformed to fulfil new needs and expectations (Buhalis et al., 2023; Triviño-Tarradas et al., 2024).

The metaverse also fosters imaginative and interactive engagement. Visitors can design unique travel plans, reconnect virtual simulations with real-world visits, and participate in gamified activities. Gamification elements such as badges, points, and prizes provide a sense of achievement and recognition. It encourages continued interaction and motivation in virtual environments and with other participants while exploring other destinations (Murti et al., 2023). By blending creativity and interactivity, metaverse tourism complements rather than replaces physical travel. It motivates real-world visits while enhancing destination experiences, as visitors have already virtually visited and know what to expect (Buhalis et al., 2023; Koo et al., 2023; Suanpang et al., 2022).

An essential aspect of metaverse tourism is the use of avatars. An avatar represents the visitor's immersive identity. It encapsulates a visitor's expectations, behaviours, and outcomes within the digital environment as a human would in the real world. It also serves as the primary means for visitors to interact through verbal and non-verbal cues, and physical senses within the environments (Koo et al., 2023). Visitors can dynamically shift their identities between human and avatar throughout their travel journey. It can create a fluid interplay between their real and virtual selves. This duality necessitates the integration of both personas' experiences to fully understand and evaluate the visitor's overall experience. Despite their potential to transform tourism experiences, avatars remain underexplored, particularly in assessing the extent to which they can authentically represent and enact a visitor's role. It is essential to examine the interaction between human and avatar identities to understand the personalised, interactive, and immersive nature of metaverse tourism. It sets the stage for further enhancing these experiences through technologies such as VR, AR, MR, and digital twins.

1.4 Expanding Use Cases and Applications of the Metaverse

Several metaverse tourism case studies show the practical implementation of immersive and interactive platforms in tourism and cultural heritage. These examples demonstrate the use of advanced digital technologies to enhance visitor engagement, provide educational experiences, and support the preservation and management of heritage sites across diverse international contexts.

Thailand has implemented the "Amazing Thailand Metaverse: Amazing Durian" project to promote tourism (TAT News, 2022). The initiative enables visitors to explore virtual durian orchards, offering immersive experiences that bridge the virtual and physical worlds. By integrating these technologies, the project enhances tourism engagement, supports local business operators, and demonstrates the use of a metaverse platform in delivering interactive cultural experiences.

In South Korea, the central and local governments have developed Incheon as a smart tourism city with the implementation of metaverse services (Um et al., 2022). The initiative integrates AR applications and the virtual platform "Incheoncraft". It enables visitors to navigate the city with AR maps, historical guides, and immersive storytelling. "Incheoncraft" was developed using Minecraft. It enables users to virtually explore the city and its rich heritage, including historic events and notable figures. These services enhance accessibility, cultural engagement, and the interpretive experience for both local and remote tourists.

The Royal Commission for AlUla has implemented a metaverse representation of Hegra's Tomb of Lihyan, marking the first UNESCO World Heritage Site recreated in the metaverse (Royal Commission for AlUla, 2024). It is hosted on the Decentraland platform. Visitors can tour the tomb and its surrounding desert landscape, entering areas that are normally inaccessible. The immersive environment features interactive information points that provide historical context and cultural interpretation, thereby extending access and engagement to global audiences.

In Spain, the locality of Montilla has explored the use of innovative technologies for cultural heritage engagement through the creation of 3D digital models, such as the perfume burner of Montilla Castle (Triviño-Tarradas et al., 2024). These models can be integrated into the metaverse as part of virtual museums, connecting exhibition spaces with tourism opportunities via digital platforms. By incorporating augmented and VR, the initiative enhances accessibility, supports the preservation and interpretation of cultural assets, and stimulates cultural participation by encouraging both virtual and physical museum visits.

Digital twin technology has been implemented in several Chinese heritage sites, including the Shanghai History Museum, Longmen Grottoes, Yellow Emperor's Native Place, and the Palace Museum (Su et al., 2024). The Shanghai History Museum provides high-resolution 3D restorations, enhancing management, relic protection, and visitor experience. The Longmen Grottoes' Smart Culture and Tourism Digital Twin Platform integrates digital twin, cloud computing, IoT, AI, and VR/AR, offering immersive exploration and multifunctional management. The Palace Museum combines digital twin with intelligent computing to optimise operations and engage visitors. These initiatives demonstrate the role of digital twin technologies in enhancing accessibility, preserving cultural assets, and promoting cultural tourism through interactive and educational experiences.

These case studies demonstrate that metaverse and digital twin technologies have been successfully applied to enhance cultural heritage engagement, tourism, and user experiences. Projects in Thailand, South Korea, Saudi Arabia, Spain, and China demonstrate how immersive platforms, 3D modelling, and intelligent computing can enhance accessibility, support heritage preservation, and offer interactive educational experiences. These initiatives highlight the potential of digital technologies to integrate physical and virtual environments, transform museum and tourism management, and foster cultural participation while promoting sustainable tourism development.

1.5 Insights and Perspectives on the Future of Immersive Metaverse Experiences

The metaverse in tourism offers more than innovative digital experiences as it aligns with broader objectives of environmental protection and responsible development. It provides the tourism industry with opportunities to reimagine tourism and cultural heritage. An indirect advantage of metaverse tourism lies in its ability to reduce travel footprints, thereby enabling efficient resource use and promoting ecotourism practices. Case studies from various countries, covering aspects ranging from travel planning to heritage education, demonstrate the effectiveness of immersive platforms and intelligent technologies in enhancing accessibility, preserving culture, and strengthening the connection between physical and virtual environments. In addition, the combination of informative content and games in metaverse tourism shows its versatility and influence in tourism practices.

Metaverse tourism is showing significant potential for growth, with its evolution highly dependent on personalisation and interactivity to create authentic and emotionally resonant experiences. These insights suggest that the future of tourism lies not in replacing physical travel but in complementing it with creative, sustainable, and technologically enriched encounters that broaden access and participation worldwide.

References

Bandyopadhyay, A., Sarkar, A., Swain, S., Banik, D., Hassanien, A. E., Mallik, S., Li., A. & Qin, H. (2023). A game-theoretic approach for rendering immersive experiences in the metaverse. *Mathematics, 11*(6), 1286. https://doi.org/10.3390/math11061286

Bhattacharya, P., Verma, A., Prasad, V. K., Tanwar, S., Bhushan, B., Florea, B. C., Taralunga, D. D., Alqahtani, F., & Tolba, A. (2023). Game-o-meta: Trusted federated learning scheme for P2P gaming metaverse beyond 5G networks. *Sensors, 23*(9), 4201. https://doi.org/10.3390/s23094201

Buhalis, D., & Karatay, N. (2022). Mixed reality (MR) for generation Z in cultural heritage tourism towards metaverse. *ENTER22 e-Tourism Conference* (pp. 16–27). Springer International Publishing. https://doi.org/10.1007/978-3-030-94751-4_2

Buhalis, D., Leung, D., & Lin, M. (2023). Metaverse as a disruptive technology revolutionising tourism management and marketing. *Tourism Management, 97*, 104724. https://doi.org/10.1016/j.tourman.2023.104724

Go, H., & Kang, M. (2023). Metaverse tourism for sustainable tourism development: Tourism agenda 2030. *Tourism Review*, 78(2), 381–394. https://doi.org/10.1108/TR-02-2022-0102

Guidi, B., & Michienzi, A. (2022). Social games and blockchain: Exploring the metaverse of Decentraland. *International Conference on Distributed Computing Systems Workshops* (pp. 199–204). IEEE. https://doi.org/10.1109/ICDCSW56584.2022.00045

Jungherr, A., & Schlarb, D. B. (2022). The extended reach of game engine companies: How companies like epic games and Unity technologies provide platforms for extended reality applications and the metaverse. *Social Media + Society, 8*(2). https://doi.org/10.1177/20563051221107641

Kaitane, W. S., Shrestha, S., Lean, C. P., Purnshatman, T., Ng, P. K., Kong, F. Y., & Khan, M. R. B. (2024). Immersive horizons exploring virtual reality, augmented reality, and the metaverse in game development – a comprehensive review. *Malaysian Journal of Science and Advanced Technology*, 222–234. https://doi.org/10.56532/mjsat.v4i3.309

Kim, J. S. (2024). Action recognition system using full-body XR devices for sports metaverse games. *International Conference on Information and Communication Technology Convergence* (pp. 1962–1965). IEEE. https://doi.org/10.1109/ICTC62082.2024.10827474

Koo, C., Kwon, J., Chung, N., & Kim, J. (2023). Metaverse tourism: Conceptual framework and research propositions. *Current Issues in Tourism, 26*(20), 3268–3274. https://doi.org/10.1080/13683500.2022.2122781

Murti, K. G. K., Darma, G. S., Mahyuni, L. P., & Gorda, A. N. E. S. (2023). Immersive experience in the metaverse: Implications for tourism and business. *International Journal of Applied Business Research*, 187–207. https://doi.org/10.35313/ijabr.v5i02.329

Nendya, M. B., Senapartha, I. K. D., Santoso, H. B., Delima, R., Wibisono, M., Antono, J. A., & Wuttisittikulkij, L. (2025). The metaverse as a game ecosystem: Evaluating player interaction through mini-game integration and experience analysis. *International Conference on Electrical Engineering/Electronics, Computer, Telecommunications and Information Technology* (pp. 1–6). IEEE. https://doi.org/10.1109/ECTI-CON64996.2025.11100450

Nordin, N., Tiew, B. W. K., & Lun, L. K. (2026). Fundamentals of the metaverse. *From Smart Cities to the Metaverse* (pp. 25–34). CRC Press. https://doi.org/10.1201/9781003619819

Oliveira, A., & Cruz, M. (2023). Virtually connected in a multiverse of madness? – perceptions of gaming, animation, and metaverse. *Applied Sciences*, 13(15), 8573. https://doi.org/10.3390/app13158573

Ramezani, D., Jaferian, G., & Wagner, M. G. (2024). Metaverse potentials for the gaming industry. *International Conference on Blockchain Computing and Applications* (pp. 580–585). IEEE. https://doi.org/10.1109/BCCA62388.2024.10844488

Royal Commission for AlUla. (2024). Tomb of Lihyan, Hegra. https://decentraland.org/places/place/?position=-122.-149

Shamim, N., Gupta, S., & Shin, M. M. (2025). Evaluating user engagement via metaverse environment through immersive experience for travel and tourism websites. International *Journal of Contemporary Hospitality Management, 37*(4), 1132–1174. https://doi.org/10.1108/IJCHM-10-2023-1590

Suanpang, P., Niamsorn, C., Pothipassa, P., Chunhapataragul, T., Netwong, T., & Jermsittiparsert, K. (2022). Extensible metaverse implication for a smart tourism city. *Sustainability, 14*(21), 14027. https://doi.org/10.3390/su142114027

Su, Y., Zhou, Z., Zhao, L., & Wang, Y. (2024). China's exploration and experience in digital twinning of tangible cultural heritage. *Intelligent Computing for Cultural Heritage* (pp. 176–202). Routledge. https://doi.org/10.4324/9781032707211-11

TAT News. (2022). TAT Launces 'Amazing Thailand Metaverse: Amazing Durian' Project. https://www.tatnews.org/2022/04/tat-launches-amazing-thailand-metaverse-amazing-durian-project.

Triviño-Tarradas, P., Mohedo-Gatón, A., Carranza-Cañadas, P., & Hidalgo-Fernandez, R. E. (2024). The application of metaverse in the tourism sector as a tool for enhancing sustainability – case study: A medieval 'Perfume Burner' of the local historical museum of Montilla (Cordoba, Spain). *Sustainability, 16*(16), 6966. https://doi.org/10.3390/su16166966

Um, T., Kim, H., Kim, H., Lee, J., Koo, C., & Chung, N. (2022). Travel Incheon as a metaverse: Smart tourism cities development case in Korea. *ENTER22 E-Tourism Conference* (pp. 226–231). Springer International Publishing. https://doi.org/10.1007/978-3-030-94751-4_20

Zawish, M., Dharejo, F. A., Khowaja, S. A., Raza, S., Davy, S., Dev, K., & Bellavista, P. (2024). AI and 6G into the metaverse: Fundamentals, challenges and future research trends. *IEEE Open Journal of the Communications Society, 5*, 730–778. https://doi.org/10.1109/OJCOMS.2024.3349465

2

The Convergence of Game Development and Immersive Technologies

Tan Chin Ike, John Hii Ing Kieng, Juha Huhtakallio, Jacob Sow Tian You, Sophie Azlan, Siti Azreena Mubin, and Zubaida Nila

2.1 Evolution of Game Development

Video games, an interactive digital entertainment platform, are not only a mainstream form of entertainment, but they have also become one of the most popular recreational activities, moving closer and closer to our reality of life and, in some cases, developing into an extension of ourselves through the virtual world (Saucier, 2022). The term "video games," which originated in the mid-1970s and 1980s, was used to describe electronic or digital games played on arcade machines or consoles, utilising the technology behind television screens (or the screen itself) as a visual output. Through the availability of affordable personal computers (PCs) with cathode ray tube (CRT) monitors as their primary visual output, the term "computer games," or "PC games," gained more prominence (Novak, 2022). There were also alternative nomenclatures being used, such as the term "electronic games." When combined with mechanical engineering, electromechanics was born, and this helped introduce the first electronic game, the pinball machine (Soderman & Boellstorff, 2023).

Another term, digital games, was also used, which is technically a more inclusive and flexible term that implies games can be played on televisions, computers, laptops, consoles, smartphones, or tablets. The term "video games," however, dates back easily to the time when the first video game was technically created. In the 1950s, Willy Higginbotham created the first interactive game using an oscilloscope, a device that utilises a CRT as its display element. This analogue interactive game became the first "video" game as it used a video screen display. Hence, the term is tied to the identity of gamers for generations, from the rise of early arcade machines to modern-day consoles (Novak, 2022). The term "video games" has now become the preferred terminology, replacing "computer, electronic, or digital games," due to the evolution of the medium and its associated technology over the years,

 DOI: 10.1201/9781003662433-3

including the diversity of game platforms (Jackson & Games, 2015). To a certain extent, the term "video games" is deeply ingrained in popular culture and the history of modern games. Games are no longer restricted to just computers. Faster processors, advanced manufacturing methods, and newer technology have enabled the power of computers to reside in mobile and handheld devices, further democratising gameplay and making it accessible to hundreds of thousands of people without PCs. In fact, the rise of immersive technologies like augmented reality (AR) and virtual reality (VR) as entertainment platforms further detaches the gameplay medium from being exclusively computer-based.

While the term "video games" or "video games industry" is commonly used to refer to the entire industry ecosystem, which includes all aspects of video game production, marketing, distribution, and sales for both hardware and software (the games themselves), "game development" refers solely to the development and production of video games. Game development refers to the processes, techniques, theories, and practices involved in creating video games, although it can also be expanded to encompass the development of serious games, educational games, and tabletop games (Berg Marklund et al., 2019; Malaysian Qualification Agency, 2015). Game development, a sophisticated and technical field, is a combination of three major specialisations: game technology, game art, and game design (Malaysia Digital Economy Corporation, 2024; Malaysian Qualification Agency, 2015; Tunnel & Norbisrath, 2023).

2.1.1 Game Development Roles

While used as a singular term, the nomenclature game developers cover any of these three areas of specialisation, each area has its own focus in the whole game development pipeline. Here is the breakdown of each role:

a. Game technology specialises in writing code and systems that govern how a video game should function and interact with the players. It is the technical backbone of game development, where programmers and engineers bring the game world to life.
b. A game designer specialises in the art and science of crafting meaningful and immersive player experiences in a video game.
c. Game artists specialise in creating everything visual in the game, from characters to the interface and the environment that players interact with.

There are other supporting roles in the game development process, which are referred to as creative support services, operational support services, and technical support services. Figure 2.1 illustrates the comprehensive scope of roles for each specialisation and the support services.

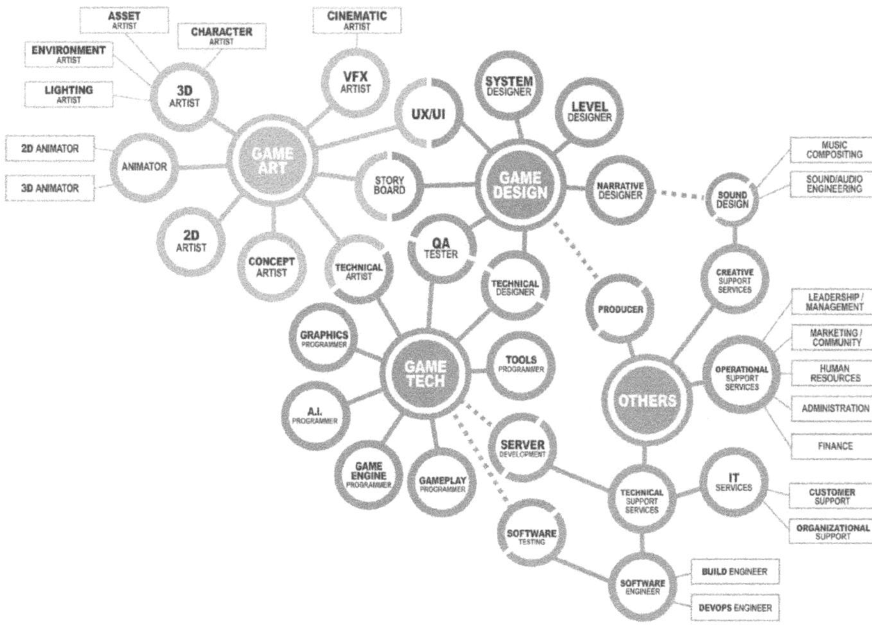

FIGURE 2.1
Revised breakdown of game development specialisation and roles (Malaysia Digital Economy Corporation, 2024).

2.1.2 Video Game Genres and Game Types

There are three recognised game types, or tiers as they are sometimes termed – independent (indie), double-A (AA), and triple-A (AAA) games. Indie video games (sometimes also known as single-A or A/B games) are typically developed and crafted by small, self-funded, or budget-constrained studios comprising no more than ten developers (Grabarczyk, 2016; Zolotarenko, 2024). Triple-A games are typically high-budget, highly anticipated, and highly marketed games developed by large studios with substantial budgets. Double-A games are video games that fall between the triple-A category and the indie category, showcasing quality and budget on a smaller scale (Mathews & Wearn, 2016). Of course, there are cases of highly successful indie studios that produce smaller games but are financially stable. The Swedish Studio Mojang, famous for Minecraft, started out as a pure indie studio in 2008, which was sold to Microsoft for US$2.5 million in 2014 (Stuart & Hern, 2014).

Video games are classified to help define the structure, style, and experience of gameplay. These classifications, based on game viewpoints, thematic elements, and genres, are categories of video games that share similar styles, mechanics, ideologies, or characteristics. Viewpoints are camera perspectives in the game, such as first-person, third-person, top-down, platform, side-scrolling, and isometric views – each providing the player with a different camera angle (Arsenault, 2009). Traditionally video games introduced common genres like puzzle games, strategy games, shooter games, role-playing games (RPG), sports, simulation, strategy and many more, with each of them further creating sub genres related to their core functionality in the game like action, arcade, adventure, racing, fighting and more (Qaffas, 2020; Toth et al., 2021).

Then, of course, there are thematic elements as well, such as horror, science fiction (encompassing sub-genres like cyberpunk, post-apocalyptic, and steampunk), fantasy, and non-fiction (covering sub-genres like history, mystery, and war), as illustrated in Figure 2.2. Thus, games can combine multiple genres, subgenres, and thematic elements. For example, first-person fantasy shooters, third-person action-adventure horror games, and online science-fiction RPGs. All genres can be identified based on their core characteristics, which are often related to the core action, mechanics, and goals.

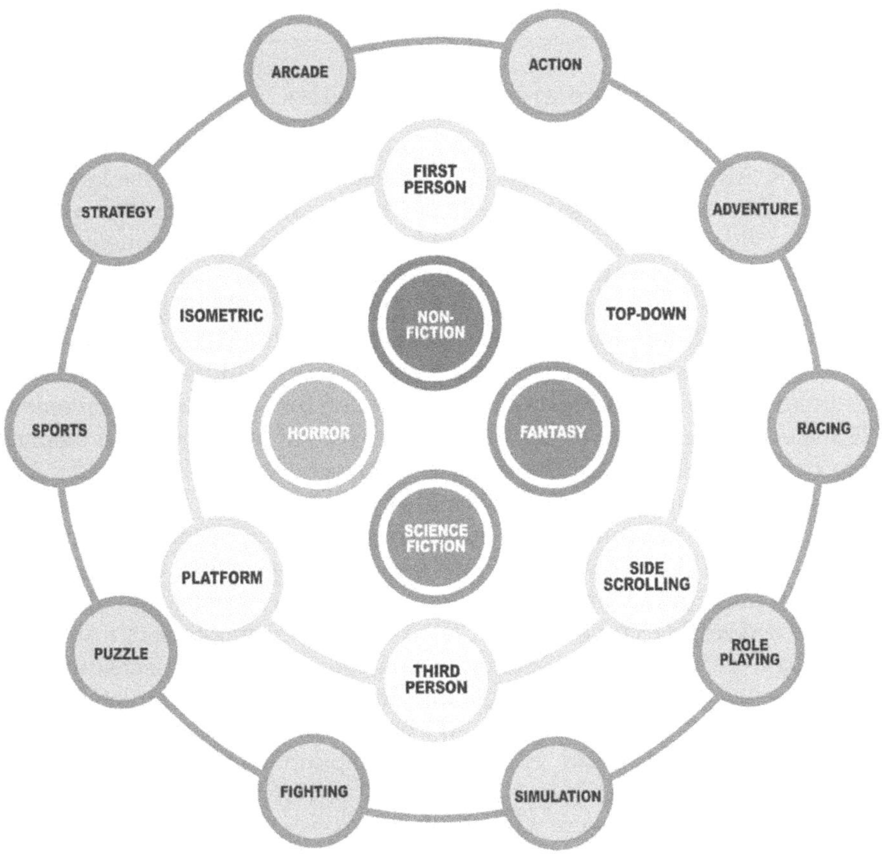

FIGURE 2.2
Video game viewpoints, genres, and themes.

Game genres are a changing and living concept. Some eight years ago, the Battle Royale genre, as seen in games like PUBG, Fortnite, and Apex Legends, did not exist, but it has since been used to identify a new type of game reaching a specific audience.

There is also one more type of gameplay genre called game modes. Game modes represent a key aspect of the gameplay experience, defining how video game players interact with the game environment and with one another. These can be broadly categorised into single-player, split-screen, and multiplayer modes, and each of these categories can be further classified based on player interaction styles, including cooperative, competitive, or social gameplay experiences. Multiple other sub-genres encompass gameplay modes that might fit into the broader picture of genres, themes, and game modes – for example, sandbox, survival, battle royale, and Roguelike, to name a few.

2.2 Exploration of Immersive Technologies

Immersive technology, often referred to as extended reality (XR), encompasses VR, AR, and mixed reality (MR), collectively reshaping the landscape of digital interaction. These technologies have evolved in parallel with the growth of video games, redefining the boundaries of entertainment, education, healthcare, and various other industries. Immersive technologies boast a rich and evolving history, significantly impacting fields such as education, healthcare, and entertainment. The concept dates to the 1800s with the invention of the Wheatstone stereoscope, which provided a 3-D perspective using still images. This innovation laid the foundation for future advancements in VR and AR (Simpkins et al., 2020). By the 1960s, AR head-mounted displays were being developed, and by the late 20th century, the US Air Force had advanced AR with heads-up displays in aircraft cockpits. The term "immersive technology" encompasses a broad spectrum of applications, including VR, AR, and MR, each offering unique ways to enhance user experiences by either creating entirely artificial environments or overlaying digital content onto the real world (Simpkins et al., 2020). VR, as a cornerstone of immersive technology, creates fully realised digital environments where users can experience a sense of presence and agency, interacting with a simulated world in ways previously unimaginable. AR, on the other hand, overlays digital content onto the real world, enhancing perception by seamlessly blending virtual and physical realities. MR, situated between VR and AR, enables dynamic interactions where virtual objects coexist and interact with the physical environment in real time, offering new dimensions of engagement and collaboration (Nila et al., 2022). As immersive technologies become more ubiquitous, their potential to revolutionise various industries continues to grow, driven by advancements in display technologies and interaction techniques (Spittle et al., 2022; Wang & Yan, 2024).

Often, both game developers and XR developers share common skill sets due to the similarities in their job nature. For example, both roles require strong programming skills to develop the interactive and immersive environment for users to experience, to produce creative content for an engaging and smooth user experience, and to utilise similar game engines for the simulated environment. Nonetheless, they also have some obvious differences. XR applications are generally used in non-entertainment industries (such as in the education or marketing sectors), and the use of additional equipment (VR headsets, AR glasses), a blend of both physical and virtual worlds.

Jobs for the Future collaborated with Meta to develop a new framework of occupations and career paths enabled by XR technology (Naik et al., 2023). In this new framework, four main XR roles and characteristics have been outlined. Different specific job positions may fall under one of these groups.

a. XR Technical Support Specialists ensure the smooth transition and process of XR hardware and software, addressing user issues and providing technical support. It is closely related to IT helpdesk support in the current industry.
b. XR Technology Enablers listen to clients' problems and help them develop product requirements, identify technological limitations, and propose solutions. It can be closely related to sales engineers in the current technology realm.
c. XR Facilitators and Solution Architects are akin to content creators or designers in the current market, primarily responsible for back-end content development. They are involved in translating requirements into virtual spaces and designing immersive learning and work environments.
d. XR Experience Builder and Developers are like the system engineers or programmers who work on the back-end development mostly. They design and build the hardware and software necessary for XR experiences, according to the system requirements.

2.3 Transformative Applications of Games and Immersive Experiences beyond Entertainment

Beyond the realm of entertainment, both video games and immersive technologies have been further explored and utilised in other areas, fully leveraging their ability to engage users and provide real-time or near-real-time feedback. While video games and XR systems are considered as entertainment constructs, there is a specialised field of study that applies video game concepts and technologies for purposes beyond entertainment, known as serious games (Wong et al., 2025). The term "serious games" encompasses a wide array of instructional applications that incorporate game elements, including educational games, game-assisted learning, and simulated training. These are usually also enhanced through the application of XR systems and immersive technologies. Gamification, which involves the application of video game principles, particularly gameplay mechanics such as reward systems, in non-game-related environments or contexts, falls outside the umbrella of serious games, as it does not utilise an actual game or game engine (Pappas, 2023; Tan et al., 2021).

In the field of education and training, immersive technologies like VR and AR create interactive and engaging virtual learning environments. Educators can make the sessions more engaging to retain students' attention and achieve better learning outcomes (Che Abdul Rani et al., 2023; Kasinathan et al., 2019; Tan et al., 2021). Students can explore historical sites or cultural heritage at their comfort (Khor & Mubin, 2024; Lee & Mubin, 2022), conduct virtual science experiments (Chitra et al., 2024), empowering marginalised to learn (Mubin et al., 2022; Mubin et al., 2024), and participate in realistic simulations that enhance understanding and retention while having an enjoyable, fun experience (Wong et al., 2024). On the other hand, industries such as healthcare, aviation, and the military have heavily leveraged these immersive technologies to maximise benefits for their respective trainees (TrainBeyond, 2024). Military training simulations (Inveris, 2023), medical training for trainee surgeons (Laspro et al., 2023), and flight simulators for trainee pilots (Guthridge & Clinton-Lisell, 2023) are common examples of serious games used for professional training and skill development.

In the field of healthcare and therapy, several emerging approaches have been introduced to patients to complement their treatment courses. VR has been used for exposure therapy, helping patients confront and manage phobias, post-traumatic stress disorder, and anxiety in a controlled environment (Hawajri et al., 2023). Meanwhile, gamification has been used in treatments that require patients' discipline and determination, such as physical therapy. Patients tend to be discouraged in therapy, for instance, due to a lack of visible improvement in a short time. They can be motivated to complete the course via a crafted gamified therapy or game-based therapy (Ferreira & Menezes, 2020; Tan et al., 2025).

From the marketing perspective, both video games and immersive technologies have transformed the shopping and buying experience. Customers can experience the items virtually before purchasing them, with discounts or additional rewards (Wong et al., 2024). The experience of purchasing in brick-and-mortar stores has been transformed into a service experience, where customers are served with an immersive and engaging experience.

2.4 Cultural and Technological Fusion of Games and Immersive Technologies

Video games and immersive technologies are reshaping the way users/players interact with learn from, and experience content, creating a convergence of culture and technology. This convergence will be able to blend narrative as we know it together with cultural and societal norms with cutting-edge advancements in game technology, XR, artificial intelligence (AI), and even raw computing processing power to create transformative experiences that transcend traditional boundaries of entertainment, education and our everyday lives (Martínez-Cano, 2024). Video games, while serving as an entertainment medium, have always had the potential to be a powerful and interactive storytelling platform that reflects and preserves cultural identities through virtual experiences and gameplay (Egea-Vivancos & Arias-Ferrer, 2021). Due to their inherent ability to transcend language and location, video games promote international communities of players with similar interests.

Immersive technologies can create shared virtual spaces where people from different backgrounds can collaborate, compete, and co-create, strengthening this cross-cultural bond through shared experiences. With XR technology becoming increasingly advanced, these experiences can evolve from mere gameplay narratives into dynamic and highly interactive experiences that allow users to experience countries and cultures, or even live through iconic moments in history, without ever leaving their physical space (Innocente et al., 2023). Users have the fantastic potential to gain a deeper understanding of other cultures, a greater sense of empathy, and – above all – a greater appreciation for them through these immersive experiences. This technology provides an opportunity to support heritage preservation and promotion in the digital age in various ways. Looking ahead, the fusion of games and immersive technologies holds significant potential for creating culturally inclusive and rich experiences that bridge the gap between technology and culture. Opportunities for people to experience and interact with culture, history, and society in meaningful ways will be further expanded by emerging trends, such as AI-driven adaptive storytelling, blockchain systems for cultural content ownership, and a working metaverse concept serving as a hub for cultural exchange (Martínez-Cano, 2024).

2.5 Innovations and Impacts in Games and Immersive Technologies

Recent innovations in games and immersive technologies have significantly transformed the game development industry and beyond. The integration of

VR and AR has created more immersive and interactive game experiences, allowing players to engage with game environments in unprecedented ways. These advancements have not only enhanced entertainment but also opened new avenues for advanced technological applications beyond normal training and education – in a world where realistic and immersive environments are crucial for effective learning and function (George, 2020). While platforms that incorporate VR and AR are being used to teach subjects ranging from history to science, providing students with hands-on experiences that traditional teaching methods cannot offer (George, 2020), the use of game engines and immersive technologies has led to significant innovations. In architecture and construction, game engines like Unreal Engine and Unity are used to create detailed and interactive visualisations of buildings and spaces, allowing architects and clients to explore designs in a virtual environment before construction begins (Jakobsson & Carney, 2023). It not only improves the design process but also helps in identifying potential issues early on, saving time and resources. These examples illustrate the broad impact that games and immersive technologies have in driving innovation and enhancing processes across various domains.

The evolution of entertainment technologies, from oral storytelling to immersive digital experiences, highlights humanity's quest for engagement and education. Over time, video games have evolved into a sophisticated medium combining art, technology, and design, transcending entertainment to impact education, healthcare, and business. The terminology of video games has evolved in tandem with technological advancements, making games more accessible across platforms, from PCs to mobile devices and later to XR. Game development, encompassing technology, design, and art, has matured into a dynamic industry catering to diverse markets. The rise of immersive technologies such as VR, AR, and MR has further blurred the lines between physical and digital realities, enhancing engagement and offering new possibilities. Beyond entertainment, games and immersive technologies are driving innovation across industries, fostering learning, training, and interaction. As AI, blockchain, and the metaverse continue to shape the future, collaboration among developers, policymakers, and institutions will be crucial in unlocking the full potential of these advancements.

References

Arsenault, D. (2009). Video game genre, evolution and innovation. *Eludamos: Journal for Computer Game Culture, 3*(2), 149–176. https://doi.org/10.7557/23.6003

Berg Marklund, B., Engström, H., Hellkvist, M., & Backlund, P. (2019). What empirically based research tells us about game development. *The Computer Games Journal, 8*(3), 179–198. https://doi.org/10.1007/s40869-019-00085-1

Che Abdul Rani, M. F., Md Yunus, M., & Kasinathan, V. (2023). QRdice: QR-based gamification tool to gamify formative assessment in higher education. In *International Workshop on Learning Technology for Education Challenges* (pp. 17–29). Cham: Springer Nature Switzerland. https://doi.org/10.1007/978-3-031-34754-2_2

Chitra, E., Mubin, S. A., Nadarajah, V. D., Se, W. P., Sow, C. F., Er, H. M., Mitra, N. K., Thiruchelvam, V. & Davamani, F. (2024). A 3-D interactive microbiology laboratory via virtual reality for enhancing practical skills. *Scientific Reports, 14*(1), 12809. https://doi.org/10.1038/s41598-024-63601-y

Egea-Vivancos, A., & Arias-Ferrer, L. (2021). Principles for the design of a history and heritage game based on the evaluation of immersive virtual reality video games. *E-learning and Digital Media, 18*(4), 383–402. https://doi.org/10.1177/2042753020980103

Ferreira, B. & Menezes, P. (2020). Gamifying motor rehabilitation therapies: Challenges and opportunities of immersive technologies. *Information, 11*(2), 88. https://doi.org/10.3390/info11020088

George, S. (2020). Games, simulations, immersive environments, and emerging technologies. In A. Tatnall (Ed.) *Encyclopedia of Education and Information Technologies*. Cham: Springer. https://doi.org/10.1007/978-3-030-10576-1_36

Grabarczyk, P. (2016). Is every indie game independent? Towards the concept of independent game. *Game Studies, 16*(1). https://gamestudies.org/1601/articles/Gardagrabarczyk/

Guthridge, R. & Clinton-Lisell, V. (2023). Evaluating the efficacy of virtual reality (VR) training devices for pilot training. *Journal of Aviation Technology and Engineering,* 12(2), 1–14. https://doi.org/10.7771/2159-6670.1286

Hawajri, O., Lindberg, J., & Suominen, S. (2023). Virtual reality exposure therapy as a treatment method against anxiety disorders and depression: A structured literature review. *Issues in Mental Health Nursing, 44*(4), 245–269. https://doi.org/10.1080/01612840.2023.2190051

Innocente, C., Ulrich, L., Moos, S., & Vezzetti, E. (2023). A framework study on the use of immersive XR technologies in the cultural heritage domain. *Journal of Cultural Heritage, 62*, 268–283. https://doi.org/10.1016/j.culher.2023.06.001

Inveris (2023). *Military Simulation Training Using VR, AR, and Projection: Which Simulation Technology Is Best for Your Training Needs?* https://www.inveristraining.com/military-simulation-training-vr-ar-projection/

Jackson, L. A., & Games, A. I. (2015). Video games and creativity. In G. P. Green, & J. C. Kaufman (Eds.) *Video Games and Creativity* (pp. 3–38). San Diego, CA: Academic Press (Elsevier).

Jakobsson, M., & Carney, L. (2023). *Games & Innovation: The Role of Games in Societal Innovation*. Cambridge, MA: MIT Game Lab.

Kasinathan, V., Mustapha, A., Fu, C. K., Rani, M. C. A., & Manikam, S. (2019). Gamification concept for encouraging lecture attendance. *Indonesian Journal of Electrical Engineering and Computer Science, 16*(1), 482. https://doi.org/10.11591/ijeecs.v16.i1.pp482-490

Khor, C. Y. & Mubin, S. A. (2024). AR mobile application for enhancing national museum heritage visualisation. *International Journal of Software Engineering and Computer Systems, 10*(1), 1–19. https://doi.org/10.15282/ijsecs.10.1.2024.1.0119

Laspro, M., Groysman, L., Verzella, A. N., Kimberly, L. L., & Flores, R. L. (2023). The use of virtual reality in surgical training: Implications foreEducation, patientsSafety, and global health equity. *Surgeries*, *4*(4), 635–646. https://doi.org/10.3390/surgeries4040061

Lee, S. Y. & Mubin, S. A. (2022). Interactive multimedia for promoting cultural heritage tourism in Penang. In *2022 International Visualization, Informatics and Technology Conference (IVIT)*, Kuala Lumpur, Malaysia, 2022, pp. 17–23. https://doi.org/10.1109/IVIT55443.2022.10033383

Martínez-Cano, F. J. (2024). A look at the crossroads of artificial intelligence, films, video games, and virtual reality. In Revolutionizing Communication (pp. 26–36). CRC Press. https://doi.org/10.1201/9781003473633

Mathews, C. C., & Wearn, N. (2016). How are modern video games marketed? *The Computer Games Journal*, *5*(1), 23–37. https://doi.org/10.1007/s40869-016-0023-2

Malaysia Digital Economy Corporation. (2024). *Southeast Asia Game Development Industry Talent Economics Report 2024*. Kuala Lumpur: Malaysian Digital Economy Corporation. https://platform.mdec.com.my/cmscdn/v1.aspx?GUID=c042b3b2-b1bc-40a2-aa8b-fddff7749ab4&file=SEA%20Game%20Talent%20Economics%20Report%202024_FINAL_compressed.pdf

Malaysian Qualification Agency. (2015). *Malaysian Qualifications Agency (MQA) Programme Standards: Creative Multimedia*. Kuala Lumpur: Malaysian Qualifications Agency. https://www2.mqa.gov.my/qad/PS/PS%20CMM%20(BI).pdf

Mubin, S. A., Sow, J. T. Y., Samiraj, E. P.R. & Jaafar, S. P. (2022). A framework for supporting deaf and mute learning experience through extended reality. In *2022 IEEE International Conference on Computing (ICOCO)*, Kota Kinabalu, Malaysia, 2022, pp. 80–83. https://doi.org/10.1109/ICOCO56118.2022.10031865

Mubin, S. A., Sow, J. T. Y., Samiraj, E. P.R. & Jaafar, S. P. (2024). Supporting and improving deaf and mute learners learning experience. In *AIP Conference Proceedings* (Vol. 2802, No. 1, p. 040001). AIP Publishing LLC. https://doi.org/10.1063/5.0183824

Naik, M., Barbosa, R. & Swartsel, A. (2023). *Immersive Learning & XR Technology Skill and Careers*. https://info.jff.org/immersive-learning-careers-skills

Nila, Z., Abdul Hamid, H., & Permadi, D. (2022). Implication of extended reality in visual effects industry for virtual production. In *2nd International Conference on Creative Multimedia 2022 (ICCM 2022)* (pp. 212–221). https://doi.org/10.2991/978-2-494069-57-2_23

Novak, J. (2022). *Game Development Essentials: An Introduction*. Santa Monica: Novy Publishing.

Pappas, C. (2023). *What Are the Differences between Serious Games and Gamification?* https://tinyurl.com/3z2xm3xs

Qaffas, A. (2020). An Operational Study of Video Games' Genres. *International Journal of Interactive Mobile Technologies (iJIM)*, *14*(15), 175–194. https://doi.org/10.3991/ijim.v14i15.16691

Saucier, J. K. (2022). The video game age: A brief history. *IEEE Potentials*, *41*(2), 7–16. https://doi.org/10.1109/MPOT.2021.3104638

Simpkins, S. D., Allen, P. D., & DeMatt, N. W. (2020). Overview of immersive technology: Terminology, state of the art, and APL efforts. *Johns Hopkins APL Technical Digest*, *35*(3), 161–168.

Soderman, B., & Boellstorff, T. (2023). Toys, video games, platforms, and Mattel Electronics's Intellivision. In *Abstract Proceedings of DiGRA 2023 Conference: Limits and Margins of Games*. Seville: Digital Games Research Association (DiGRA).

Spittle, B., Frutos-Pascual, M., Creed, C., & Williams, I. (2022). A review of interaction techniques for immersive environments. *IEEE Transactions on Visualization and Computer Graphics, 29*, 3900–3921. https://doi.org/10.1109/TVCG.2022.3174805

Stuart, K., & Hern, A. (2014). Minecraft sold: Microsoft buys Mojang for $2.5bn. *The Guardian*.https://www.theguardian.com/technology/2014/sep/15/microsoft-buys-minecraft-creator-mojang-for-25bn

Tan, C. I., Wong, B. K. M., & Campbell, A. (2025). Enhancing digital healthcare through gamification: Cyber psychology advancements in the Asia Pacific. In Digital Healthcare, Digital Transformation and Citizen Empowerment in Asia-Pacific and Europe for a Healthier Society. (pp. 99–119). Academic Press. https://doi.org/10.1016/B978-0-443-30168-1.00007-4

Tan, C. I., Wong, C. Y., Abdullah, A., & Lee, J. E. K. (2021). Investigating the effects of social gameplay elements in gamifying online classes. In *European Conference on Games Based Learning* (pp. 709–XXII). Academic Conferences International Limited. https://www.proquest.com/conference-papers-proceedings/investigating-effects-social-gameplay-elements/docview/2616227911/se-2

Toth, A. J., Conroy, E., & Campbell, M. J. (2021). Beyond action video games: Differences in gameplay and ability preferences among gaming genres. *Entertainment Computing, 38*, 100408. https://doi.org/10.1016/j.entcom.2021.100408

TrainBeyond (2024). *Top Virtual Reality Platforms for Immersive Experiences*. https://www.trainbeyond.com/top-virtual-reality-platforms-for-immersive-experiences/

Tunnel, R.-H., & Norbisrath, U. (2023). Classification of video games bachelor's curricula. *Journal of Education and Learning, 12*(2), 39–51. doi:10.5539/jel.v12n2p39

Wang, K., & Yan, W. (2024). An introduction to immersive display technologies. *IEEE Open Journal on Immersive Displays, 1*, 79–85. https://ieeexplore.ieee.org/abstract/document/10487022

Wong, B. K. M., Law, F. L., & Tan, C. I. (2024). Modern consumerism and retailing: The metaverse bound. In *Augmenting Retail Reality, Part A: Blockchain, AR, VR, and the Internet of Things* (pp. 143–166). Emerald Publishing Limited. https://doi.org/10.1108/978-1-83608-634-520241020

Wong, B. K. M., Tan, C. I., & Bastrygina, T. (2025). Advancing healthcare digitalization through games and gamification in the Asia. In *Digital Healthcare, Digital Transformation and Citizen Empowerment in Asia-Pacific and Europe for a Healthier Society* (pp. 73–97). Academic Press. https://doi.org/10.1016/B978-0-443-30168-1.00016-5

Zolotarenko, J. (2024). Indie, AA, and AAA games: The ultimate guide. *The Medium*. https://hitberrygames.medium.com/indie-aa-and-aaa-games-the-ultimate-guide-4147c393ca72

3

Technological Foundations in Transforming Games and Immersive Realities

Rehab Albeladi

3.1 Introduction

Digital entertainment has been fundamentally transformed by the rapid advancement of technology, blurring the lines between reality and virtual worlds. With immersive technologies, including virtual reality (VR), augmented reality (AR), and mixed reality (MR), user engagement has been redefined by providing interactive and lifelike environments that respond dynamically to human actions. In addition to reshaping the gaming industry, these innovations are also influencing other fields such as education, healthcare, training, and design.

This chapter explores the fundamental technologies driving the evolution of games and immersive realities. It discusses the key software and hardware components that enable these experiences, the role that artificial intelligence (AI) and machine learning (ML) play in enhancing interactivity and realism, and the broader applications and impacts of immersive technologies across industries.

3.2 Technological Foundations of Immersive Experiences

Immersive experiences enabled by VR and AR technologies have foundations in many other fields. One of the very relevant technologies is special computing. It represents a paradigm shift in human-computer interaction by enabling devices and systems to interact seamlessly with the physical environment through spatial awareness and context. Spatial computing was originally defined by Greenwold (2003) as "human interaction with a machine in which the machine retains and manipulates referents to real objects and spaces". From Global Positioning System and location-based services, spatial

DOI: 10.1201/9781003662433-4

computing can facilitate the shift from a traditional global data network to a dynamic immersive data ecosystem (Yenduri et al., 2024). Spatial computing nowadays integrates elements of computer vision, sensor networks, ML, and AR/VR to bridge the gap between the physical and digital world. The three core principles of spatial computing are enabling technologies to understand and interpret three-dimensional (3D) concepts, facilitating interaction with digital 3D elements, and providing a robust framework for effective 3D user experience design (Balakrishnan et al., 2021).

At the core of spatial computing is the ability to map and localise objects and environments in real time. Technologies such as simultaneous localisation and mapping play a critical role by constructing 3D maps of an environment while tracking the position of a device or user within that space (Davison et al., 2007). Additionally, computer vision algorithms play a crucial role in enabling devices to interpret spatial data. These systems use cameras and depth sensors to recognise objects, surfaces, and spatial relationships. Spatial computing also enables interaction through natural modalities such as gestures, voice, and eye tracking. This approach aligns with the concept of embodied interaction, where digital systems respond to human actions in a manner that feels intuitive and natural (Dourish, 2001).

Spatial computing underpins the functionality of AR and MR systems by enabling virtual elements to be precisely integrated into the physical world. For example, AR applications use spatial mapping to place digital annotations over real-world objects, while MR systems allow users to interact with holographic elements in 3D space. While VR operates in fully digital environments, spatial computing ensures accurate tracking of user movements and interactions. By creating spatially consistent virtual spaces, VR systems enhance the sense of immersion and presence. The development of immersive technologies such as VR, AR, and MR is heavily reliant on foundational supporting systems. Among these, the Internet of Things (IoT), cloud computing, and 5G serve as critical enablers, providing the infrastructure, computational power, and connectivity necessary for seamless and realistic immersive experiences.

The IoT refers to a network of interconnected devices that communicate, collect, and exchange data with minimal human intervention (Rose et al., 2015). IoT networks are characterised by their low-latency sensor communication, edge computing processing, and distributed computation architectures. In the context of immersive experiences, IoT plays a crucial role in enhancing realism, interactivity, and contextual awareness by enabling the collection of real-time environmental data. IoT-enabled VR and AR applications can access and utilise information from connected devices, enabling more dynamic and responsive immersive experiences. Furthermore, by processing data closer to the source, edge computing reduces latency and conserves bandwidth, enhancing the performance of immersive applications.

As rendering high-quality visuals can require significant computational resources, VR and AR applications can also leverage cloud computing. Cloud computing is a paradigm that enables on-demand access to shared computing resources, such as storage, processing power, and software, over the internet. Major technical characteristics of cloud computing include large-scale computing resources, high scalability, and dynamic resource scheduling (Qian et al., 2009). Immersive technologies rely on cloud infrastructures to overcome the limitations of local devices, such as limited processing capabilities and storage, and to enable collaborative, scalable experiences.

The fifth generation (5G) of mobile network technology offers significantly enhanced connectivity, characterised by ultra-low latency, high bandwidth, and massive device connectivity. These features make 5G an essential enabler for immersive experiences that require real-time responsiveness and high data throughput (Hazarika & Rahmati, 2023).

3.3 Software Foundations for Immersive Game Development

The software foundations for immersive game development provide the technical backbone for creating engaging, interactive, and realistic virtual worlds. These foundations combine tools, frameworks, and libraries designed to handle 3D graphics, physics, interactivity, sound, and other advanced features. This section provides a brief overview of the most relevant technologies, including game engines, graphics APIs, and VR/AR toolkits.

3.3.1 Game Engines

Game engines have facilitated the creation of immersive games by offering a suite of tools that enable developers to construct realistic and interactive virtual worlds. A game engine can be defined as a set of simulation code modules that do not directly specify the game's logic or the game's environment (Lewis & Jacobson, 2002). Game engines typically offer real-time rendering capabilities, dynamic physics engines, and sophisticated lighting systems, which enable the seamless integration of visual and auditory elements, thereby enhancing realism and player engagement. These features, coupled with the engines' adaptability to diverse platforms, have significantly expanded the scope of what is achievable in virtual environments, cementing their role in advancing immersive digital experiences.

Game engines are considered a cornerstone of modern game development, offering a software framework for creating interactive digital experiences. Their origins can be traced back to the early days of video gaming in the 1980s and 1990s, where game developers began reusing code from earlier projects to streamline development. One notable example is the *id Tech 1* engine, used in the iconic game *Doom* (1993), which introduced modularity and tools for level editing, laying the groundwork for modern engines

(Lowood, 2014). This modular approach soon became a defining characteristic of game engines, enabling developers to focus on design and creativity rather than building core functionalities from scratch.

The architecture of game engines is typically designed to provide flexibility and efficiency across a wide range of game types and platforms. Key components include the rendering engine, physics engine, animation system, audio engine, scripting module, and tools for asset management and level design. The rendering engine handles the real-time visualisation of 2D or 3D scenes, leveraging advancements such as ray tracing for realistic lighting to enhance visual fidelity (Zhang, 2024). The physics engine simulates interactions such as gravity, collisions, and rigid body dynamics, enabling lifelike behaviour of objects in the game. Meanwhile, scripting modules allow developers to define game logic using programming or visual scripting languages, ensuring adaptability to diverse gameplay scenarios (Gregory, 2018). In addition, modern engines, such as Unreal Engine and Unity, incorporate robust toolsets for AI, networking, and cross-platform compatibility. These advancements cater to the growing demand for immersive and multiplayer experiences. The scalability of these engines also enables their use in industries beyond gaming, such as film, architecture, and simulation training.

Several research papers studied the features of different game engines and provided comparative analysis for them (Gazis & Katsiri, 2023; Barczak & Woźniak, 2019; Christopoulou & Xinogalos, 2017). In terms of developing immersive applications, Unreal Engine offers high-fidelity graphics and advanced rendering capabilities, making it ideal for applications that require detailed visualisation (Krüger et al., 2024). On the other hand, Unity Engine offers flexibility and ease of use, particularly for mobile and web applications (Gazis & Katsiri, 2023). Unity is also generally considered more user-friendly, with extensive documentation and community support, facilitating quicker onboarding for new developers (Barczak & Woźniak, 2019).

3.3.2 The Immersive Web

By combining web technologies with AR, VR, and MR, the web can become an ideal platform for delivering immersive experiences (Kamal & Andujar, 2022). By integrating 3D graphics, spatial computing, and real-time interactivity into the browser, it democratises access to immersive content, removing the barriers of standalone applications and dedicated hardware. The immersive web enables users to interact with spatially aware environments on devices ranging from desktops and smartphones to advanced VR headsets, potentially leading to widespread adoption and innovation.

The technological specifications of the immersive web are based on standards such as WebXR and WebGL. WebXR, developed by the World Wide Web Consortium, provides a unified API for creating AR and VR content that adapts to user devices and environments. WebGL, a graphics library that enables the direct rendering of 3D content in the browser, provides high-quality visual experiences without the need for plugins (Macario, 2024). These technologies work together to support real-time interactivity, spatial tracking, and rich visualisations, making the web a viable platform for immersive applications.

Over the past decade, advancements in browser capabilities have significantly contributed to the development of the immersive web. Early web-based VR efforts relied on experimental plugins and limited browser support, but modern solutions offer seamless integration and performance optimisation. With the adoption of WebXR by major browsers like Chrome, developers now have the tools to create diverse applications, from virtual showrooms in retail to collaborative virtual workspaces in business. Its continued evolution promises even greater potential, particularly with the integration of AI and 5G connectivity, which will further enhance its capabilities. Using web technologies like WebXR can lead to an alternate kind of Metaverse (Martí-Testón et al., 2023).

3.3.3 AR/VR Toolkits

AR and VR Software Development Kits (SDKs) play an essential role in the development of immersive applications. These SDKs are collections of tools, libraries, and APIs provided by hardware manufacturers or platform providers, designed to interface directly with AR and VR devices. They enable developers to leverage features such as spatial tracking, gesture recognition, environment mapping, and rendering on head-mounted displays (HMDs) or mobile devices (Vakaliuk & Pochtoviuk, 2021). Key AR/VR SDKs include ARKit (iOS), ARCore (Android), Oculus SDK, and Microsoft's Mixed Reality Toolkit (MRTK). Each provides unique functionalities tailored to its respective platform.

These SDKs often complement game engines like Unity and Unreal Engine, which integrate them to simplify the development process. While game engines provide a general-purpose framework for creating immersive applications, AR/VR SDKs specialise in enabling device-specific functionality, making them indispensable for utilising the full potential of AR and VR hardware.

3.4 Hardware Innovations Powering Immersive Realities

The rapid advancement of immersive technologies, including VR, AR, and MR, has been made possible by significant innovations in hardware. These hardware developments are essential for enabling realistic, responsive, and engaging experiences. This section explores key hardware components and innovations, including display technologies, haptic feedback devices, sensing technologies, and processing units, that power immersive realities.

3.4.1 Display Technologies

Different types of displays are currently being used for immersive applications. These include handheld, projection-based and HMDs (Liu et al., 2021). Handheld displays, such as tablets and smartphones, as well as projection-based displays, are typically used for AR applications. Handheld devices have the advantage of being widely accessible and easy to carry, while using projectors enables users to experience AR without having to wear or hold any device. However, both types of display have the restriction of a limited field of view (FoV). On the other hand, HMDs such as Meta Quest, Microsoft HoloLens, and Google Glass can enable fully immersive experiences such as VR and MR with a wide FoV.

3.4.2 Haptic Feedback Devices

Haptic technologies allow users to experience tactile sensations, adding a physical dimension to immersive realities. In general, haptic interaction entails transmitting human actions, such as motion and force, to a virtual or remote environment (haptic input) while simultaneously recreating tactile feedback sensations from that environment (haptic output) (Bai et al., 2021). Devices in this technology include haptic gloves, suits, and controllers that provide force feedback and tactile sensations through vibration. Haptic gloves and wearables, such as the HaptX Gloves and Teslasuit, integrate microfluidics and electroactive polymers to simulate a wide range of textures and forces. These systems enhance interaction by enabling users to "feel" virtual objects. Furthermore, innovations in controllers, such as those used in the PlayStation VR2, utilise adaptive triggers and precise haptic feedback to simulate resistance and pressure, thereby enriching the gaming and training experience.

3.4.3 Sensing Technologies

Advanced sensor systems represent another critical domain of hardware innovation. Sensors are critical for tracking motion, detecting gestures, and enabling spatial awareness in immersive systems. Modern VR and AR systems leverage a combination of inertial measurement units, depth sensors, and cameras. Advances in inside-out tracking, where cameras and sensors on the device map the environment and track the user's position, have reduced the need for external tracking setups. This innovation enhances portability and usability. Eye-tracking technology, which can also be integrated into HMDs, enhances realism by enabling foveated rendering, a technique that reduces computational load by focusing processing power on the areas where the user is looking (Kim et al., 2024). Depth-sensing cameras, such as LiDAR and time-of-flight sensors, enable accurate spatial mapping for AR applications. These sensors enable devices to overlay virtual elements onto physical objects with seamless precision.

3.4.4 Processing Units

Immersive applications require significant computational power to render high-quality visuals, process interactions, and manage real-time spatial tracking. Innovations in processors and graphics processing units (GPUs) have enabled the achievement of these demands within compact and energy-efficient systems. For example, high-performance GPUs, such as NVIDIA's RTX series, enable real-time ray tracing and advanced rendering techniques, creating visually realistic immersive environments. In addition, devices that leverage edge computing distribute processing workloads between the device and nearby servers, reducing latency and enhancing responsiveness (Shi et al., 2016), which are critical requirements, especially in multi-user immersive environments.

3.5 AI and ML in Immersive Gaming

AI and ML have revolutionised the gaming industry, particularly in immersive technologies like VR, AR, and MR. AI-driven techniques enhance realism, generate dynamic content, personalise gameplay, and improve real-time interactions in virtual environments. This section examines four key areas where AI and ML enhance immersive gaming experiences.

3.5.1 Non-player Character Behaviour and Decision-Making

Traditional gaming AI relied on Finite State Machines and Behaviour Trees, but immersive technologies require more complex behaviour modelling. Reinforcement learning enables non-player characters to learn and adapt based on player interactions, resulting in more dynamic and lifelike engagements (Jaderberg et al., 2019). For example, in a VR role-playing game, AI-controlled merchants might adjust their prices based on supply and demand, or enemy AI could change tactics based on the player's previous combat patterns. It enhances the sense of realism, making interactions feel more natural.

3.5.2 Procedural Content Generation

Procedural Content Generation utilises AI and ML to automatically create game elements such as levels, quests, and entire worlds, reducing the need for manual design and ensuring unique experiences for players. This ability is crucial for the evolution of open-world games and other genres that depend on vast, immersive environments (Gomez-Alvarez et al., 2024). Generative Adversarial Networks and deep learning are often applied to content creation (Mittalella et al., 2021).

3.5.3 Personalised and Adaptive Gameplay

AI and ML help tailor gameplay experiences by analysing player preferences, skill levels, and engagement patterns, ensuring a customised experience. For instance, AI can monitor player performance and adjust game difficulty dynamically. ML enables adaptive difficulty adjustment by analysing player behaviour and adjusting the game's challenge level in real time. AI models learn from player actions and can adjust the pace, complexity, and difficulty to match the player's skill level, thereby improving engagement and player retention (Silva et al., 2015). A VR combat simulator, for example, might increase enemy intelligence if the player is excelling or introduce more health packs if they are struggling.

3.5.4 Real-Time Object and Gesture Recognition

For VR/AR applications, AI is used to enhance interactivity and realism through real-time object tracking, gesture recognition, and spatial awareness. AI algorithms process input from sensors in immersive environments, enabling virtual objects to interact seamlessly with real-world elements. AI-driven computer vision enables real-time hand, face, and body tracking, allowing for more intuitive interactions in immersive environments. A VR game might use convolutional neural networks to analyse gestures and translate them into in-game actions (Kang et al., 2020). For example, AI-powered hand tracking in VR fitness games ensures accurate movement detection, thereby enhancing the realism of workouts.

3.6 Applications and Impact of Games and Immersive Technologies across Industries

Games and immersive technologies, such as VR, AR, and MR, have expanded far beyond entertainment to industries like education, healthcare, business, and training. These technologies create highly engaging, interactive, and experiential environments, enhancing productivity and learning while fostering innovation. Below is an exploration of their applications and impact across different fields.

3.6.1 Education and Training

The integration of games and immersive technologies is significantly transforming education and training by enhancing engagement and providing experiential learning opportunities. These technologies enable interactive environments that foster a deeper understanding and skill acquisition. In interactive classrooms, VR enhances learning experiences by allowing students to explore historical sites, conduct virtual science experiments, and engage with interactive simulations. Studies have shown that VR enhances knowledge retention and engagement compared to traditional teaching methods (Krokos et al., 2019; Jensen & Konradsen, 2018). In addition, these technologies support personalised learning experiences, accommodating diverse learning styles and paces (Tsymbaliuk & Fedasyuk, 2024). AR and VR are also utilised for workforce training in industries such as aviation, construction, and manufacturing. These technologies provide employees with realistic, risk-free simulations that enable them to learn complex skills.

While the potential of immersive technologies in education is vast, concerns regarding accessibility and the digital divide remain critical issues that need to be addressed to ensure equitable learning opportunities for all students. Challenges such as high costs and technological complexity might hinder widespread implementation (Bosman et al., 2024).

3.6.2 Healthcare

Immersive technologies, such as VR and AR, have been utilised in healthcare to train healthcare professionals and advance therapeutic methods. VR simulations are widely used in medical education to train students and professionals in surgical procedures and patient care. A systematic review by Alaker et al. (2016) concluded that proficiency-based VR training, when conducted under supervision with clear instructions and haptic feedback, has been shown to be the most effective method for delivering VR training. Immersive technologies have also been used in therapeutic applications. Exposure therapy using VR has been effective in treating phobias and post-traumatic stress disorder by allowing patients to confront fears in controlled settings (Rizzo et al., 2009). Serious games designed for cognitive training can aid in treating conditions such as Alzheimer's and attention-deficit/hyperactivity disorder (McCallum & Boletsis, 2013). VR is also utilised in physical rehabilitation, enabling stroke patients to regain motor functions through interactive exercises (Laver et al., 2018).

3.6.3 Other Industries

Immersive technologies are increasingly used in business and retail sectors. For example, applications like IKEA allow customers to visualise how furniture fits in their homes. Studies show AR enhances decision-making and improves customer satisfaction (Pandey & Pandey, 2025). The tourism industry has also adopted immersive technologies to create virtual experiences that inspire travellers and aid them in planning trips (Yung & Khoo-Lattimore, 2019). For instance, immersive technologies are used to create digital reconstructions of historical sites, allowing people to explore ancient ruins or museums virtually. Furthermore, immersive technologies are used in smart city planning by simulating future cityscapes to optimise transportation, infrastructure, and public services based on predictive models (Liu et al., 2024).

In conclusion, games and immersive technologies have found applications across diverse industries, enhancing engagement, efficiency, and creativity. However, challenges such as accessibility, ethical considerations, and data privacy must be addressed to maximise their benefits and ensure inclusive adoption (Rachmawati & Tornando, 2024). As these technologies evolve, their ability to create innovative and meaningful experiences will continue to reshape industries and enhance human experiences.

References

Alaker, M., Wynn, G. R., & Arulampalam, T. (2016). Virtual reality training in laparoscopic surgery: A systematic review & meta-analysis. *International Journal of Surgery, 29*, 85–94. https://doi.org/10.1016/j.ijsu.2016.03.034

Bai, H., Li, S., & Shepherd, R. F. (2021). Elastomeric haptic devices for virtual and augmented reality. *Advanced Functional Materials, 31*(39), 2009364. https://doi.org/10.1002/adfm.202009364

Balakrishnan, S., Hameed, M. S. S., Venkatesan, K., & Aswin, G. (2021, March). Interaction of spatial computing in augmented reality. In *2021 7th International Conference on Advanced Computing and Communication Systems (ICACCS)* (Vol. 1, pp. 1900–1904). IEEE. https://doi.org/10.1109/ICACCS51430.2021.9442010

Barczak, A. M., & Woźniak, H. (2019). Comparative study on game engines. *Studia Informatica. Systems and Information Technology. Systemy i Technologie Informacyjne, 23*(1–2), 5–24. https://doi.org/10.34739/si.2019.23.01

Bosman, I. D. V., Smith, A. E., Wong, Y. L., Ka, K. S. D., Alemneh, D., & Chow, A. (2024). Immersive technology in education. *Proceedings of the Association for Information Science and Technology, 61*(1), 721–724. https://doi.org/10.1002/pra2.1086

Christopoulou, E., & Xinogalos, S. (2017). Overview and comparative analysis of game engines for desktop and mobile devices. *International Journal of Serious Games, 4*(4), 21–36. https://doi.org/10.17083/ijsg.v4i4.194

Davison, A. J., Reid, I. D., Molton, N. D., & Stasse, O. (2007). MonoSLAM: Real-time single camera SLAM. *IEEE Transactions on Pattern Analysis and Machine Intelligence, 29*(6), 1052–1067. https://doi.org/ 10.1109/TPAMI.2007.1049

Dourish, P. (2001). *Where the Action Is: The Foundations of Embodied Interaction* (Vol. 210). MIT Press.

Gazis, A., & Katsiri, E. (2023). Serious games in digital gaming: A comprehensive review of applications, game engines and advancements. arXiv preprint arXiv:2311.03384. https://doi.org/10.48550/arXiv.2311.03384

Gomez-Alvarez, D., Lopez-Franco, M., Carranza, D. B., Lopez-Franco, C., & Lopez-Franco, L. (2024). The future of gaming: How artificial intelligence is revolutionizing the industry. *ReCIBE, Revista electrónica de Computación, Informática, Biomédica y Electrónica, 13*(3), E6–10. https://doi.org/10.32870/recibe.v13i3.373

Greenwold, S. (2003). Spatial computing. *Master thesis.* Massachusetts Institute of Technology.

Gregory, J. (2018). *Game Engine Architecture.* AK Peters/CRC Press.

Hazarika, A., & Rahmati, M. (2023). Towards an evolved immersive experience: Exploring 5G-and beyond-enabled ultra-low-latency communications for augmented and virtual reality. *Sensors, 23*(7), 3682. https://doi.org/10.3390/s23073682

Jaderberg, M., Czarnecki, W. M., Dunning, I., Marris, L., Lever, G., Castaneda, A. G., ... & Graepel, T. (2019). Human-level performance in 3D multiplayer games with population-based reinforcement learning. *Science, 364*(6443), 859–865. https://doi.org/10.1126/science.aau6249

Jensen, L., & Konradsen, F. (2018). A review of the use of virtual reality head-mounted displays in education and training. *Education and Information Technologies, 23,* 1515–1529. https://doi.org/10.1007/s10639-017-9676-0

Kamal, A., & Andujar, C. (2022). Designing, testing and adapting navigation techniques for the immersive web. *Computers & Graphics, 106,* 66–76. https://doi.org/10.1016/j.cag.2022.05.015

Kang, T., Chae, M., Seo, E., Kim, M., & Kim, J. (2020). DeepHandsVR: Hand interface using deep learning in immersive virtual reality. *Electronics, 9*(11), 1863. https://doi.org/10.3390/electronics9111863

Kim, J., Kim, J., Jung, M., Kwon, T., & Kim, K. (2024). Individualised foveated rendering with eye-tracking head-mounted display. *Virtual Reality, 28*(1), 25. https://doi.org/10.1007/s10055-023-00931-8

Krokos, E., Plaisant, C., & Varshney, A. (2019). Virtual memory palaces: Immersion aids recall. *Virtual Reality, 23*(1), 1–15. https://doi.org/10.1007/s10055-018-0346-3

Krüger, M., Gilbert, D., Kuhlen, T. W., & Gerrits, T. (2024). Game engines for immersive visualisation: Using Unreal Engine beyond entertainment. *PRESENCE: Virtual and Augmented Reality,* 1–25. https://doi.org/10.1162/pres_a_00416

Laver, K. E., Lange, B., George, S., Deutsch, J. E., Saposnik, G., & Crotty, M. (2018). Virtual reality for stroke rehabilitation. *Stroke, 49*(4), e160–e161. https://doi.org/10.1161/STROKEAHA.117.020275

Lewis, M. & Jacobson, J. (2002). Game engines in scientific research: Introduction. *Communications of the ACM, 45*(1), 27.

Liu, R., Peng, C., Zhang, Y., Husarek, H., & Yu, Q. (2021). A survey of immersive technologies and applications for industrial product development. *Computers & Graphics, 100,* 137–151. https://doi.org/10.1016/j.cag.2021.07.023

Liu, Z., He, Y., Demian, P., & Osmani, M. (2024). Immersive technology and building information modeling (BIM) for sustainable smart cities. *Buildings, 14*(6), 1765. https://doi.org/10.3390/buildings14061765

Lowood, H. (2014). Game engines and game history. *Kinephanos. Revue d'études des médias et de* culture *populaire,* 179–198.

Macario, G. (2024). An open, cross-platform, web-based metaverse sing WebXR and A-Frame. arXiv preprint arXiv:2408.13520.

Martí-Testón, A., Muñoz, A., Gracia, L., & Solanes, J. E. (2023). Using WebXR metaverse platforms to create touristic services and cultural promotion. *Applied Sciences, 13*(14), 8544. https://doi.org/10.3390/app13148544

McCallum, S., & Boletsis, C. (2013). Dementia games: A literature review of dementia-related serious games. In *Serious Games Development and Applications: 4th International Conference, SGDA 2013*, Trondheim, Norway, September 25–27, 2013. Proceedings 4 (pp. 15–27). Springer Berlin Heidelberg. https://doi.org/10.1007/978-3-642-40790-1_2

Mittalella, N., Singh, P. P., & Sharma, P. (2021). Generative adversarial networks based PCG for games: A comprehensive study. In *Deep Learning in Gaming and Animations* (pp. 137–156). CRC Press.

Pandey, P. K., & Pandey, P. K. (2025). Unveiling the transformative power of augmented reality in retail: a systematic literature analysis. *Journal of Strategy and Management.* https://doi.org/10.1108/JSMA-05-2023-0101

Qian, L., Luo, Z., Du, Y., & Guo, L. (2009). Cloud computing: An overview. *In Cloud Computing: First International Conference, CloudCom 2009*, Beijing, China, December 1–4, 2009. Proceedings 1 (pp. 626–631). Springer Berlin Heidelberg. https://doi.org/10.1007/978-3-642-10665-1_63

Rachmawati, A. K., & Tornando, H. (2024). Challenges in consumer adaptation to immersive technologies: A comprehensive literature review. *eCo-Buss, 7*(1), 317–328. https://doi.org/10.32877/eb.v7i1.1461

Rizzo, A., Reger, G., Gahm, G., Difede, J., & Rothbaum, B. O. (2009). Virtual reality exposure therapy for combat-related PTSD. *Post-traumatic Stress Disorder: Basic Science and Clinical Practice,* 375–399. https://doi.org/10.1007/978-1-60327-329-9_18

Rose, K., Eldridge, S., & Chapin, L. (2015). The Internet of things: An overview. *The Internet Society (ISOC), 80*(15), 1–53.

Shi, W., Cao, J., Zhang, Q., Li, Y., & Xu, L. (2016). Edge computing: Vision and challenges. *IEEE Internet of Things Journal, 3*(5), 637–646. https://doi.org/10.1109/JIOT.2016.2579198

Silva, M. P., do Nascimento Silva, V., & Chaimowicz, L. (2015, November). Dynamic difficulty adjustment through an adaptive AI. In *2015 14th Brazilian symposium on computer games and digital entertainment (SBGames)* (pp. 173–182). IEEE. https://doi.org/10.1109/SBGames.2015.16

Tsymbaliuk, T., & Fedasyuk, D. (2024). Use of immersive technologies in the educational process: Advantages of the approach, analysis of commercial systems, classification of educational environments. *Vìsnik Nacìonal'nogo Unìversitetu L'vìvs'ka Polìtehnìka Serìâ Ìnformacìjnì Sistemi Ta Merežì, 15,* 219–237. https://doi.org/10.23939/sisn2024.15.219.

Vakaliuk, T. A., & Pochtoviuk, S. I. (2021, July). Analysis of tools for the development of augmented reality technologies. *CEUR Workshop Proceedings.* https://ceur-ws.org/Vol-2898/paper06.pdf

Yenduri, G., Maddikunta, P. K. R., Gadekallu, T. R., Jhaveri, R. H., Bandi, A., Chen, J., … & Wang, W. (2024). Spatial computing: Concept, applications, challenges and future directions. arXiv preprint arXiv:2402.07912. https://doi.org/10.48550/arXiv.2402.07912

Yung, R., & Khoo-Lattimore, C. (2019). New realities: A systematic literature review on virtual reality and augmented reality in tourism research. *Current issues in tourism, 22*(17), 2056–2081. https://doi.org/10.1080/13683500.2017.1417359

Zhang, Q. (2024). Advanced techniques and high-performance computing optimisation for real-time rendering. *Applied and Computational Engineering, 90*(1), 14–19. https://doi.org/10.54254/2755-2721/90/2024melb0061

4

The Evolution of Gaming in the Metaverse

Juncheng Wang

4.1 Immersive Worlds and Gameplay in the Metaverse

The metaverse is rapidly evolving, with gaming as its most widely utilised service. As the metaverse gains traction globally, there are notable differences in how it is perceived by news media, academia, and the general public (Kim and Kim, 2024). Games developed for virtual reality (VR), mixed reality (MR), and augmented reality (AR) platforms fall under the umbrella term "metaverse games" (MGs). These games enhance immersion and allow players to interact with real-world settings. Recent successes like Sandbox, Axie Infinity, Horizon World, and Decentraland illustrate the high user engagement and financial viability of MGs. A current trend is the enhancement of social features in these games, enabling real-time conversations and activities through extended reality (XR) technologies, fostering a sense of social presence among users. Indeed, understanding the evolution of metaverse gaming requires a holistic perspective that considers its multifaceted opportunities and challenges (Koohang et al., 2023).

The metaverse provides a modern immersive environment where people can work, socialise, and entertain themselves in virtual settings. Key factors driving user acceptance and market expansion for MGs include their increasing popularity and decreasing costs. XR applications extend beyond gaming and entertainment, reaching various sectors such as public services, education, marketing, and healthcare. For example, virtual and AR technologies have been employed to create social learning environments, demonstrating the metaverse's potential for collaborative education (Scavarelli et al., 2021). Platforms like Roblox, for instance, have been used in educational contexts to engage learners through interactive metaverse experiences (Han, Liu and Gao, 2023). According to Gartner (2022), by 2027, 30% of users will engage with the metaverse for social interaction, work, entertainment, and education for an average of two hours daily. The user experience (UX) of presence and immersion is becoming vital in the gaming industry as XR technologies mature.

DOI: 10.1201/9781003662433-5

As gaming experiences become increasingly immersive, individuals from diverse regions are forming digital communities and cultivating lasting social connections in virtual environments. The metaverse represents a convergence of social connections, virtual worlds, and limitless creative possibilities, allowing users to navigate various virtual settings with ease. This environment enables travel to distant places, collaboration in shared virtual offices, and interaction with people globally, satisfying fundamental human needs for artistic expression, intellectual stimulation, and social engagement. Notably, game design elements in AR experiences can be leveraged to promote cooperative behaviour among players, thereby strengthening community bonds (Morschheuser et al., 2017).

Despite the extensive use of VR in gaming and entertainment, research on modern MG experiences—especially regarding affordances—remains limited. There are unresolved questions about what users seek from MGs and how different aspects are experienced. Existing literature suggests that media attributes, such as virtuality, connection, and modality, influence user behaviour. VR technology is revolutionising interactions within the metaverse and among game users. It immerses players in engaging virtual worlds, enhancing the gaming experience by blending reality with fiction. VR contributes to creating immersive 3D environments in the metaverse, optimising resource allocation through game-theoretic approaches, and ensuring robust user virtual service provider mappings. VR gesture interfaces can further enhance immersion and participation, especially in educational contexts, aiding learning outcomes for children with attention disorders.

Procedural storytelling is an emerging strategy within Procedural Content Generation (PCG). This approach utilises artificial intelligence (AI) to generate unique characters, locations, and narratives in response to user input. Procedural Narrative Generation (PNG) enables AI to dynamically generate characters and storylines, presenting users with varied scenarios. Advanced Natural Language Generation (NLG) capabilities ensure effective communication between software and users. Akimoto and Ogata's (2012; 2014) work demonstrates how narrative theories can be integrated with programming to create responsive narratives, resulting in emergent storytelling that transcends traditional frameworks.

The metaverse's growth is at a critical juncture, with significant investments from businesses and tech giants aimed at creating immersive virtual worlds. Platforms like Facebook Horizon, Roblox, and Decentraland are driving this expansion. The convergence of blockchain technology, AI, and advanced graphics is generating renewed interest in the metaverse, promising innovative avenues for social interaction, work, education, and entertainment (Kshetri, 2023). Future research should address challenges such as integrating different game versions, enhancing GPS and collision detection capabilities, and ensuring flexible content management. Expanding user assessments with larger sample sizes will yield more accurate insights into user preferences, thereby enhancing the AR gaming experience. AR represents a transformative technology that merges digital and physical realms, offering opportunities for immersive and health-focused gaming experiences (Baranowski and Lyons, 2020).

Historically, gaming has been a pioneer in utilising the metaverse for entertainment, facilitated by various technologies such as smartphones, tablets, and AR devices. Gaming has evolved from a simple pastime to a complex life experience, blurring the lines between gaming and the metaverse. This relationship highlights how technology and game features contribute to immersive experiences. The metaverse's focus on social engagement, immersive experiences, and economic opportunities is set to transform gaming. By developing and exchanging virtual assets, it can create new economic dimensions, strengthen community ties through social interactions (Hollensen, Kotler and Opresnik, 2022), and enhance UXs by merging the real and virtual worlds. However, potential issues such as addiction, privacy, and ethical concerns also arise.

Factors influencing immersion include social features, technological devices, game design, and UX. Social interactions in AR and VR can enhance immersion, while high-quality equipment provides a more realistic experience. The interactivity, storyline, and visual effects of games significantly impact players' engagement, and the usability of interfaces also plays a crucial role. Developers should prioritise social features and interactive design to attract players, but they must also consider the potential adverse effects of immersion, such as addiction and social isolation. Striking a balance between immersion and players' mental health and social needs is essential in MG design.

In summary, the dynamic relationship between the metaverse and gaming communities is anticipated to shape gaming experiences in innovative ways. As the metaverse evolves, it presents new opportunities for engagement, creativity, and community building, while also addressing the challenges of responsible usage and the potential mental health impacts (Whang, Chang, and Lee, 2023).

4.2 Narrative and Storytelling in MGs

Procedural narrative is a strategy within PCG, an important aspect of modern software design. This approach utilises AI to create unique characters and environments, ensuring that elements like faces, bodies, and vegetation in a game are distinct. This leads us to PNG, where AI goes beyond randomising pre-written scripts. Instead, it creates dynamic narratives by generating characters, backgrounds, events, and more, responding to user inputs with varied stories. To effectively implement PNG, advanced NLG capabilities are essential. NLG enables characters and narrators to exhibit non-logical behaviours, facilitating effective communication between the software and users. This technology has found applications in virtual assistants like Siri, which simulate human-like responses. However, the potential of PNG in specific contexts, such as Papua New Guinea, remains largely unexplored.

Researchers Akimoto and Ogata (2012; 2014) have built upon narrative theories developed by scholars such as Barthes, Propp, and Genette. They have designed programs that generate random narratives while adapting to user input. Their work integrates established narrative frameworks with cutting-edge programming, drawing on examples from digital humanities to illustrate their findings. They propose three stages of PNG that mirror the human creative process:

a. Framework establishment—The system begins by creating a general story framework, outlining a sequence of markers that form a tree structure to predict potential outcomes.
b. Discourse construction—In this stage, the narrative takes shape as the system selects elements to present to users, defining which aspects can change based on user interactions.
c. Textual-audiovisual expression—Ultimately, the narrative is presented in a format that allows users to see, hear, and interact with it, effectively bringing the story to life.

This AI-driven creative process parallels human storytelling, offering the advantage of systematic and continuous adaptation. AI can respond to unexpected user interactions, crafting new narratives in an ever-evolving landscape with limitless combinations. The emergence of such narratives challenges traditional storytelling constraints while emphasising the importance of a coherent structure. Predicting emotional responses remains difficult, and failures in narrative engagement do not negate the value of those experiences. Digital service algorithms analyse user data to tailor content, enhancing the predictive power of narrative design.

The metaverse exemplifies a virtual space that fosters interaction and collaboration. Users navigate diverse environments with avatars, engaging in co-creation and shared experiences. Within the metaverse, spatial storytelling flourishes, supported by various media forms. This evolution can be traced from comic books to animated shows, films, video games, and immersive virtual worlds. The growth of digital technology has facilitated the creation of expansive digital narrative spaces. Effective spatial storytelling enhances interactive narratives across different locations, merging historical visuals to create immersive experiences. Users often prefer familiar settings; thus, engaging spatial applications in gaming can draw players deeper into the narrative world (Pulver et al., 2020). Spatial storytelling also plays a significant role in tourism, particularly in theme parks that curate visitor experiences through sensory and emotional immersion (Agustina et al., 2022).

In recent years, immersive storytelling opportunities in VR have surged, with spatial audio contributing to users' feelings of presence and immersion. Audiences can navigate virtual environments, making choices about their viewing direction, which poses challenges for cinematic VR playback (Chaurasia and Majhi, 2022). Museums also leverage spatial storytelling, integrating technology to enrich visitor experiences. By assembling historical narratives through visual narratives, museums create transcendent experiences that utilise location, architecture, and human stories. Techniques such as interactive panels and animations engage visitors more deeply (Trisno et al., 2022). Gamified elements, like role-playing games, can enhance immersion as visitors explore exhibits.

Audiovisual technology and spatial storytelling serve as frameworks for museums to convey the significance of artworks. The architecture itself becomes a storytelling medium, helping visitors grasp concepts through spatial and sensory experiences. Research shows that the arrangement of architectural elements can convey profound narratives, demonstrating architecture's role in spatial storytelling and cultural context. Gamified narrative techniques can blend traditional museum experiences with modern technology, creating vibrant learning environments. Through AR and VR, visitors can engage with historical events as if they were present, turning museum spaces into interactive games where design and layout enhance exploration and puzzle-solving. Spatial and cinematic photography methods are also valuable in creating and evaluating spatial narratives (Kretzer, 2021).

Moreover, spatial storytelling emphasises landscapes, recognising their role in crafting artistic spaces. Landscape-centred narratives enrich storytelling, allowing visitors to engage with exhibitions through challenges and quests that enhance their experience. This approach not only makes narratives more engaging but also fosters creativity and involvement. Spatial skills, essential for everyday tasks, can be integrated into educational settings, allowing children to explore these techniques and access more engaging learning opportunities (Baykal et al., 2018). As technology evolves, the convergence of the metaverse and spatial storytelling is likely to deepen, providing more prosperous and more diverse experiences. It is crucial to find a balance between leveraging technology and ensuring authentic UXs to maintain narrative depth and interactivity.

4.3 Game Engines and Technologies for Metaverse Development

The essential infrastructure that speeds up the creation of digital games, including video and computer games, is provided by game engines like

Unreal and Unity. An engine is a piece of software that provides developers with pre-made solutions and tools for basic programming tasks in the creation of virtual worlds, games, and digitally augmented settings. It enables game creators to build upon a standard foundation. A small community of outside developers and service providers has developed around game engines over time. Game engines have recently been utilised in industries beyond gaming, including manufacturing, AI, architecture, urban planning, and filmmaking. This has made companies that develop, provide, and maintain game engines (such as Epic Games [EG] and Unity Technologies [UT]) influential players across all social and economic domains, which are beginning to rely on game engines for software or services.

Game engines are platforms that provide developers with tools containing ready-made solutions for foundational programming tasks in games, virtual, and digitally enhanced environments. These solutions include graphic rendering, environmental physics, object collision detection, and AI (Gregory, 2018). It shortens development time, enabling many small game developers to deliver games with complex looks and feels. Over time, this allows for the emergence of an open ecosystem of third-party developers and service providers that enrich and support the shared use of the underlying engine. EG and UT now dominate the market for game engines. EG controls the market for expensive console games thanks to the Unreal Engine. Conversely, UT's Unity Engine has made it the industry leader in independent game creation and mobile gaming (Chia et al., 2020). However, their impact extends well beyond gaming; they are currently found in industries including manufacturing, AI, architecture, filmmaking, and public planning. In fact, by providing platform-based services for XR, gaming engines are poised to emerge as one of the most important components of the future digital infrastructure.

Game engine companies are also gradually reshaping the entertainment landscape by building digital environments that seamlessly integrate brands and narrative worlds, breaking down traditional intellectual property silos by allowing users to interact across devices. Currently, this is manifested in gaming environments, but it is expected to evolve into broader, digitally enhanced social environments. A prominent example of this is the Fortnite game offered by EG. Thus, game engine companies provide platforms that allow seamless interaction between users, as well as the seamless integration of brands and narrative worlds.

Game engines are evolving into digital platforms that are becoming more and more prevalent in social, cultural, and economic spheres (Freedman, 2020). An increasingly networked digital environment can be created by simply integrating these digital shadows into different apps that are powered by their own engines. As a result, gaming engines serve as crucial platforms for the subsequent phase of social digitalisation, laying the groundwork for applications in virtual and AR, which some critics have started to call the "metaverse." Long regarded as an unmanageable aspect of digital transformation, XR (a term that includes VR, AR, and MR) (Greengard, 2019, p. 17;

Lanier, 2017). However, as sensor technology and software continue to advance, XR has become increasingly significant in various domains, including gaming, industrial design, and the development of AI for driverless cars (Bailenson, 2018).

Businesses like Microsoft, Apple, Meta/Facebook, and Alphabet/Google are also making strides in the XR space. They frequently concentrate on exclusive hardware products, such as the Oculus Rift, Google Glass, and iPhones (Egliston and Carter, 2022). The underlying software, which renders virtual settings and objects and maps the physical movements of hands, eyes, bodies, and senses into digital space, is crucial to the success of XR. Consequently, hardware developers are turning to game engines for ready-made solutions in these areas, but only a few companies (such as EG and UT) provide sufficiently flexible engines that can be implemented on a large scale across product lines. This alone positions game engine providers as key players in the platform market, with their power only increasing as the importance of XR capabilities continues to rise.

The emergence of game engines as platforms for the increasingly digitalisation of economic, social, and political life, combined with the rise of the metaverse, represents a transformation. As we have demonstrated in this article, current developments not only align with the analytical framework of platform research but also necessitate further expansion. These expansions can be achieved through broader interdisciplinary efforts, particularly in the field of digital game research. As the scope and diversity of platforms expand, research on platforms will receive increasing attention. Still, it must also recognise the growing demand for interdisciplinary research and remain open to new developments related to the digitalisation of social, economic, and political life, along with new participants, infrastructures, business models, and practices.

4.4 The Role of User-Generated Content in Shaping MGs

Co-creation in video games differs significantly from social media content production, which is primarily focused on marketing or communication. It involves participatory and iterative design processes closely linked to game mechanics and UXs, fostering engagement and creativity in ways that other digital environments do not. User-generated content (UGC) plays a crucial role in MGs, enabling players and creators to collaboratively craft shared digital experiences, including game worlds and narratives. This interactive creation enhances user engagement, reduces marketing costs, boosts revenues through virtual economies, and encourages the formation of vibrant communities. In metaverse environments, players are not just participants; they are also content creators whose insights and feedback shape the game's development, leading to diverse and dynamic experiences.

UGC encompasses any content produced by users rather than professionals, including posts, images, and videos. Over recent years, UGC has become integral to the evolving video game industry, influencing both game culture and community dynamics. This shift transforms gaming from a one-sided entertainment experience into a collaborative, user-driven ecosystem. Furthermore, research suggests that UGC is perceived as more helpful when creators actively interact with their audience, underlining the importance of creator engagement in the community (Zhuang et al., 2023). As such, it underscores the need to summarise the current developments in UGC within the gaming sector. The rise of the internet has significantly contributed to the growth of UGC, responding to user demands for more personalised and diversified content. The rapid adoption of digital technologies has further accelerated this trend, resulting in vast quantities of knowledge generated on social media platforms every second. This growth has prompted increased interest in rapid product innovation techniques that align with customer preferences, emphasising the importance of user involvement in product design. Researchers have explored various ways to open the design process, encouraging user engagement and leading to interactive innovation that emphasises collaboration among users, designers, and businesses to develop products effectively. For instance, a structured framework has been proposed to turn consumer-generated ideas into an innovation resource within online user communities, highlighting the innovative potential of user contributions (Lin et al., 2022).

In the metaverse, UGC is anticipated to revolutionise immersive internet experiences by enabling access to high-fidelity environments that blend realistic and virtually reflected experiences. Various industries, including gaming, social media, education, and tourism, have begun to leverage the capabilities of the metaverse. This digital space enables the seamless integration of digital identities, virtual avatars, and real-world interactions, offering a wealth of features and endless opportunities. UGC in the metaverse plays a crucial role in product development, facilitating widespread user participation and offering practical solutions to existing challenges. Ultimately, UGC drives game evolution and fosters deep interactions between users and platforms, infusing MGs with unprecedented creativity and engagement.

"Interactive innovation" refers to the active collaboration among customers, clients, and businesses to foster product design and innovation. This process generates a wealth of knowledge on real-world internet platforms, encompassing various content forms, including UGC, professionally created content, and occupationally generated content. Such content originates from diverse social media platforms, resulting in dynamic, unstructured data that requires businesses to adopt multiple strategies to effectively balance content quantity and quality. In such collaborative development settings, effectively acquiring user knowledge is crucial for guiding the design process (Tan and Zhang, 2021).

In the metaverse, UGC propels game evolution and enhances user-platform interactions, driving product innovation. Different content creators focus on various scenarios, prompting businesses to seek valuable knowledge that enables MGs to thrive creatively and engagingly. Through technologies such as XR, holograms, brain-computer interfaces (BCIs), and sensors, users are immersed in a sensory "connection" within the metaverse. This environment extends UGC beyond traditional formats to include real-time images, thoughts, and actions, facilitated by technologies like blockchain, AI, and network computing.

In practical terms, virtual office spaces can be created within the metaverse using existing platforms like Facebook Creator Studio, Roblox, and NVIDIA. These spaces allow user groups, designers, and business departments to collaborate and innovate. Despite the vast and diverse nature of creative knowledge, metaverse technologies can convert this information into structured data in real time, enhancing its application in product innovation. Users can utilise their digital identities to access "virtual labs," "workshops," and "factories," where they can design and develop virtual products based on their preferences.

The metaverse also enables the recording of design parameters for statistical analysis, allowing designers to perceive user needs from the user's perspective. This collaborative approach fosters a synergy among user groups, designers, and business departments within the metaverse, resulting in high-quality interactive innovation knowledge for product development.

As the gaming industry and the metaverse continue to evolve, the role of UGC will likely expand, driving further innovations and enhancing UXs. The participatory nature of co-creation in video games not only reshapes how content is produced but also influences community dynamics, resulting in richer and more diverse interactions. The integration of advanced technologies will further enhance the potential of UGC, making it an essential component of the future digital landscape.

In conclusion, the interplay between UGC and the metaverse is reshaping the gaming industry. As players become active contributors, their involvement leads to more vibrant and engaging gaming experiences. The continuous advancement of technology will only amplify these trends, creating new opportunities for creative expression and community building in virtual spaces.

4.5 The Future of Gaming and Innovation in the Metaverse

Short-term trends (1–3 Years)—The metaverse in gaming aims to enhance player immersion and interactivity. Players can explore virtual worlds, complete tasks, and socialise with others. In the short term, advancements such as AI-driven non-player characters, enhanced VR controllers, and cloud gaming technology are expected to enhance interactivity and realism significantly. The metaverse has the potential to transform game design, enabling developers to create persistent worlds that evolve in response to player actions, resulting in a dynamic gaming experience where players influence the game's direction. Beyond gaming, the metaverse has the potential to fundamentally transform education, entertainment, communication, business, and social interaction (Daneshfar and Jamshidi, 2023). It offers opportunities for people to connect in a virtual environment that feels almost as real as the physical world, enabling imagination and discovery (Knox, 2022). As the metaverse evolves, its importance and impact will grow.

Mid- to long-term trends (5–10 Years)—In the mid- to long-term, the metaverse is expected to undergo profound changes. For instance, the application of BCIs will allow players to interact with virtual environments using their thoughts. Fully immersive gaming will provide heightened realism and interactivity. The integration of digital twins will enable virtual worlds to reflect real life, opening new avenues for accurate exploration (Rakic et al., 2023). Digital twin frameworks thus serve as a critical link between physical and virtual realms, and are expected to play an integral role in future metaverse developments (Singh et al., 2021).

The future metaverse may evolve into a decentralised open-source platform, empowering users to create and own virtual assets. This democratic and accessible platform could attract global contributors. By combining advanced technologies such as AR, VR, and AI, the metaverse will offer immersive benefits, potentially reducing the costs associated with physical infrastructure (Anshari et al., 2022). Despite its potential, the future of metaverse gaming faces challenges, including technological barriers, legal issues, and ethical concerns:

a. Technological limitations—VR technology creates immersive experiences, but it has limitations, including high hardware requirements, latency, and a lack of haptic feedback. A combination of advanced technology and low-latency networks is necessary for seamless user interaction. Edge computing can address latency by processing data closer to the user, enabling real-time experiences that are crucial for immersive experiences.
b. User security and privacy—With the rise of cyber threats, including cryptocurrency theft and data breaches, ensuring user privacy and security is crucial. AI can help mitigate cyber threats, but criminals can also exploit it. There are significant risks to critical infrastructure and social cohesion. Establishing consistent security and privacy boundaries within the metaverse is essential, although shared norms and practices are still in development. A recent survey on the metaverse highlights similar security and privacy concerns that must be addressed (Wang et al., 2023).

c. Health concerns—Virtual environments may lead to physical health issues like eye strain and motion sickness, as well as mental health problems such as social isolation and addiction. Addressing these issues requires mandatory research and testing regarding mental health, emphasising the need for legal and regulatory compliance.

In summary, while the metaverse presents transformative potential across various domains, it must navigate significant technological, security, and health-related challenges to realise its full capabilities.

References

Agustina, I. A., Noegroho, N., Ardiani, Y. M., & Avida, C. (2022, February). Resilient COVID-19 village: The application of healthy housing in densely populated areas in Surabaya. Study case: Kampung Pradah, Surabaya. In *IOP Conference Series: Earth and Environmental Science* (Vol. 998, No. 1, p. 012038). IOP Publishing. https://doi.org/10.1088/1755-1315/998/1/012038

Akimoto, T., & Ogata, T. (2012). Macro structure and basic methods in the integrated narrative generation system by introducing narratological knowledge. In *Proceedings of the 11th IEEE International Conference on Cognitive Informatics & Cognitive Computing*, Kyoto, Japan, 22–24 August. IEEE, pp. 253–262. Available at: https://ieeexplore.ieee.org/document/6331482 (Accessed: 2 September 2025).

Akimoto, T., & Ogata, T. (2014). An information design of narratology: The use of three literary theories in a narrative generation system. *International Journal of Visual Design, 7*(3), pp. 31–61. Available at: https://www.researchgate.net/publication/317920470 (Accessed: 2 September 2025).

Anshari, M., Syafrudin, M., Fitriyani, N. L., & Razzaq, A. (2022). Ethical responsibility and sustainability (ERS) development in a metaverse business model. *Sustainability, 14*(15), 15805. https://doi.org/10.3390/su142315805

Bailenson, J. (2018). *Experience on demand: What virtual reality is, how it works, and what it can do*. W. W. Norton.

Baranowski, T., & Lyons, E. J. (2020). Scoping review of Pokémon Go: Comprehensive assessment of augmented reality for physical activity change. *Games for Health Journal, 9*(2), 71–84.

Baykal, G. E., Alaca, I. V., Yantaç, A. E., & Göksun, T. (2018). A review on complementary natures of tangible user interfaces (TUIs) and early spatial learning. *International Journal of Child-Computer Interaction, 16*, 104–113. https://doi.org/10.1016/j.ijcci.2018.01.003

Chaurasia, H. K., & Majhi, M. (2022). Sound design for cinematic virtual reality: A state-of-the-art review. In *International Conference of the Indian Society of Ergonomics* (pp. 357–368). Cham: Springer. https://doi.org/10.1007/978-3-030-94277-9_31

Chia, A., Keogh, B., Leorke, D., & Nicoll, B. (2020). Platformisation in game development. *Internet Policy Review, 9*(4), 1–28. https://doi.org/10.14763/2020.4.1515

Daneshfar, F., & Jamshidi, M. B. (2023). An octonion-based nonlinear echo state network for speech emotion recognition in the metaverse. *Neural Networks, 163*, 108–121. https://doi.org/10.1016/j.neunet.2023.03.026

Egliston, B., & Carter, M. (2022). Oculus imaginaries: The promises and perils of Facebook's virtual reality. *New Media & Society, 24*, 70–89. https://doi.org/10.1177/1461444820960411

Freedman, E. (2020). *The persistence of code in game engine culture*. Routledge.

Gartner. (2022). Predicts 2022: 4 technology bets for building the digital future. https://www.gartner.com/en/documents/4009206

Gregory, J. (2018). *Game engine architecture*. 3rd edn. A K Peters/CRC Press. Available at: https://doi.org/10.1201/9781315267845 (Accessed: 2 September 2025).

Greengard, S. (2019). *Virtual reality*. The MIT Press.

Han, J., Liu, G., & Gao, Y. (2023). Learners in the metaverse: A systematic review on the use of Roblox in learning. *Education Sciences, 13*(3), 296.

Kim, Y., & Kim, B. (2024). How do the news media, academia, and the public view the metaverse? Evidence from South Korea. *Technological Forecasting and Social Change, 198*, 122980.

Koohang, A., Nord, J. H., Ooi, K. B., Tan, G. W. H., Al-Emran, M., Aw, E. C. X., Baabdullah, A. M., Buhalis, D., Cham, T. H., Dennis, C., & Dutot, V. (2023). Shaping the metaverse into reality: A holistic multidisciplinary understanding of opportunities, challenges, and avenues for future investigation. *Journal of Computer Information Systems, 63*(3), 735–765.

Kretzer, A. (2021). Beyond the haze of carnival candles: Cinematic space in architectural design education. In *Handbook of research on methodologies for design and production practices in interior architecture* (pp. 21–43). IGI Global. https://doi.org/10.4018/978-1-7998-7254-2.ch002

Knox, J. (2022). The metaverse, or the serious business of tech frontiers. *Postdigital Science and Education, 4*, 207–215. https://doi.org/10.1007/s42438-022-00300-9

Kshetri, N. (2023). Metaverse technologies in product management, branding, and communications: Virtual and augmented reality, artificial intelligence, non-fungible tokens, and brain-computer interface. *Central European Management Journal, 31*, 511–521.

Lanier, J. (2017). *Dawn of the new everything: Encounters with reality and virtual reality*. Macmillan.

Lin, J., Wang, C., Zhou, L., & Jiang, X. (2022). Converting consumer-generated content into an innovation resource: A user ideas processing framework in online user innovation communities. *Technological Forecasting and Social Change, 174*, 121266.

Morschheuser, B., Riar, M., Hamari, J., & Maeche, A. (2017). How games induce cooperation? A study on the relationship between game features and we-intentions in an augmented reality game. *Computers in Human Behavior, 77*, 169–183.

Pulver, Y., Merz, C., Koebel, K., Scheidegger, J., & Cöltekin, A. (2020). Telling engaging interactive stories with extended reality (XR): Back to 1930s in Zurich's main train station. *ISPRS Annals of Photogrammetry, Remote Sensing & Spatial Information Sciences, 5*(4). https://doi.org/10.5194/isprs-annals-V-4-2020-171-2020

Rakic, S., Medic, N., Leoste, J., Vuckovic, T., & Marjanovic, U. (2023). Development and future trends of digital product-service systems: A bibliometric analysis approach. *Applied Systems Innovation, 6*, 89.

Hollensen, S., Kotler, P., & Opresnik, M. O. (2022). Metaverse: The new marketing universe. *Journal of Business Strategy*. https://doi.org/10.1108/JBS-01-2022-0014

Scavarelli, A., Arya, A., & Teather, R. J. (2021). Virtual reality and augmented reality in social learning spaces: a literature review. *Virtual reality, 25*(1), 257–277. https://doi.org/10.1007/s10055-020-00444-8

Singh, M., Fuenmayor, E., Hinchy, E., Qiao, Y., Murray, N., & Devine, D. (2021). Digital twin: Origin to future. *Applied Systems Innovation, 4*, 36.

Tan, L., & Zhang, H. (2021). An approach to user knowledge acquisition in product design. *Advances in Engineering Information, 50*, 101408.

Trisno, R., Wibisono, A. Y., Lianto, F., & Sularko, V. U. (2022). The narration layer of Fatahillah Museum based on narratology model analysis. *International Journal on Advanced Science, Engineering and Information Technology, 12*(2), 2088–5334.

Wang, Y., Su, Z., Zhang, N., Xing, R., Liu, D., Luan, T. H., & Shen, X. (2023). A survey on metaverse: Fundamentals, security, and privacy. *IEEE Communications Surveys & Tutorials, 25*, 319–352.

Whang, J.-B., Chang, W., & Lee, J.-H. (2023). Interactive and synergistic relationships among different types of innovations. *Journal of Retailing and Consumer Services, 74*, 103422.

Zhuang, W., Zeng, Q., Zhang, Y., Liu, C., & Fan, W. (2023). What makes user-generated content more helpful on social media platforms? Insights from the creator interactivity perspective. *Information Processing & Management, 60*, 103201.

Section II

Games Technology and Immersive Experiences in Action

5

Augmented Reality Storytelling: Re-Living the 1821 Kedah-Siam War at Kota Kuala Kedah

Noradila Nordin, Husniza Husni, Fakhrul Anuar Aziz, and Azizi Ab Aziz

5.1 Introduction

Cultural heritage is a legacy of traces of the past that is important to see the social-cultural conditions of the past society, the strengthening of the nation's history in understanding the identity and wealth of the nation, as a trace of knowing the migration of the past, and a trace of the geographical change of a region. UNESCO defines cultural heritage as artefacts, monuments, groups of buildings and sites, and museums that possess a diversity of values, including symbolic, historic, artistic, aesthetic, ethnological, anthropological, scientific, and social significance (UNESCO Institute of Statistics, 2009). Malaysia is one of the countries in Southeast Asia with a rich and diverse history, marked by complex interactions with various cultures and colonial powers, which have resulted in a diverse array of cultural heritage sites. However, many of the cultural heritage sites lack formal historical documentation, and thus, they lack understanding and appreciation of the region's cultural and historical legacy. Cultural heritage is also emerging as a key element that can stimulate the national tourism industry.

Kota Kuala Kedah in Malaysia, also known as Kuala Kedah Fort, is one of the cultural heritage sites that holds historical and cultural significance, particularly in relation to the history of Kedah and its interactions with Siam, now known as Thailand. At Kota Kuala Kedah, a significant event in the history of the state of Kedah occurred, where a Siamese attack took place, leading to a series of important events in the formation of modern Kedah. The Kacapuri Gateway, one of the gateways that was built on the eastern wall, holds historical significance in relation to the Kedah-Siam War as part of the fort's defensive structure and stands as a historical symbol of Kedah's resistance against foreign invasion. The fort was gazetted by the Department of

DOI: 10.1201/9781003662433-7

Museums and Antiquities, currently known as the Department of Museums Malaysia, on 31 August 1978 as a historic site under the Antiquities Act 1976, Act 165. In November 2000, the Department of Museums and Antiquities carried out conservation work on the eastern and southern walls, including the reconstruction of the Kacapuri Gateway, which had collapsed in 1970. Despite the presence of ancient artefacts and building remains at the fort, the exhibition remains static and lacks interactivity, limiting its appeal to younger generations. Museums continuously innovate methods and tools for knowledge communication and dissemination. Storytelling and interactive exhibitions are among the most common approaches used to enhance visitor engagement, allowing interaction with artefacts and objects. Digital technologies, particularly augmented reality (AR), offer an effective means of creating interactive content. When integrated into museum exhibitions, AR supports both storytelling and visitor interaction (Spadoni et al., 2022).

The motivation for this research stems from the fact that not all historical events are included in school curricula. This raises the question of how such histories can be communicated to the public, regardless of age, in a relaxed, engaging and unconventional manner beyond traditional reading materials. Furthermore, the Kota Kuala Kedah fort is the actual site where the 1821 conflict unfolded. By visiting the location and viewing the remains in conjunction with AR-driven video storytelling, visitors are provided with a more impactful and immersive means of learning about the history, enhancing both understanding and retention.

This chapter proposes the application of AR technology to transform static historical displays at the Kota Kuala Kedah Museum into immersive storytelling experiences. The current exhibition, which primarily consists of physical artefacts and site remains, lacks interactivity and narrative depth. While these displays may appeal to historians or those already familiar with the 1821 Kedah–Siam War, they often fail to engage wider audiences, particularly younger visitors with limited historical knowledge. The absence of contextual storytelling limits the exhibition's ability to convey the significance of the events that took place at the site. To address this, the proposed approach leverages AR technology through readily accessible platforms such as smartphones and mobile devices. Historical narratives are embedded in the environment through video-based storytelling, with the aim of increasing visitor engagement and fostering a deeper understanding of the war through immersive, location-specific experiences.

AR technology enables real-time overlays of computer-generated content, such as graphics, animations, and videos, onto the real-world environment. By integrating AR, additional historical information about the Kedah-Siam War can be presented without altering the physical displays at Kota Kuala Kedah. The work aims to educate and attract the general public, particularly the younger generation, to understand and appreciate the historical event of the Kedah-Siam War through the use of AR technology. This enhances visitor engagement by allowing them to explore, interact with real-world objects, and gain knowledge in an immersive and informative manner. By integrating AR to preserve and present historical narratives and artefacts through storytelling, this initiative aims to transform the appreciation of the region's cultural and historical legacy into a more engaging and immersive experience. The widespread use of mobile devices presents an opportunity for seamless integration of AR applications in museums. Visitors can use their smartphones as interactive screens, turning the surrounding space into a dynamic stage for historical storytelling (Banfi et al., 2023; Fanini et al., 2023). AR not only enriches the available information but also provides an engaging way to visualise and experience key historical events, making the visit more interactive and educational (Banfi et al., 2023; Prihandini et al., 2023).

5.2 Immersive Storytelling and AR in Cultural Heritage

A museum is a building where historical, scientific, artistic, or cultural objects are stored and exhibited. The development of museums aims to preserve regional culture, ensuring that it is well documented and can be studied by future generations. Traditionally, museums have displayed replicas or original objects. However, this concept requires further innovation. In some cases, visitors may not always have the opportunity to view the objects in person. Therefore, museums must integrate technology, such as AR, to enhance the experience. Digital technologies can bridge the gap between artefacts and the contexts in which they were found, creating immersive experiences. Furthermore, these technologies enhance interaction between visitors and museum artefacts, making the exhibits feel 'alive' and virtually interactive (Cesário & Campos, 2024). AR can be effectively integrated into museum exhibitions to enhance both storytelling and interaction. As hybrid realities become more familiar, AR is increasingly accessible for public events and cultural heritage applications. AR can present information in both 3D and 2D forms, including text, audio, and gamification elements (Prihandini et al., 2023). Numerous examples demonstrate the use of this technology in museum exhibitions (Spadoni et al., 2022).

Storytelling in museum exhibitions captivates visitors and shapes their understanding of historical events. Digital storytelling enhances this experience by allowing visitors to engage with characters' experiences through personalised narratives that integrate personal accounts with historical events. Museums preserve historical artefacts by passing down stories, and visitors expect these narratives to be presented in unique, era-appropriate ways. Through digital media, such as video, audio, and images, digital storytelling immerses visitors in historical events, transforming the traditional museum experience into a dynamic and interactive journey. In this context, the historical event itself serves as the story, while the video acts as the medium to bring it to life. Narrative structure, creativity, and multimedia are key components that contribute to the effective recreation of historical events, offering innovative ways to convey the past (Hutson & Hutson, 2024).

A storytelling approach fosters deeper understanding across cultural and historical divides. Museums aim to bridge these gaps by bringing past epochs, civilisations, and events to life, making them more tangible and relatable. Digital representation enhances this process through virtual reality, AR, interactive exhibits, and mobile applications, transforming the traditional museum visit into a more accessible and engaging experience. With technological advancements, storytelling has evolved from print and cinema to television, smartphones, and public displays. Social media platforms such as Twitter, Instagram, and TikTok enable real-time storytelling, contributing to the rise of immersive experiences and promoting inclusivity in cultural heritage. Museums have incorporated gaming elements and structured narratives to foster emotional connections with visitors, positioning audiences at the centre of cultural narratives. The integration of AR with storytelling further intertwines the narrative and the audience, creating immersive and memorable experiences (Cesário & Campos, 2024).

There have been numerous AR experiences across various museum projects and exhibitions worldwide, some of which are temporary. For example, the Design Museum in London features an AR experience as part of the 'The World of Tim Burton' exhibition, running from 25 October 2024 to 26 May 2025 (The Design Museum, n.d.). Studies by Fanini et al. (2023) and Spadoni et al. (2022) listed many other temporary AR experiences in museums worldwide, including those in Miami, Ontario, London, and Singapore. Permanent exhibitions, such as those at the Muséum National d'Histoire Naturelle in Paris, enable visitors to encounter extinct animals brought back to life through AR. This AR experience brings extinct or endangered animal species back to life (Muséum National d'Histoire Naturelle, n.d.).

In Singapore, the AR City offers an immersive way to explore the city through location-based AR experiences in Google Maps. Visitors can discover iconic landmarks and hidden gems across various areas, including the Civic District, Chinatown, Orchard Road, and Sentosa. Whether onsite in Singapore or anywhere in the world, users can launch AR experiences by scanning their surroundings or viewing them on Street View in Google Maps (Visit Singapore, n.d.). Previously, an app called the Visit Singapore Travel Guide app was used, but it has since been removed.

The National Museum of Malaysia offers the Muzium Negara AR application, allowing visitors to access information on 28 selected collections in 2D and 3D AR. However, this AR experience is only available to visitors at the National Museum, who must download the app before or during their visit and scan the provided QR code to access the experience (Muzium Negara, n.d.). At Casa Batlló in Barcelona, an AR guide enhances the visitor experience by offering a dynamic, semi-immersive journey. The guide leads visitors through a narrative exploration of the space's original appearance,

Gaudí's childhood, and his sources of inspiration. The SmartGuide has been integrated into the tour since 2013, offering AR to enhance understanding of Gaudí's genius (Casa Batlló, n.d.). These examples demonstrate the growing interest in using AR within the cultural heritage sector and highlight the potential impact of augmented and mixed reality applications on enhancing the attractiveness of museums.

5.3 Designing and Evaluating an Immersive AR Heritage Experience

This study focuses on two important parts. The first is the development of an AR application using the Agile development approach (Jacobson et al., 1999), which allows for continuous iteration throughout the work process, as illustrated in Figure 5.1. This includes (i) planning and designing the required content, (ii) developing and implementing the application using AR technology, and (iii) testing the application to ensure the content and AR function are as intended. The second part of this study is to evaluate the impact of digitising cultural heritage, using the Short User Experience Questionnaire (UEQ-S) as the evaluation instrument.

5.3.1 Plan and Design of AR Content

In describing the Kedah-Siam War of 1821, short videos with narration were chosen as the primary content for the AR experience. One key reason is that re-enacting the event is more effective in engaging the public and helping them learn about history, rather than relying on imagination. This approach, which the project seeks to explore in terms of its impact on visitors, is supported by recent films such as Mat Kilau: Awakening of Heroes (Yusof et al., 2022) and Warrior Awang and Master Tok Gajah (Shukor et al., 2024). Visual

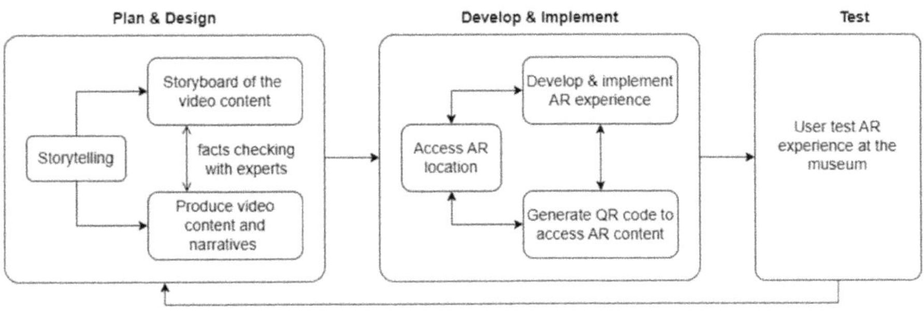

FIGURE 5.1
The project process.

perception through videos, complemented by narration, helps visitors understand the historical event. This is further supported by Mayer's Cognitive Theory of Multimedia Learning, which emphasises the value of short videos in museums in enhancing the visitor experience, evoking emotions, and fostering deeper connections with the content (Mayer, 2024; Aziz et al., 2024).

5.3.2 Develop and Implement AR Experience

AR Storytelling: Kedah-Siam War 1821 is a location-based and web-based interactive application designed for mobile accessibility. It is developed using HTML, CSS, JavaScript, Photoshop, and WebAR tools, where QR codes are used to redirect users to specific URLs to engage with AR content. The QR code is one of the most straightforward and efficient technologies, considering public access and readiness to use it. The museum's location at Kota Kuala Kedah, featuring outdoor artefacts, further enhances accessibility, requiring minimal learning effort for users. The QR codes serve as AR markers positioned at six key locations, each selected for its historical significance and proximity to key events or artefacts. These locations include the Kota Kuala Kedah Museum, the original wall, the Kacapuri Gateway, the British Gateway, the Badak Berendam Cannon, and the Katak Puru Cannon. QR codes providing access to the AR application are available at the museum, enabling visitors to explore and gain insights into the historical events presented. At Kota Kuala Kedah, each QR code is printed on aluminium composite signboards, positioned at the six historical sites shown in Figure 5.2, to provide durable, weather-resistant access points for visitors. These strategically placed signboards ensure that historical narratives remain accessible and engaging, enhancing visitors' experience with the site's rich heritage.

FIGURE 5.2
Locations of the signboards that consist of QR codes to access the AR content at different locations in Kota Kuala Kedah.

FIGURE 5.3
Online map representing the locations of signboards with QR codes to access AR content at various locations in Kota Kuala Kedah.

To ensure broad accessibility, a web-based version has been developed, enabling both local and international audiences to engage with the content remotely. While all versions consistently utilise QR codes for access, the website also provides an option to view the content without AR components. Additionally, an online map version of AR Storytelling: Kedah-Siam War 1821 is available through the website, as shown in Figure 5.3. This version includes brief information about Kota Kuala Kedah and the 1821 Kedah-Siam War, along with a map featuring six QR codes linked to AR materials. The online map serves two key functions: at the museum, it acts as a guide directing visitors to AR locations, while remotely, it allows users to access the AR content from anywhere, ensuring engagement beyond the physical site.

At each of the QR codes that redirect to the specific AR materials in the form of video, as shown in Figure 5.4, there are two versions available by tapping on the Malaysia flag or the Union Jack to choose the narration in Malay or English. The video as AR content will be displayed accordingly. The video's location can be rearranged by simply tapping the screen, allowing the user to move to the next location while watching. This was to ensure that if the visitor is there, they have covered the entire area of the Kota Kuala Kedah Museum grounds, visiting all the main spots or sites that make up the whole history of Kota Kuala Kedah and the remaining artefacts.

5.3.3 Data Collection and Analysis

The project evaluated the impact of AR technology using the UEQ-S, which was conducted during the Semarak @ Muzium Kota Kuala Kedah programme,

FIGURE 5.4
An example of AR content in the form of a video when the QR code is scanned at a specific location in Kota Kuala Kedah.

organised by the Department of Museums Malaysia, on 14–15 October 2023. The primary objectives were to assess the AR application's effectiveness in attracting visitors, raising awareness of the historical event, and enhancing the museum's offerings. Visitors accessed the AR content through QR codes placed throughout the museum, allowing them to engage with the historical narrative interactively. The initiative aimed to educate the public, increase awareness of the region's history, and foster a sense of identity and patriotism, particularly among younger generations. To evaluate the effectiveness of the AR application, the UEQ-S was employed to measure its impact on knowledge enhancement and its role as an effective information channel. A random sample of 159 visitors participated in the study, accessing the AR content via their own mobile devices or those provided at the museum. Participants completed the UEQ-S after their visit, reflecting on their experiences. To support this initiative, the Kota Kuala Kedah Museum provided open Internet access for visitors using the AR application. The collected data was analysed using the UEQ-S

Data Analysis Tool (Schrepp et al., 2017), and the findings were shared with the museum to inform future improvements, particularly in AR integration. This initiative demonstrates the potential of AR technology to attract visitors by offering an immersive and engaging experience that deepens their connection to the historical events of Kota Kuala Kedah.

5.4 Immersive Impact: Visitor Responses to AR Storytelling

UEQ-S assesses two key aspects of quality: pragmatic and hedonic. It consists of eight items measured on a 7-point Likert scale. Pragmatic quality focuses on usability-related aspects, including hindrance-supportive, complicated-easy, inefficient-efficient, and confusing-clear. Hedonic quality evaluates aesthetics, engagement, and innovation, encompassing boring to engaging, unattractive to attractive, conventional to innovative, and usual to leading-edge. All item scores are rescaled to a range from −3 (most negative) to 3 (most positive) to ensure consistency in interpretation.

The results in Figure 5.5 indicate a positive impact on visitors, with measurement scales showing a pragmatic quality score of 1.210, suggesting good usability, a hedonic quality score of 1.535, reflecting an engaging and innovative experience, and an overall quality mean value of 1.372. In the UEQ-S assessment, scores above 0.8 indicate a positive experience based on the eight measured items. These findings were derived from the responses of 159 participants, whose feedback was successfully collected and analysed.

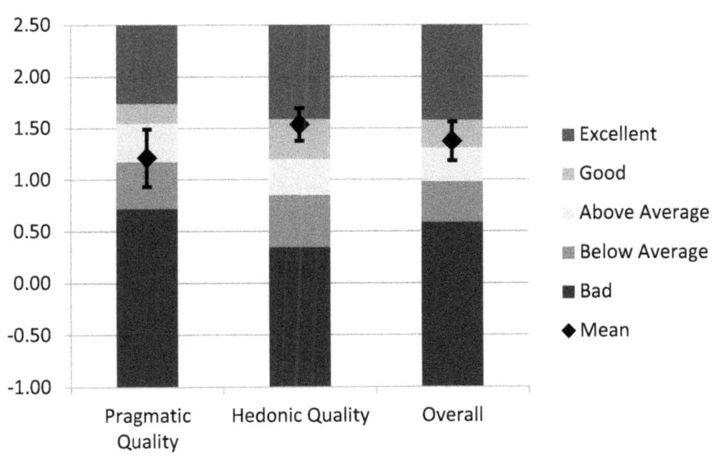

FIGURE 5.5
UEQ-S benchmark results.

The mean and standard deviation (SD) values for each item are presented in Figure 5.6. The mean scores suggest that respondents generally held positive perceptions across all items, with all scores exceeding 5.00 on the 1–7 scale. The highest rated item was obstructive-supportive, with a mean value of 5.55 (SD 1.50), indicating that respondents found the AR application to be more supportive than obstructive. The SD of 1.50 suggests some variation in responses, but the overall sentiment remained positive. Another notable item, which was conventional-inventive, received a mean value of 5.40 (SD 1.23), indicating that respondents viewed the system as leaning towards the inventive rather than the conventional. The relatively low SD indicates a high level of agreement among respondents on this item. The item of interest (not interesting-interesting) scored a mean of 5.35 (SD 1.35), showing moderate variation in responses, with most finding the AR application interesting. This project contributes to inclusive and quality education by providing accessible historical war information through AR, available to anyone with a smartphone by simply scanning QR codes placed around the museum. It supports lifelong learning, enabling visitors of all ages to appreciate one of the significant historical events in the Malay world. The use of AR technology promotes the museum's sustainability, acting as a catalyst for preserving Malaysia's cultural and historical heritage while fostering patriotism, noble values, and national identity. The majority of visitors expressed excitement about the AR application, finding it provided a more engaging and interactive experience compared to merely exploring Kota Kuala Kedah without knowing the stories and historical context behind the artefacts.

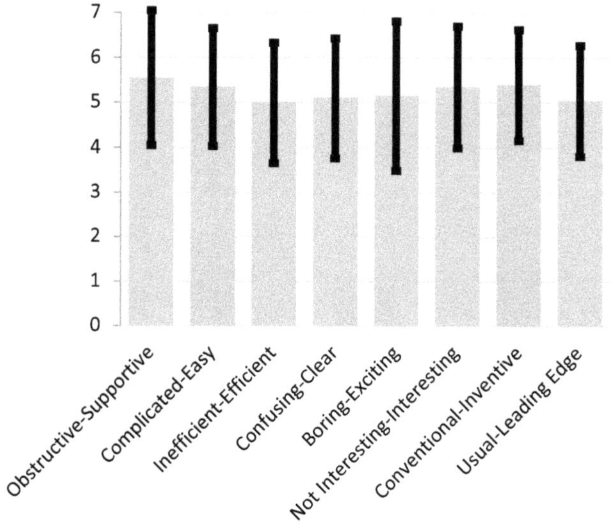

FIGURE 5.6
Items mean and SD values.

The lowest-rated item was inefficient, with a mean value of 5.00 (SD 1.34), suggesting that efficiency was perceived as slightly lower than other aspects. Although still leaning towards efficiency, this result suggests that there may be opportunities to enhance the system's operational efficiency. The item 'confusing-clear' scored a mean value of 5.10 (SD 1.33), suggesting that the clarity of the content and AR application could be further improved. The item with the leading edge, having a mean value of 5.05 (SD 1.23), was one of the lower-rated items, indicating that the innovation of the AR experience did not strongly stand out as a leading-edge feature. The project's primary challenges focused on identifying the most effective methods to implement AR technology within the museum environment, which features large-scale outdoor artefacts, such as those at Kota Kuala Kedah. Additionally, the AR system needed to be user-friendly and accessible to anyone with a smartphone and data connection. To address these concerns, the simplest and most stable form of AR, scanning QR codes, was selected. These QR codes are displayed on signage, designed to withstand the weather conditions in Kota Kuala Kedah, which is located near the mouth of the Kedah River.

There was variation in responses for the item 'boring-excited,' with an SD of 1.66, indicating that respondents had mixed opinions about the level of engagement with the AR application. While some found the experience exciting, others felt it was less engaging. The project progressed smoothly during its implementation, including the development of AR technology and the installation of AR signage around Kota Kuala Kedah. However, several challenges arose during the AR content development phase, particularly in depicting key historical events. These challenges were influenced by factors such as time constraints and weather conditions. Organising filming sessions with professional martial artists and other participants was difficult due to their individual careers and commitments. Moreover, unpredictable weather disrupted the filming and editing processes; sessions had to be conducted in half-day intervals, and some were postponed due to heavy rain, resulting in logistical difficulties, such as limited provisions beyond the initial two days of filming.

Furthermore, considering that this AR project requires smartphones and QR codes, visitors from outside Kedah who cannot physically visit Kota Kuala Kedah Museum can still experience the AR content and appreciate one of the significant war stories of the Malay world. By creating mock exhibitions in other museums across Malaysia, QR codes can be displayed to offer access to the AR application for the Kedah-Siam War 1821, enabling visitors to engage with the content remotely. However, it is important to note that the immersive experience of being physically present at the historical sites differs from experiencing the story virtually.

The use of AR through QR codes provides visitors with a more engaging and interactive experience. This AR project has the potential to be expanded to cover other key aspects of Malaysian history, not just the Kedah-Siam War. Given that the QR codes around the museum are expected to remain active for one year (from 2023 to 2024), they can serve as a tool to draw attention to ongoing museum activities that encourage lifelong learning. This initiative enables visitors of all ages to engage with and learn about the historical events that occurred in Kota Kuala Kedah. It is therefore recommended that additional programmes related to Malaysian history be held at Kota Kuala Kedah Museum to further enhance this AR project and attract broader participation.

5.5 Reimagining Cultural Heritage through AR and Immersive Interaction

Cultural heritage represents a valuable legacy that reflects the social, cultural, and historical conditions, providing insight into a nation's history. To ensure the continued relevance and engagement of museums, it is essential to integrate modern technologies such as AR. By bridging the gap between physical artefacts and their historical contexts, AR creates immersive experiences that enhance the visitor's understanding. Digital storytelling, through short videos, transforms traditional museum exhibits into dynamic and interactive journeys. In this way, historical events become the story, with AR serving as the medium to bring them to life. This chapter evaluates the integration of AR technology to transform static museum displays into immersive storytelling experiences, offering a novel way to engage visitors through widely accessible mobile devices. By overlaying digital content, such as graphics, animations, and videos, onto real-world environments, AR enriches historical narratives without altering the physical exhibits. This technology enhances visitor engagement, offering an interactive and educational approach to understanding the 1821 Kedah-Siam War, particularly appealing to younger audiences.

The study's findings indicate a positive impact on the visitor experience, with pragmatic quality demonstrating good usability and hedonic quality reflecting an engaging and innovative experience. The overall quality scores further support the effectiveness of AR in enriching museum experiences. Respondents rated the AR application highly, with the highest-rated item, 'obstructive-supportive,' indicating that visitors found AR to be more supportive than obstructive. The system was also perceived as inventive and interesting. These findings highlight AR's potential to revitalise cultural heritage interpretation. By turning smartphones into interactive storytelling tools, AR transforms museums into dynamic spaces where visitors actively engage with history rather than passively observing exhibits. This approach not only enhances learning but also fosters a deeper appreciation of historical events, making heritage sites more accessible and compelling.

Acknowledgement

This research was supported by the University for the Creative Arts Knowledge Exchange Fund (2023) and the UNESCO MNCU Contribution Grant (S/O code: P-58/666, 2023).

References

Aziz, F. A., Husni, H., Nordin, N., Suhairy, M. S., Siambaton, M. Z. & Ahmad, J. (2024). Augmented reality and short videos: transforming museum experiences for visitors. *Asian Journal of Applied Communication, 13*(2), 87–92. https://doi.org/10.47836/ajac.13.02.04

Banfi, F., Pontisso, M., Paolillo, F. R., Roascio, S., Spallino, C., & Stanga, C. (2023). Interactive and immersive digital representation for virtual museum: VR and AR for semantic enrichment of Museo Nazionale Romano, Antiquarium di Lucrezia Romana and Antiquarium di Villa Dei Quintili. *ISPRS International Journal of Geo-Information, 12*(2), 28. https://doi.org/10.3390/ijgi12020028

Casa Batlló. (n.d.). https://www.casabatllo.es/en/experience, last accessed 21 March 2025.

Cesário, V., & Campos, P. (2024). The integrated museum engagement model (IMEM): Bridging participatory design, immersive storytelling, and digital representation for enhanced museum experiences. *The International Journal of the Inclusive Museum, 17*(1), 63. https://doi.org/10.18848/1835-2014/CGP/v17i01/63-81

Fanini, B., Pagano, A., Pietroni, E., Ferdani, D., Demetrescu, E., & Palombini, A. (2023). Augmented reality for cultural heritage. In *Springer Handbook of Augmented Reality*, 391–411. Cham: Springer International Publishing. https://doi.org/10.1007/978-3-030-67822-7_16

Hutson, J., & Hutson, P. (2024). Storytelling. In *Inclusive Smart Museums*. Cham: Palgrave Macmillan. https://doi.org/10.1007/978-3-031-43615-4

Jacobson, I., Booch, G., & Rumbaugh, J. (1999). *The Unified Software Development Process*. Boston, MA: Addison Wesley Professional.

Mayer, R. E. (2024). The past, present, and future of the cognitive theory of multimedia learning. *Educational Psychology Review, 36*(1), 8. https://doi.org/10.1007/s10648-023-09842-1

Muséum National d'Histoire Naturelle. (n.d.). https://www.mnhn.fr/en/experience/revivre-extinct-animals-in-augmented-reality, last accessed 2025/3/20.

Muzium Negara. (n.d.). https://www.muziumnegara.gov.my/en/guided-tours-and-ar, last accessed 2025/3/25.

Prihandini, T. F., Triyono, M. B., Priyanto. (2023). A bibliometric analysis examining the adoption of augmented reality in tourism research. *International Journal of Interactive Mobile Technologies (iJIM), 17*(15), 135–154. https://doi.org/10.3991/ijim.v17i15.40171

Schrepp, M., Hinderks, A., & Thomaschewski, J. (2017). Design and evaluation of a short version of the user experience questionnaire (UEQ-S). *International Journal of Interactive Multimedia and Artificial Intelligence, 4*(6), 103–108. https://doi.org/10.9781/ijimai.2017.09.001

Shukor, S. R. (Director), Dali, S. (Producer), & Dali, A. R. (Producer). (2024). Warrior Awang and Master Tok Gajah [Film]. Studio Kembara.

Spadoni, E., Porro, S., Bordegoni, M., Arosio, I., Barbalini, L., & Carulli, M. (2022). Augmented reality to engage visitors of science museums through interactive experiences. *Heritage, 5*(3), 1370–1394. https://doi.org/10.3390/heritage5030071

The Design Museum. (n.d.). https://designmuseum.org/exhibitions/the-world-of-tim-burton, last accessed 2025/3/20.

UNESCO Institute for Statistics. (2009). *UNESCO Framework for Cultural Statistics.* https://unesdoc.unesco.org/ark:/48223/pf0000191061

Visit Singapore. (n.d.). https://www.visitsingapore.com/travel-tips/travelling-to-singapore/singapore-ar-experience, last accessed 2025/3/20.

Yusof, S. (Director), Dali, S (Producer), & Dali, A. R. (Producer). (2022). Mat Kilau: Awakening of Heroes [Film]. Studio Kembara & Skop Productions Sdn Bhd.

6

Virtual Reality and Environmental Innovation in Japan's Smart Cities: Illuminating the Path to Sustainability

Siti Azreena Mubin, Tan Chin Ike, Muhammad Nur Affendy Nor'a, and Yong Jie Wong

6.1 Introduction

Japan is renowned for its technological advancements and environmentally friendly stance, which makes it a leader in smart city concepts. The most promising innovation in this area is the integration of virtual reality (VR) technologies to enhance environmental initiatives. VR offers new and unique ways of viewing and interacting with the urban environment, making it a valuable tool in planning, managing, and experiencing urban environments. Thus, the smart cities in Japan that utilise VR are not only addressing current environmental issues but also preparing for the future (University of Tokyo, 2023).

The use of VR in environmental initiatives for smart cities is one piece of evidence of Japan's advanced thinking on the concept of sustainable urban development. VR technologies enable city planners, policymakers, and residents to experience and influence the shape and form of the urban environment in a way that was previously impossible. From virtual walks through parks to simulations of disaster situations, VR provides valuable information that can be used to inform decisions supporting environmentally friendly actions. Additionally, partnerships among government, business, and academia are helping to develop and apply VR technologies most effectively.

6.2 Integrating VR in Environmental Initiatives within Smart Cities

The rise of smart cities represents a transformative shift in various domains, blending advanced technology with sustainable practices to address pressing

DOI: 10.1201/9781003662433-8

societal and environmental challenges. Japan, a global leader in innovation, has embraced the concept of smart cities to enhance urban living and address its unique demographic and environmental concerns. By offering immersive simulations and fostering public engagement, VR can revolutionise environmental management within Japan's smart cities, providing a blueprint for sustainable urban development.

In Japan, one notable study that began decades ago investigates the integration of VR simulation systems to support Light Rail Transit (LRT) projects, aiming to promote sustainable urban development. By integrating VR, the research enables a detailed examination and visualisation of various aspects, such as traffic, landscapes, and city planning, facilitating a better understanding and consensus among stakeholders (Kawaguchi et al., 2009). The VR system enables the simulation of LRT vehicle movements and urban environments, helping to address issues such as traffic congestion and environmental impact. This approach aligns with the goals of smart cities to leverage advanced technologies for improved urban management and sustainability, making it a valuable tool for planning and promoting sustainable city initiatives.

Another study in Kyoto, Japan, utilises virtual city models to assess the environmental equity of access to sunlight. By employing detailed virtual urban modelling, the study examines variations in sunlight exposure. The methodology involves creating a Digital Surface Model and calculating possible sunshine duration for residential buildings, highlighting the potential of VR to model complex environmental phenomena and support urban planning and design, which aligns with the goals of smart cities to leverage advanced technologies for improved urban management and sustainability (Yasumoto et al., 2012). In the realm of education, a study explores the use of VR in a STEM project focused on renewable energy. The project involved designing and building a specialised aeroplane for wind energy, highlighting the advantages of VR in providing a flexible and immersive learning environment without the constraints of space and time (Barry et al., 2017). The VR setting allowed students to engage in engineering design processes and collaborate effectively. This integration of VR aligns with the goals of smart cities to leverage advanced technologies for improved urban management and sustainability (Barry et al., 2017).

Disaster management is another critical area where VR is making significant contributions in Japan. A study presents a VR visualisation of pre-recorded data from approximately 18,000 weather sensors across Japan, aimed at enhancing disaster management within smart cities. Utilising the HTC Vive and Unity engine, the visualisation allows users to explore sensor data in both global and local contexts, providing a "big picture" view while enabling detailed analysis of individual sensors (Ready et al., 2018). This innovative approach demonstrates how VR can be integrated into environmental initiatives, offering an immersive and interactive method for managing and interpreting large-scale environmental data, thereby supporting smart city objectives of improved urban resilience and disaster preparedness (Ready et al., 2018).

Urban design also benefits from the integration of VR. A study examines the use of VR integrated with an automatic presentation script (APS) to enhance the understanding of urban design concepts in the Tatsumi region of Tokyo Bay, Japan. This approach aims to enhance user interaction and information exchange between designers and users, thereby facilitating a better understanding of sustainable urban design schemes (Zhang et al., 2020). By creating a virtual environment and utilising APS to guide users through design concepts, the study demonstrates how VR can effectively communicate urban planning ideas and enhance public engagement in smart city initiatives (Zhang et al., 2020).

Landscape perception is another area where VR integration proves valuable, as evidenced by a study that investigates the use of VR to assess landscape perception. The study compares on-site surveys with VR simulations to evaluate aesthetic preferences and landscape cognition in Tsuchiura and Tsukuba cities, Japan. The findings indicate that VR can effectively replicate real-world experiences, making it a reliable tool for landscape assessment (Shi et al., 2020). The research highlights that "immersive VR is a reliable tool for assessing landscape cognition" and can substitute on-site surveys, offering a cost-effective and efficient alternative (Shi et al., 2020).

According to Wallace (2022), Japan's Ministry of Land, Infrastructure, Transport and Tourism is developing a digital twin (DT) of the entire country using open data 3D city models, known as Plateau, to enhance disaster simulations and urban planning. This initiative demonstrates how VR can create immersive environments that support smart city development, improve disaster preparedness, and optimise urban services, aligning with Japan's broader goals of technological innovation and sustainable urban growth.

In conclusion, the integration of VR in environmental initiatives within Japan's smart cities significantly enhances urban functionality and sustainability. By leveraging advanced technologies, Japan continues to lead in innovative urban management, setting a blueprint for sustainable urban development worldwide.

6.3 Virtual Tours of Urban Green Spaces and Natural Wonders

Immersive virtual tours are bringing Japan's urban green spaces, including Shinjuku Gyoen in Tokyo, Osaka Castle Park and Ueno Park, and its stunningly pristine natural wonders, Yakushima's ancient cedar forests, the UNESCO-listed Shiretoko Peninsula and the dramatic scenery of the Japanese Alps and the volcanic formations of Aso-Kuju National Park—closer than ever. People from all around the world can experience the multicultural landscapes and metropolitan cities through digital encounters, utilising state-of-the-art technologies such as 360-degree drone capturing, real-time GIS adjustments, LiDAR landscape terrain mapping, and AI-managed tour guides that speak different languages (Rupprecht et al., 2015).

These virtual excursions provide users with the potential to learn more dynamically about vital topics such as Japan's culture, biodiversity, climate adaptation processes, and the importance of green spaces. On the other hand, these digital experiences are also beneficial to both international and national tourists, as they serve as an introduction to the country's tourist attractions, enabling them to organise their trips effectively and serve as a marketing strategy to promote the country's less-exposed tourist attractions.

Besides that, through VR, some historical sites in Japan, such as Yakushima's Ancient Cedar Forest and the Shiretoko Peninsula's Biodiversity and Wildlife Protection, can offer a close-up look at the islands' subtropical rainforests and diverse wildlife, raising awareness about their delicate ecosystems. Rare flora and fauna can be tracked using digital conservation tools, such as virtual ecological monitoring, to assess the health of the forest (Gunarto, 2011).

On the other hand, as Japan's most famous landmark, Mt. Fuji draws millions of visitors annually, raising concerns about overtourism and environmental damage. Virtual climbing tours now allow people to explore the mountain's trails, summit views, and cultural sites, thereby easing pressure on the natural environment. These initiatives complement Japan's commitment to net-zero emissions by offering sustainable travel alternatives to traditional tourism (Jones et al., 2017).

Through these virtual tours, Japan's environmental sustainability efforts are promoted, making them accessible to a broader audience. By providing immersive experiences that reduce the carbon footprint of actual travel, especially in sensitive ecosystems, these activities can support the nation's commitment to sustainable tourism and its broader net-zero emissions targets (Soonthodu & Wahab, 2022).

6.4 Disaster Preparedness and Environmental Impact through VR Simulations in Smart Cities

The increasing rate of urbanisation has significantly impacted the physical and social landscapes of cities, resulting in more densely populated living places. Buildings are frequently constructed in proximity to maximise real estate. While growing urban centres are a great indicator of a nation's economic growth and focus on a knowledge-based economy, there is a pressing concern among emergency services that such urban centres may also pose significant challenges for disaster preparedness and response times. The high concentration of people living in such densely packed environments may complicate measures like evacuations during emergencies and disasters, making rescue and mitigation attempts logistically challenging.

To address these challenges, many urban cities around the world have implemented various methods to prepare and train their citizens for emergencies. Traditionally, disaster management has focused primarily on hazard mitigation practices by utilising physical systems, which involve using technology to enhance the resilience of structures to disasters (Prior & Roth, 2013; Yenidogan, 2021).

The use of VR technology can significantly support and even enhance disaster preparedness by providing a simulated, immersive, and interactive experience for disaster planners, first responders, and the general public (Zhu & Li, 2021). According to García et al. (2022), a VR system can be used to train occupants to detect cracks, fissures, or other pathologies in a house and relate them to potential risks. This technology can also be used to train emergency responders to observe for potential structural or environmental hazards during or after an emergency that can lead to further structural problems.

One such example is QuickAware, a VR tool that simulates a realistic environment for direct interaction with the causes of a quick clay landslide disaster (Alene et al., 2024). Not only that, but VR simulation technology is also more effective in disaster preparedness due to the retention of spatial working memory, which improves task completion time and provides feedback on errors in decision-making, compared to traditional disaster preparedness simulations (Alshowair et al., 2024). A VR-simulated environment can assist planners in evaluating crisis communication in a realistic simulation, providing insight into participants' decision-making during emergencies and enabling better planning without the associated costs and risks of injuries. When coupled with the concept of DT technology, VR can assist in the close-up and on-the-ground visualisation and interaction. DT technology is a method of creating a virtual representation or replica of a real-world system, object, and even entire environments. By creating a virtual replica of an urban environment, planners can simulate climatic conditions, traffic, people, and even simulated disasters (Ramu et al., 2022).

An example of such technology integration was carried out by Dembski et al. (2019), where a test application of a DT was implemented within a VR environment for the town of Herrenberg in Germany (population 30,000). The researchers chose the township for its high traffic and pollution, simulating much larger cities, which allowed them to test a series of scenarios with potential solutions. The VR component enables them to experience the impact from a ground-level perspective, rather than a bird's-eye view, which, in the long run, enhances democratic decision-making for planning smart, sustainable cities, as well as infrastructure development and design for disaster management and preparedness.

A study by Khanal et al. (2022) has shown that immersive technology is already being used extensively in computer simulation modelling, infrastructure assessment, and public awareness applications in disaster management. The value of immersive technologies, such as VR, extends beyond their technical applications. It can bring a positive impact and contribution to community participation and education. In addition to disaster preparedness, VR is an effective tool for analysing and mitigating environmental consequences in urban areas in the event of flooding and wildfires. In conclusion, VR simulations paired with DTs or other technologies provide a novel and inventive solution to solving the dual concerns of disaster preparedness and environmental sustainability in cities.

6.5 Collaboration and Innovations in VR Environmental Initiatives within Smart Cities

Smart cities in Japan are utilising VR to help address environmental issues and promote sustainability. These initiatives encompass not only technology but also collaboration among government agencies, tech companies, universities, and the public. This collaborative approach ensures that the VR applications are practical and widely adopted (Ryu & Lim, 2023). The collaboration between different sectors is one of the most critical factors in the success of VR-based environmental initiatives in Japan's smart cities. Government agencies provide the framework and funding, while tech companies provide the latest VR technology. Universities contribute through research and development, ensuring that applications are scientifically sound and effective. For instance, the EcoMOBILE initiative is a collaborative project between local governments, universities, and tech companies… This project uses VR to create immersive experiences that engage the public in environmental conservation and sustainable practices. By combining diverse expertise, EcoMOBILE has developed innovative solutions that are both engaging and educational (Regan, 2020).

VR is being utilised in various innovative ways to enhance environmental initiatives in Japan's smart cities. One of the most interesting applications is the production of virtual tours of urban green spaces and natural wonders. These tours enable residents and visitors to explore and appreciate how natural features are incorporated into the urban environment, thus encouraging support for conservation efforts and sustainable urban planning (Xiang et al., 2023). For example, in Tokyo, VR tours of urban parks have been created to showcase the city's green spaces. These tours offer an immersive experience in these areas. In Osaka, the VR biodiversity tours and ecological value of the waterfront emphasise the importance of preserving natural environments within the urban context (Deguchi, 2020). Figure 6.1 illustrates the eco-friendly urban development, an "Area Energy Management System

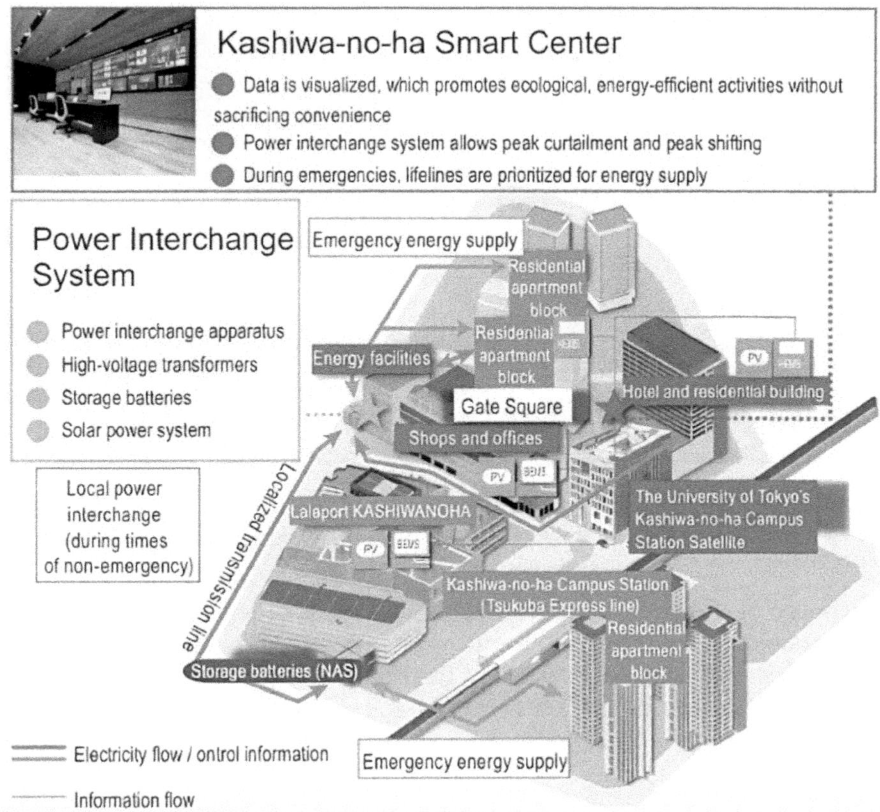

FIGURE 6.1
The AEMS was developed by Hitachi (Deguchi, 2020).

(AEMS)" introduced to manage energy supply in four zones around the stations developed by Hitachi (Deguchi, 2020).

Japan is a country that frequently experiences natural disasters, such as earthquakes and tsunamis. VR simulations are being utilised in smart cities to enhance disaster preparedness and better understand environmental impacts. These simulations offer valuable training and education on disaster response, as well as environmental consequences and the importance of sustainable practices. For instance, VR simulations have been developed to teach people how to evacuate during an earthquake. These simulations present realistic scenarios that teach people the do's and don'ts of staying safe during a disaster. Additionally, they highlight the environmental impacts of such events and emphasise the need for sustainable urban planning to mitigate these effects (University of Tokyo, 2023).

The success of the VR environmental initiatives in Japan's smart cities can also be attributed to the innovative approaches that different collaborative projects incorporate. One of these projects is a collaboration between the

FIGURE 6.2
Employee serves customer via a digital screen using avatars of their choice (University of Tokyo, 2023).

University of Tokyo and several tech companies aimed at developing VR applications for environmental education. This project has developed VR experiences that educate users about the importance of biodiversity and the impacts of climate change (University of Tokyo, 2023). Figure 6.2 shows one of the projects by the University of Tokyo.

6.6 The Future of VR in Sustainable Smart Cities

VR, with its immersive and interactive nature, presents new possibilities for addressing the challenges facing modern cities. This technology enables users to present their ideas in a more life-size and realistic way than the two-dimensional maps and models commonly used in planning. For example, VR can be used in planning to present to people how new buildings will impact traffic flow, air quality, and the quantity of green spaces. After analysing these simulations, the planners will be able to identify any potential issues and rectify them before any construction commences. It is a proactive approach to avoiding costly mistakes and ensuring that new developments are sustainable.

One of the most significant challenges of smart city initiatives is engaging residents in the urban planning process. The solution to this problem is found in VR because it makes the complex data and plans more easily understandable and accessible. Through the use of VR experiences, people can provide feedback on proposed developments based on their own experiences within the virtual environment. VR can be used to create virtual tours of new parks, public spaces and transportation systems. These tours enable residents to see the potential benefits of proposed projects and offer suggestions for how those benefits can be improved. This interactive form of engagement helps to create a sense of ownership and is an essential part of the decision-making process (IEEE Digital Reality, 2023). Figure 6.3 shows an example of a virtual walk experience in Osaka City. This project simulates a tourism planning support system and a web-based geographic information system (Web-GIS) (Koga & Yamamoto, 2023).

VR also provides a significant contribution to disaster preparedness and environmental impact assessments. In countries such as Japan, which are

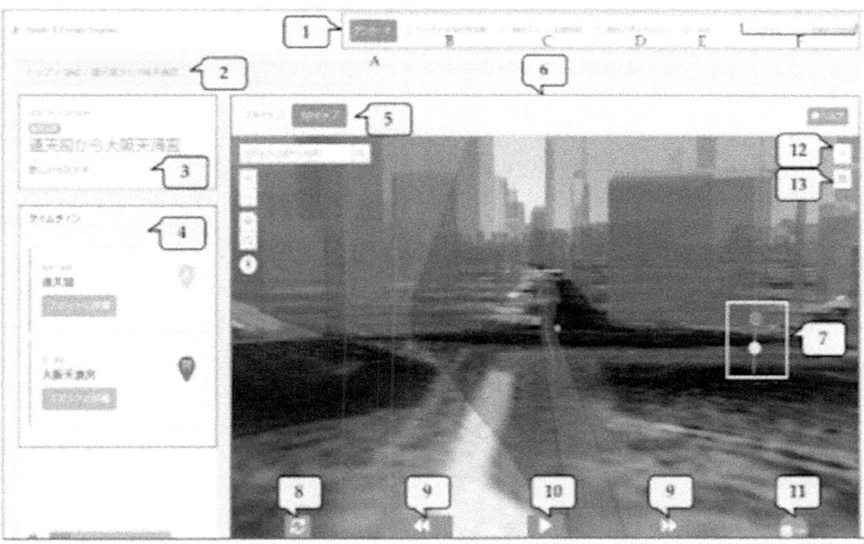

No	Description
1	Navigation bar (A: Questionnaire survey, B: Function of virtual city walk experience, C: Function of creation of sightseeing plan and record, D: Function of viewing sightseeing spot information, E: Function of sharing sightseeing plan and record, F: Log in and registration
2	Page for the function of sharing sightseeing plan and record
3	Selected sighseeing plan
4	Timeline of sightseeing plan
5	Switch between the 2D and 3D digital maps
6	Screen of virtual city walk experience
7	Reset of the perspective on the 3D map
8	Reverse of the direction of the course, and change of the perspective
9	Acceleration of the perspective movement
10	Stop
11	Insolation (Every time the button is clicked or tapped on, the time in the virtual space moves forward which changes the insolation.)
12	Change layer
13	Change of base maps (3D digital map and 3D city model)

FIGURE 6.3
Example of virtual walk city experience (3D city model) in Osaka City, Japan (Koga & Yamamoto, 2023).

vulnerable to natural disasters, VR simulations can be beneficial to emergency response teams and residents. These simulations recreate real-life situations that help users prepare for the best course of action during disasters. Moreover, VR can be used to assess the environmental impact of urban developments. Using simulation techniques, planners will be able to assess how various scenarios impact the habitat and wildlife of the area. This information is vital in making informed decisions that are environmentally friendly and support sustainable development (IEEE Innovation at Work, 2024).

Collaborative partnerships between government, tech companies, and academic institutions are developing the future of VR in sustainable smart cities. These partnerships ensure that the applications of VR are practical and widely used. These collaborations between academic research and cutting-edge technology produce highly effective educational tools (University of Tokyo, 2023). There are, however, some limitations to integrating VR in smart cities. The major constraint is the cost of VR equipment, which can limit its use.

Furthermore, concerns exist regarding data security and privacy, as many VR applications require the storage and processing of large amounts of data. To overcome these challenges, it is crucial to continue investing in research and development. Future improvements in VR technology, such as affordable hardware and enhanced data security features, will make VR applications more accessible and secure. Also, further collaboration between stakeholders will be necessary to encourage innovation and ensure that VR remains an integral part of sustainable smart cities.

6.7 Conclusion

The future of VR in sustainable smart cities is promising and has the potential to transform cities by enhancing urban planning, improving public engagement, and supporting disaster preparedness and environmental impact assessments. These innovations are being driven by collaborative efforts among government agencies, tech companies, and academic institutions, ensuring that VR applications are effective and widely adopted. This technology will undoubtedly continue to advance, and VR will play an increasingly important role in creating more sustainable and livable urban environments.

Acknowledgement

The authors would like to acknowledge Asia Pacific University of Technology & Innovation and Kyoto University of Advanced Science for the support. The authors would also like to thank the anonymous reviewers for their valuable feedback and comments.

References

Alene, G. H., Depina, I., Thakur, V., Perkis, A., & Bruland, O. (2024). QuickAware: A virtual reality tool for quick clay landslide hazard awareness. *Natural Hazards, 120*(2), 1869–1898. https://doi.org/10.1007/s11069-023-06274-6

Alshowair, A., Bail, J., AlSuwailem, F., Mostafa, A., & Abdel-Azeem, A. (2024). Use of virtual reality exercises in disaster preparedness training: A scoping review. *SAGE Open Medicine, 12,* 20503121241241936. https://doi.org/10.1177/20503121241241936

Barry, D. M., Kanematsu, H., Lawson, M., Nakahira, K., & Ogawa, N. (2017). Virtual STEM activity for renewable energy. *Procedia computer science, 112,* 946–955. https://doi.org/10.1016/j.procs.2017.08.130

Deguchi, A. (2020). From smart city to society 5.0. *Society, 5,* 43–65. https://doi.org/10.1007/978-981-15-2989-4_3

Dembski, F., Yamu, C., & Wössner, U. (2019). Digital twin, virtual reality and space syntax: Civic engagement and decision support for smart, sustainable cities. In *Proceedings of the 12th International Space Syntax Symposium* (pp. 316–1). Beijing, China.

García, S., Trejo, P., & García, A. (2022). Intelligent VR-AR for natural disasters management. In D. Cvetkovic (Ed.), *Augmented reality and its application* (pp. 99–120). IntechOpen.

Gunarto, H. (2011). Digital preservation of Borobudur World heritage and cultural treasures. *Ritsumeikan Center for Asia Pasific Studies (RCAPS) Research Report,* Japan.

IEEE Digital Reality. (2023). Virtual reality urban planning. https://digitalreality.ieee.org/publications/virtual-reality-urban-planning

IEEE Innovation at Work. (2024). How will new developments in virtual and augmented reality technology impact smart cities? https://innovationatwork.ieee.org/how-will-new-developments-in-virtual-and-augmented-reality-technology-impact-smart-cities

Jones, T. E., Yang, Y., & Yamamoto, K. (2017). Assessing the recreational value of world heritage site inscription: A longitudinal travel cost analysis of Mount Fuji climbers. *Tourism Management, 60,* 67–78. https://doi.org/10.1016/j.tourman.2016.11.009

Kawaguchi, T., Nishimura, Y., Maruhashi, A., Fukuda, T., & Yabuki, N. (2009). A Study of the virtual reality simulation system for LRT projects towards sustainable city. In *Proceedings of The 14th International Conference on Computer Aided Architectural Design Research in Asia* (pp. 23–32). Yunlin, Taiwan.

Khanal, S., Medasetti, U. S., Mashal, M., Savage, B., & Khadka, R. (2022). Virtual and augmented reality in the disaster management technology: A literature review of the past 11 years. *Frontiers in Virtual Reality, 3,* 843195. https://doi.org/10.3389/frvir.2022.843195

Koga, Y., & Yamamoto, K. (2023). Tourism support system to utilise virtual reality space reflecting dynamic information in real time. *ISPRS International Journal of Geo-Information, 12*(8), 301. https://doi.org/10.3390/ijgi12080301

Prior, T., & Roth, F. (2013). *Preparing for disasters in global cities: An international comparison*. ETH Zurich.

Ramu, S. P., Boopalan, P., Pham, Q. V., Maddikunta, P. K. R., Huynh-The, T., Alazab, M., Nguyen, T.T., & Gadekallu, T. R. (2022). Federated learning enabled digital twins for smart cities: Concepts, recent advances, and future directions. *Sustainable Cities and Society, 79*, 103663. https://doi.org/10.1016/j.scs.2021.103663

Ready, M., Dwyer, T., & Haga, J. H. (2018). Immersive visualisation of big data for river disaster management. In *Workshop on Immersive Analytics: Exploring Future Visualization and Interaction Technologies for Data Analytics*, Phoenix, AZ.

Regan, E. (2020). Smart cities in Japan: Practical innovations for conscious future living. *Tokyoesque (2021, Haziran 22)*. Erişim Adresi: https://tokyoesque.com/smart-cities-in-japan

Ryu, H., & Lim, H. (2023). Linking smart city and urban sustainability issue: A comparative study of smart City services in Japan and Korea. *Urban and Regional Planning Review, 10*, 263–293. https://doi.org/10.14398/urpr.10.263

Rupprecht, C. D. D., Byrne, J. A., Ueda, H., & Lo, A. Y. (2015). "It's real, not fake like a park": Residents' perception and use of informal urban green-space in Brisbane, Australia and Sapporo, Japan. *Landscape and Urban Planning, 143*, 205–218. https://doi.org/10.1016/j.landurbplan.2015.07.003

Shi, J., Honjo, T., Zhang, K., & Furuya, K. (2020). Using virtual reality to assess landscape: A comparative study between on-site survey and virtual reality of aesthetic preference and landscape cognition. *Sustainability, 12*(7), 2875. https://doi.org/10.3390/su12072875

Soonthodu, S., & Wahab, I. N. (2022). Innovative technology uses in sustainable destination management in Asia. In *Handbook of technology application in tourism in Asia* (pp. 1203–1225). Singapore: Springer Nature Singapore. https://doi.org/10.1007/978-981-16-2210-6_54

University of Tokyo (2023). Changing reality with virtual technologies. https://www.u-tokyo.ac.jp/focus/en/features/z0508_00036.html

Wallace, C. (2022). Japan's promotion of smart cities at home and abroad: Socioeconomic and strategic considerations. EUI RSC, 2022/11, Global Governance Programme, [EU Asia project]. https://hdl.handle.net/1814/74973

Xiang, M., Wang, R. H., Zhong, Z., Hong, C. Y., Yi, Y. W., Xiang, S. W., & Roy, D. (2023). Empowering society 5.0 through AR-VR applications: Studying the potential in Aizuwakamatsu smart city. In *AIP Conference Proceedings* (Vol. 2909, No. 1). AIP Publishing. https://doi.org/10.1063/5.0182561

Yasumoto, S., Jones, A., Yano, K., & Nakaya, T. (2012). Virtual city models for assessing environmental equity of access to sunlight: A case study of Kyoto, Japan. *International Journal of Geographical Information Science, 26*(1), 1–13. https://doi.org/10.1080/13658816.2011.570268

Yenidogan, C. (2021). Earthquake-resilient design of seismically isolated buildings: A review of technology. *Vibration, 4*(3), 602–647. https://doi.org/10.3390/vibration4030035

Zhang, Y., Shen, Z., & Liu, S. (2020). Virtual reality with the integrated automatic presentation scrip for improving concepts understanding of urban design: A case study in Tatsumi region of Tokyo Bay zone, Japan. *Multimedia Tools and Applications, 79*, 3125–3144. https://doi.org/10.1007/s11042-018-6588-y

Zhu, Y., & Li, N. (2021). Virtual and augmented reality technologies for emergency management in the built environments: A state-of-the-art review. *Journal of Safety Science and Resilience,* 2(1), 1–10. https://doi.org/10.1016/j.jnlssr.2020.11.004

7

Augmented Reality in Social Welfare: Designing Immersive Donation Experiences

Azizah Che Omar, Norhana Yusof, and Mohd Adib Abd Muin

7.1 Introduction

Islam divides the group of Asnaf (those in need) into categories of *fakir* and *miskin* as groups eligible for donations, along with six other asnaf categories such as *amil, muallaf, al-riqab, al-gharimin, fisabilillah,* and *ibnu sahil* (Hairunnizam et al., 2009; Rodin, 2015; Ahmad & Yahaya, 2023; Abu Bakar, 2012; Lokman, 2022). According to Imam Abu Hanifah and Imam Malik, a *fakir* is defined as someone who is extremely poor and has no wealth or resources to support their daily life. *Miskin,* on the other hand, refers to someone who has limited wealth or resources (Abu Bakar, 2012). Imam Syafie and Imam Hambali defined *fakir* as someone with no wealth at all, while *miskin* refers to someone who has some wealth but cannot meet all of their needs. Therefore, a *fakir* can be defined as someone who is extremely poor, while *miskin* is someone who is still able to manage, even though they face financial difficulties (Abu Bakar, 2012; Lokman, 2022).

Referring to the advice of Prophet Muhammad SAW to Abu Dzar RA, which means: "love the poor and be close to them," this is an encouragement to seek ways to help the poor and bring them out of poverty. It is the essence of the contributions for the poor and needy in Islam (Abu Bakar, 2012). As part of the effort to assist the Asnaf group, the Kedah State Zakat Board (in Malay *Lembaga Zakat Negeri Kedah* – LZNK) has initiated the development of a web-based system called AsnafCare (Lembaga Zakat Negeri Kedah, 2020), as shown in Figure 7.1. It is a crowdfunding platform operated by the LZNK that channels fast and transparent aid, such as food and cash vouchers, to eligible Asnaf in need.

AsnafCare is a platform that offers numerous opportunities for the public to support those in need. Interestingly, AsnafCare also focuses on individuals who have been severely affected by the COVID-19 pandemic. AsnafCare offers several campaign options for the public to participate in, including food campaigns, voucher campaigns, online learning campaigns, and more

DOI: 10.1201/9781003662433-9

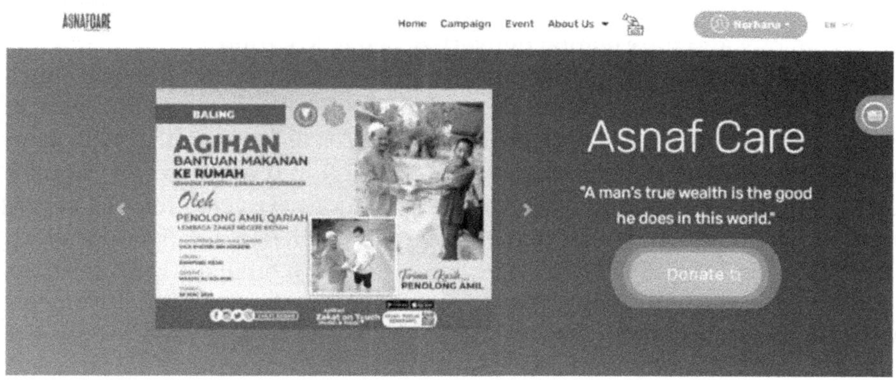

FIGURE 7.1
AsnafCare web-based system.

TABLE 7.1
AsnafCare Fund Record (Updated August 2024)

Items	Amount in Ringgit Malaysia (RM)
Target fund amount	RM 68,660,450.00
Total funds collected	RM 1,730,458.63
Amount still needed	RM 66,929,991.37

(Lembaga Zakat Negeri Kedah, 2021). The activities carried out and the total funds collected through donations are also shared on AsnafCare to raise public awareness and encourage donations to those in need (Lembaga Zakat Negeri Kedah, 2021). Table 7.1 shows the most recent fundraising record conducted by AsnafCare in 2024 (Nor et al., 2024). Based on this record, it is clear that the funds collected are insufficient to cover the distribution needed for the Asnaf group. It suggests that public awareness and contributions to the Asnaf group are still predominantly from individuals in a lower socioeconomic position (Abd Muin et al., 2022).

To further enhance public awareness of donating to the Asnaf group, this study proposes intensifying the promotion of AsnafCare to the public, especially the people of Kedah, by utilising mobile augmented reality (AR) technology. It is believed that the use of mobile AR technology will increase public awareness in contributing through AsnafCare. This, in turn, will help increase the amount of donations that can be channelled to the Asnaf group in need of assistance. The use of AR technology will make it easier for users to browse and access information about AsnafCare. Additionally, the developed AsnafCare AR mobile application also includes a link to the Zakat on Touch app. This is to make it easier for the public to report overlooked Asnaf individuals and ensure that donations received from AsnafCare are directed to the proper beneficiaries. It also enhances the efficiency and effectiveness of technology and information delivery (Chen & Ko, 2019).

Currently, mobile AR applications are widely used in various fields such as teaching and learning (Mulyani et al., 2021; Saputra et al., 2015; Umam & Susandi, 2024), business (Alves et al., 2024; Prodea & Constantin, 2023), manufacturing (Melo et al., 2023; Ramalho et al., 2023), and social media (Sinha & Srivastava, 2023). Moreover, mobile AR applications are very effective in promoting products and tourist destinations (Dieck et al., 2024; Spallone et al., 2023; Yawised et al., 2023). This is because the use of mobile AR applications can attract users with their unique features by combining digital elements with the real-world environment interactively and in real time (Akçayır & Akçayır, 2017; Nesterov et al., 2017; Saidin et al., 2015; Le et al., 2015; Huang & Liao, 2015; Hassan & Jung, 2018).

Moreover, although AR technology has been implemented on a widespread scale today, the application of AR specifically focusing on the Asnaf group is still very limited. While zakat organisations in Malaysia have started to utilise technology-enabled platforms, their usage is still restricted (Salleh & Chowdhury, 2020; Meerangani et al., 2021). Based on studies conducted by these researchers, it was found that most zakat organisation in Malaysia utilise technology-based systems that are primarily focused on online payment of zakat (Majlis Agama Islam Wilayah Persekutuan, 2020; Tabung Baitulmal Sarawak, 2021; Al Athar & Al Arif, 2021, Hamzah et al., 2021), website systems, and mobile applications such as Zakat on Touch (Lembaga Zakat Negeri Kedah, 2021), Mobile Jejak Asnaf MAIWP (Majlis Agama Islam Wilayah Persekutuan, 2020), and Jejak Asnaf (Tabung Baitulmal Sarawak, 2021), as displayed in Figure 7.2.

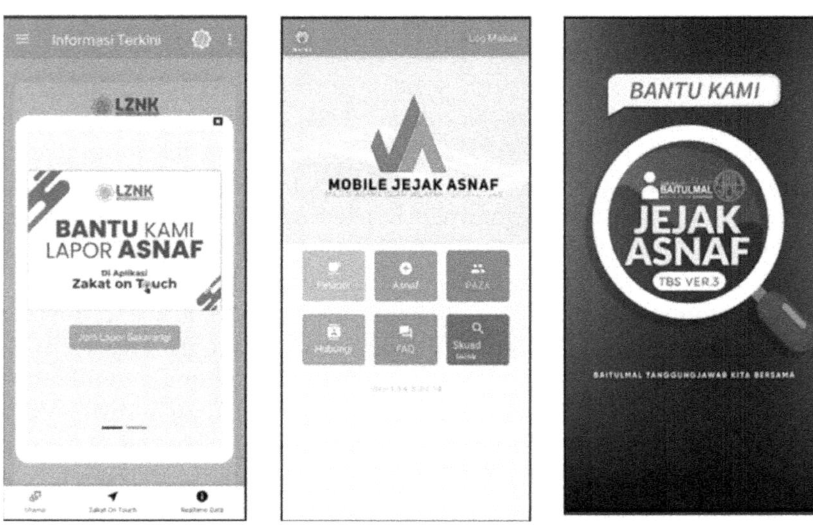

FIGURE 7.2
Examples of Mobile Applications: Zakat on Touch (LZNK), Mobile Jejak Asnaf MAIWP, and Jejak Asnaf (Tabung Baitulmal Sarawak).

An early consultation with subject matter experts also revealed that the implementation of technology for other purposes, such as disbursing zakat and increasing awareness of the Asnaf community, is still poorly addressed (Azarudin, 2021). Hence, it is understandable that the implementation of AR technology within Malaysian zakat organisations is still minimal.

The preliminary study also found that most mobile applications developed for the Asnaf group are primarily intended to create a platform for the public to report overlooked Asnaf to the zakat authorities. As a result, the functionality of these mobile applications for the Asnaf group is quite limited and not diversified for public use in assisting the Asnaf. Furthermore, as shown in Table 7.1, public awareness of donating to the Asnaf group remains significantly underdeveloped. Therefore, this study aims to promote the AsnafCare fund system to boost further the collection of donations for the affected Asnaf group through the development of the AR4AsnafCare mobile application.

7.2 AR as an Immersive Enabler for Social Innovation

The use of AR as an immersive technology has been widely adopted in various fields, including marketing (Egieya et al., 2023), education (Al-Ansi et al., 2023), and cultural heritage (Suyuti & Setyanto, 2023). AR can be defined as a simulated environment where physical and digital entities are combined with the aid of sensory input made by computer technology. The combination of these two entities can boost users' perception and collaboration with their surroundings. Therefore, it is unsurprising that AR technology can significantly improve users' perception (Bekele et al., 2018), encouraging a more immersive experience with AR content.

In AR technology, the use of a camera is essential to visualise models in either 2D or 3D form. AR technology can use websites as a medium for delivery. However, nowadays, digital mechanisms such as smartphones, tablets, or AR glasses are increasingly popular as access mediums because they enhance the level of immersion among users (Barta et al., 2023). AR technology can be classified into several categories based on the technology and practices used. Two main categories of AR technology are marker-based AR and markerless AR. Marker-based AR, also known as image identification AR, utilises special objects or markers, such as cards or images, to generate a virtual representation of 3D objects, as shown in Figure 7.3 (El Filali & Krit, 2019).

Meanwhile, markerless AR depends on environmental cues to verify the placement and orientation of virtual objects (Hidayat & Wardat, 2024). However, the virtual objects displayed do not provide any specific information about the user's environment. Markerless AR systems are capable of defining and identifying objects and locations in the real world without

FIGURE 7.3
Examples of marker-based AR. (Source: El Filali and Krit, 2019.)

FIGURE 7.4
Example of markerless AR. (Source: Mitsuhara et al., 2021.)

relying on markers or images (Wanti et al., 2022). Therefore, the operation of markerless AR systems differs significantly from that of marker-based AR systems. Currently, location-based AR technology is widely used for recreational activities such as games or training. An example of a markerless AR system is illustrated in Figure 7.4, which is used to train users on how to respond during evacuation procedures in the event of a disaster (Mitsuhara et al., 2021).

Compared to the two types of AR technology discussed above, marker-based AR is the easiest to use and develop. This is because marker-based AR offers greater accuracy and control to users compared to markerless AR, which focuses more on adaptability and spontaneous interaction. Since the target users of the AR4AsnafCare Mobile Application include adults and older people, this study has decided to adopt marker-based AR technology. The next section presents a comparative analysis of the existing marker-based AR mobile applications.

7.2.1 Learning from Marker-Based AR Applications: Insights for Social Good

Currently, marker-based AR systems are widely used in the form of mobile applications. This aligns with the rapid advancement of mobile technology today. In this section, several examples of marker-based AR mobile applications are presented to provide a clearer understanding of how these applications function. All of these application examples are then analysed through a comparative analysis displayed in Table 7.2. Meanwhile, Table 7.3 displays the elements found in the discussed applications.

TABLE 7.2

The Advantages and Limitations of the Existing AR Applications

Application	Advantages	Limitation
Virtual Blood Donation	• User-friendly AR application • A very attractive and neat interface with smooth animation.	• Not much interaction from the user; it only shows an animation and fills the blood bag • No pictures or videos to give more knowledge about blood donation
AR Brochure for Alnwick Garden	• Easy-to-use AR application • Have interaction between the user and the app.	• Just shows a video. • It lacks additional multimedia features, such as animation and pictures.
AR Charity Card	• Can be utilised on both Android and iOS devices • It is available for download on the Play Store or Apple Store	• It only displays a video. • It lacks additional media such as animations and images.

TABLE 7.3

The Elements in Existing Applications and AR4AsnafCare Application

Application	Text	Graphics	Video	Audio	Button	Animation	Total
Virtual Blood Donation	✓	-	-	✓	-	✓	3
AR Brochure for Alnwick Garden	✓	–	✓	✓	✓	-	4
AR Charity Card	✓	-	✓	✓	✓	-	4
AR4AsnafCare Mobile App	✓	✓	✓	✓	✓	✓	6

7.2.2 NSH Virtual Blood Donation

The Virtual Blood Donation Application, shown in Figure 7.5, is a campaign designed to raise awareness about the life-saving power of blood and encourage people to donate blood through an AR mobile application. This AR app connects to a large outdoor advertising screen that displays an empty blood bag and an image of a sick patient, as viewed through an iPhone (Thomas, 2016).

7.2.3 Aircards AR Brochure for Alnwick Garden

The AR brochure is an app made to promote unique tourist attractions in the United Kingdom. The brochure features videos of stunning views at Alnwick Garden, utilising AR technology. It also features a "LEARN MORE" button located in the bottom-right corner of the AR app, which directs users to the website to book tickets online, as shown in Figure 7.6.

7.2.4 Overlay AR Charity Card

The AR Greeting Card is a charity donation card that uses AR technology. It is an AR project where scanning the card plays a video about the company and displays a donation button, allowing users to contribute money to support a youth charity. This can be seen in Figure 7.7.

Based on Tables 7.2 and 7.3 and Figure 7.8, it can be concluded that the AR4AsnafCare mobile application to be developed will include all multimedia elements such as text, video, audio, graphics, buttons, and animations, which some existing AR applications do not cover.

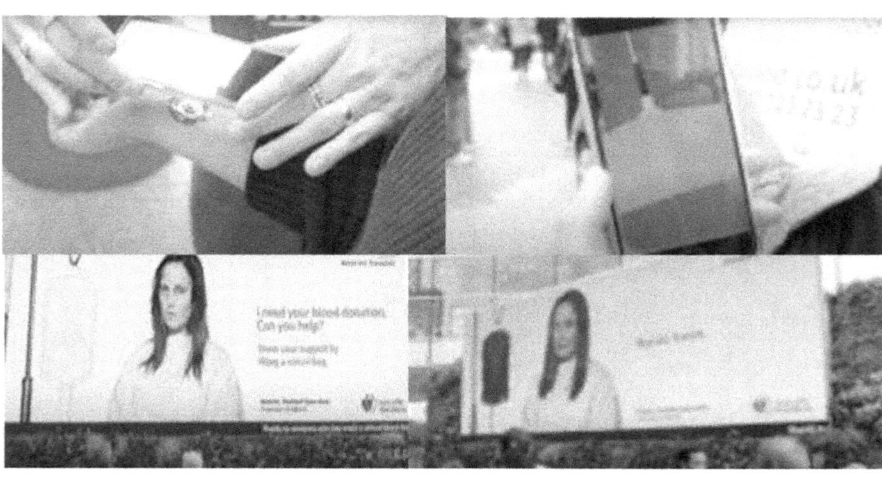

FIGURE 7.5
AR application –Virtual Blood Donation. (Source: NHS Blood and Transplant, 2016.)

FIGURE 7.6
AR application – AR Brochure for Alnwick Garden. (Source: Aircards, 2020.)

FIGURE 7.7
AR Charity Card. (Source: Fectar, 2020.)

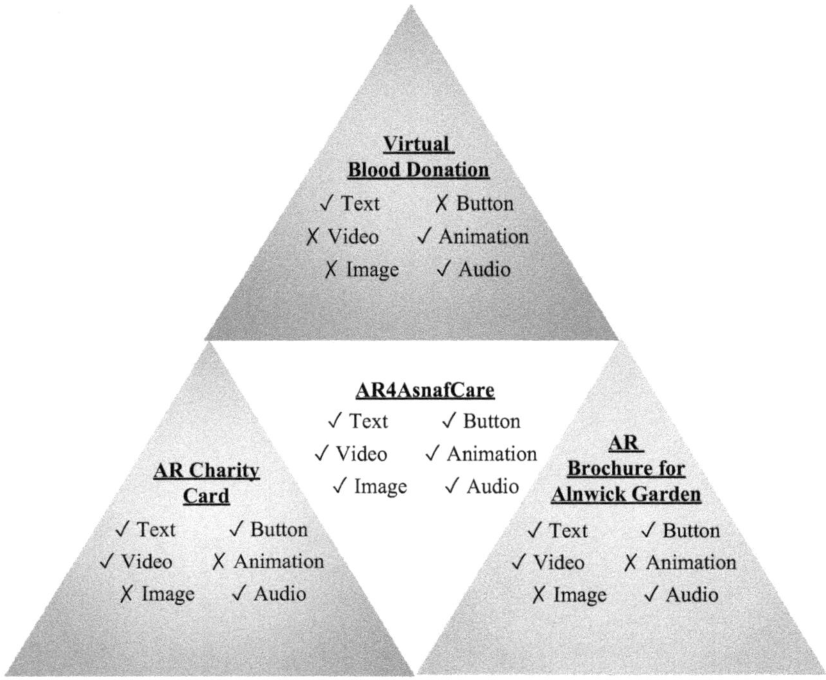

FIGURE 7.8
Comparative analysis between the existing AR applications and AR4AsnafCare mobile application.

7.2.5 Digital Transformation in Zakat Institutions: From Online Platforms to AR and Beyond

Based on the literature analysis, it was found that most state-level zakat institutions in Malaysia only use mobile technology and websites in their payment systems. The use of AR technology is almost non-existent. Most mobile applications developed by state zakat institutions focus on three primary functions: zakat calculation, zakat verification, and zakat payment. For example, the Terengganu Islamic Religious Council and Malay Customs (MAIDAM) use a web and mobile application system to facilitate zakat payers in Terengganu. The application developed is called Sahabat MAIDAM (Majlis Agama Islam dan Adat Melayu Terengganu, 2024) as shown in Figure 7.9. The Sahabat MAIDAM app has several functions, including reporting Asnaf, a calculator, online zakat payment, a list of registered Amils, and other features developed in the application.

The Selangor Zakat Board (Lembaga Zakat Selangor, 2023) has also developed its own mobile application, known as Zakat Selangor. This mobile application also features functions similar to those of the Sahabat MAIDAM app, developed by the Terengganu Islamic Religious Council and the Malay

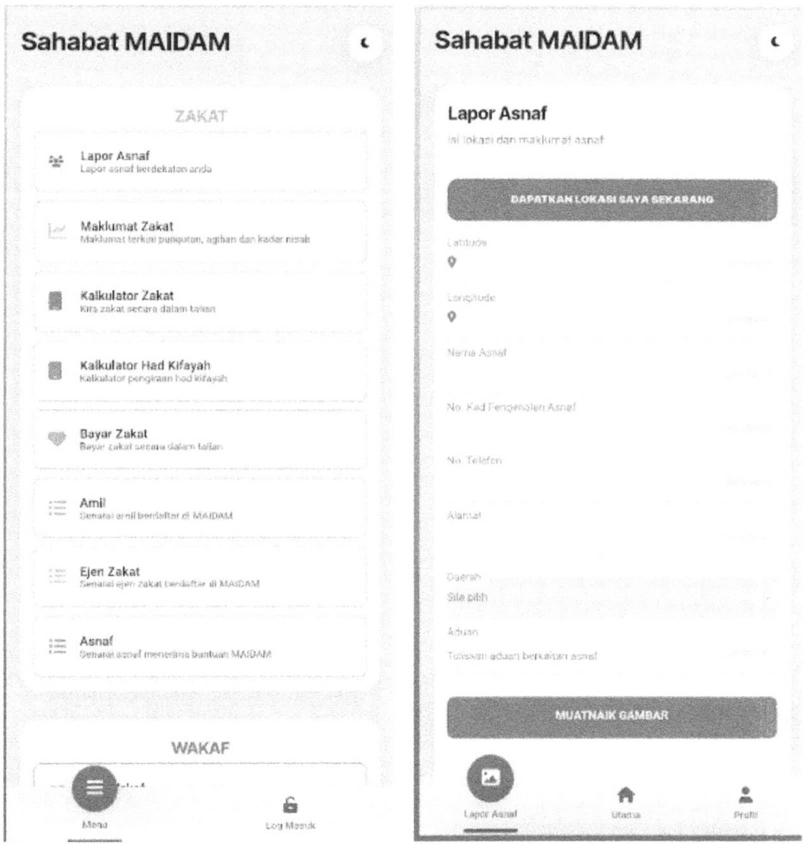

FIGURE 7.9
Sahabat MAIDAM mobile application.

Customs Department. This is clearly evident in Figure 7.10, which displays the Zakat Selangor mobile application's interface.

According to a study conducted by Rosele et al. (2022), in this rapidly evolving digital era, every zakat institution must educate capable individuals on fulfilling their zakat obligations. This can be achieved by further diversifying the use of available digital technologies to increase awareness among zakat payers, such as Artificial Intelligence, AR, and the Metaverse. The use of appropriate technologies not only helps increase zakat collection but also encourages the well-off members of society to contribute beyond zakat to the Asnaf groups. For instance, the LZNK introduced the AsnafCare application to encourage the community, particularly in Kedah, to make generous contributions to the Asnaf who are affected. Research by Abdul Haniff et al. (2021) shows that the AsnafCare application has received positive feedback from the public.

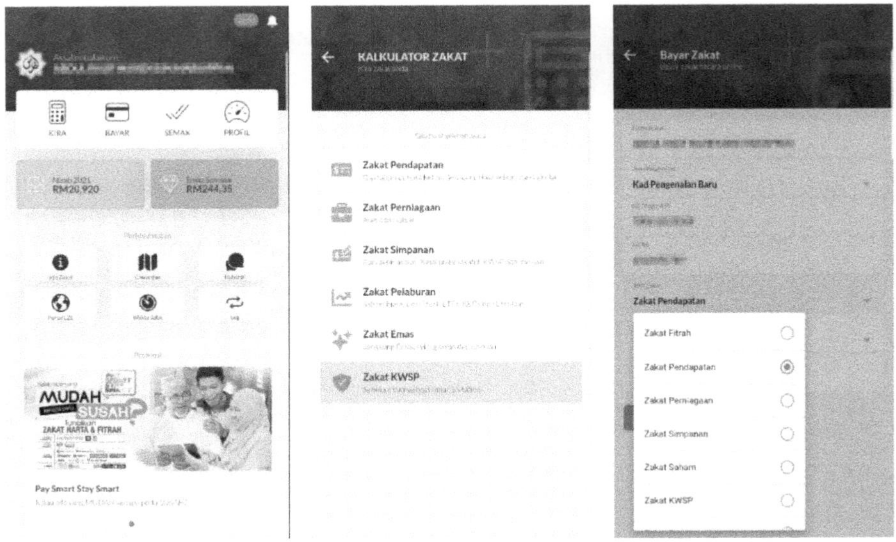

FIGURE 7.10
Zakat Selangor mobile application.

Additionally, Saro et al. (2023) have demonstrated that the use of digital technology in zakat institutions in Malaysia is steadily increasing. The acceptance and usage rate of digital applications is notably high in Kedah among zakat payers and the local community. This acceptance rate is comparable to that of Selangor and Kuala Lumpur. The findings from this study highlight a significant potential for zakat organisations in Malaysia to further enhance the use of digital applications, such as Artificial Intelligence, AR, the Metaverse, and various other technologies, in managing zakat and special fund donations.

7.3 Designing and Validating a User-Centred AR Donation Platform

As illustrated in Figure 7.11, this study consists of two phases: prototype development and prototype validation. The first phase involved the development of the prototype, which was designed in collaboration with content experts (Hameed, 2020). This approach ensured that the needs of the target audience, specifically the public, were met. Continuous user feedback was integrated into the design process to refine the prototype, particularly in relation to AR components and multimedia elements. The prototype was developed using Unity 2020. In the second phase, the prototype underwent validation through an expert review process, which provided valuable insights, identified

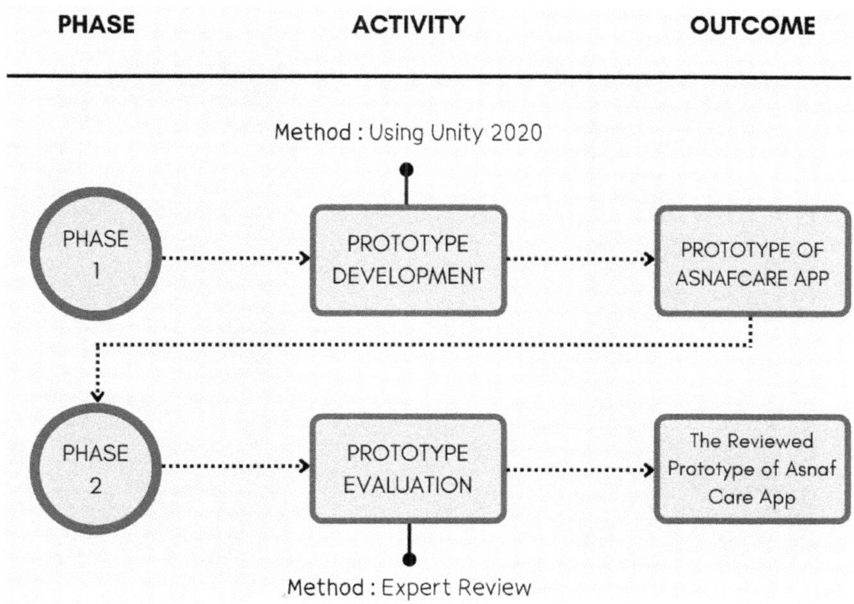

FIGURE 7.11
The research process.

potential issues, and led to recommended improvements (Aziz et al., 2020; Omar et al., 2021). Five experts, each with at least five years of experience in mobile-human computer interaction and AR, were selected to evaluate the prototype. Feedback from these experts was collected through interview questions, analysed qualitatively, and used to improve the application.

7.4 AR4AsnafCare: Prototype for Immersive Fundraising and Engagement

AR4AsnafCare mobile application uses an interactive design to help users explore its features. In Figure 7.12, the Home page shows several buttons: "About Us," "Campaign," "Events," and "Exit." The application also displays the LZNK and AsnafCare logos on every page. When users click the "About Us" button, they see three more options: "Info," "Website," and "AR Button." If users choose "Info," they are directed to a page (Figure 7.13) that explains how AsnafCare was established. A Home icon at the bottom left of each page allows users to return to the Home page at any time. There are also left and right arrows to move between pages. The "Website" button (Figure 7.14) opens the AsnafCare website. Users can learn more and make donations on the site. The "AR Button" (Figure 7.15) asks users to scan a QR code. After

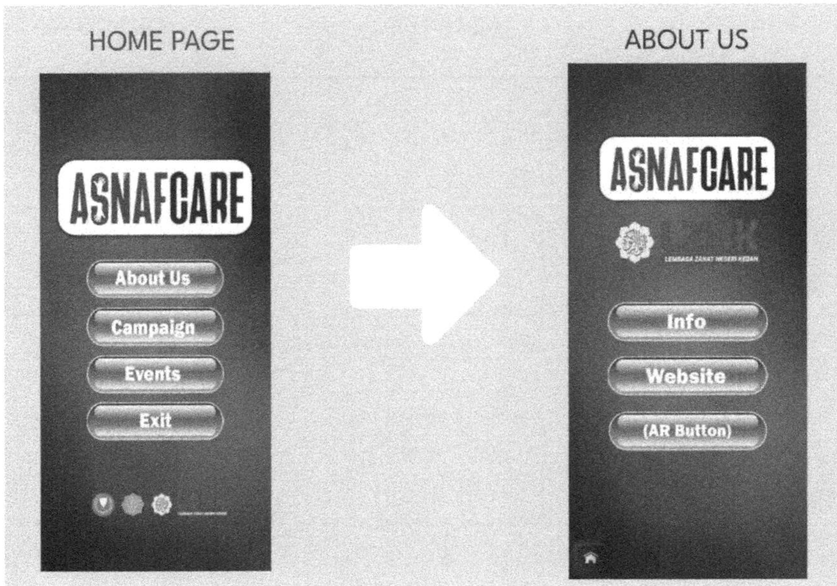

FIGURE 7.12
"About Us" button on the home page directs users to the "About Us" section.

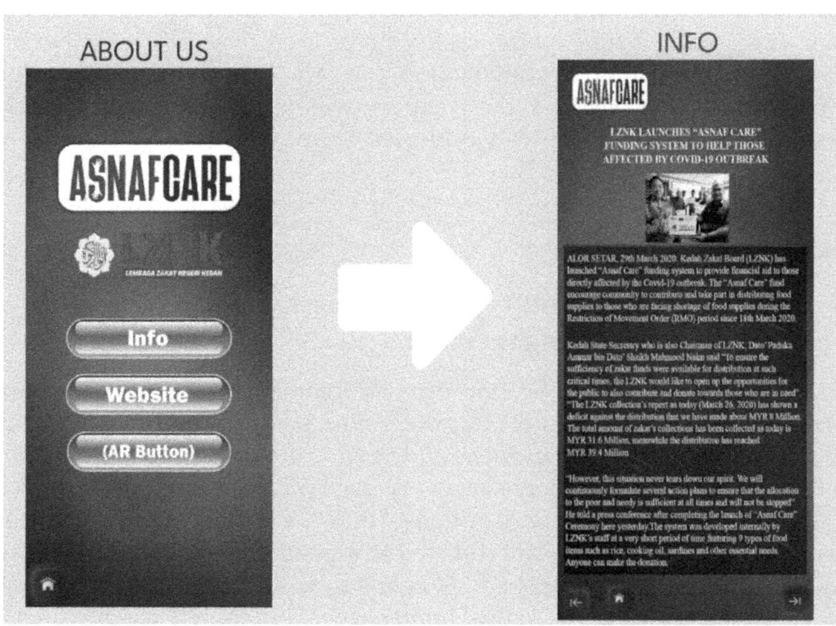

FIGURE 7.13
Information about the background of AsnafCare in the "Info" page.

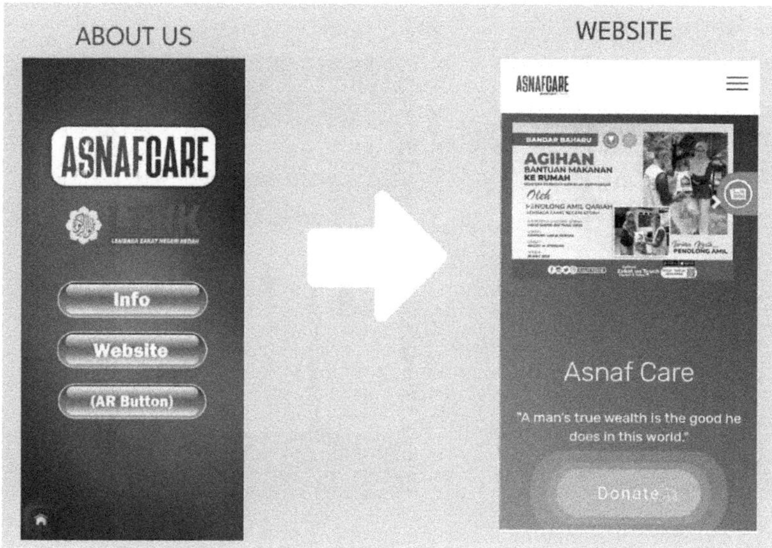

FIGURE 7.14
A "Website" button that takes users to AsnafCare's official website.

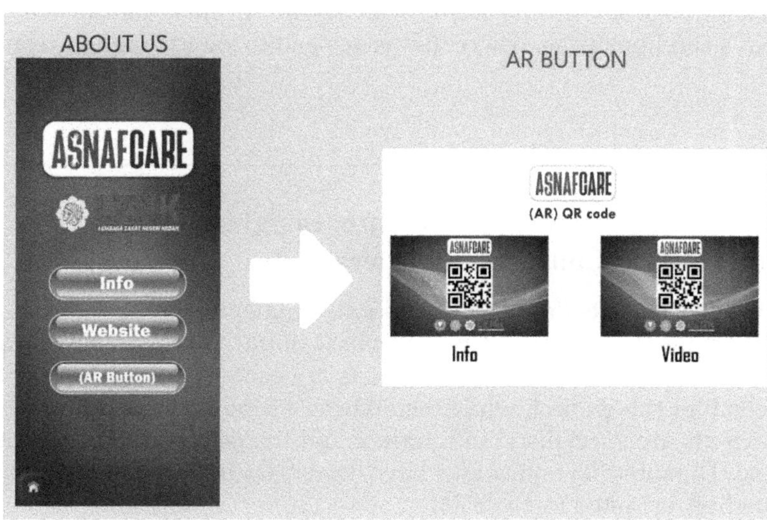

FIGURE 7.15
"AR Button" for QR code scanning.

scanning, they see details about how to donate items such as food, cash vouchers, school supplies, clothes, or help to build and repair houses. They also watch a short AR video about AsnafCare's work.

On the Home page, clicking "Campaign" (Figure 7.16) displays donation campaigns that require support. These include food, school tools, and

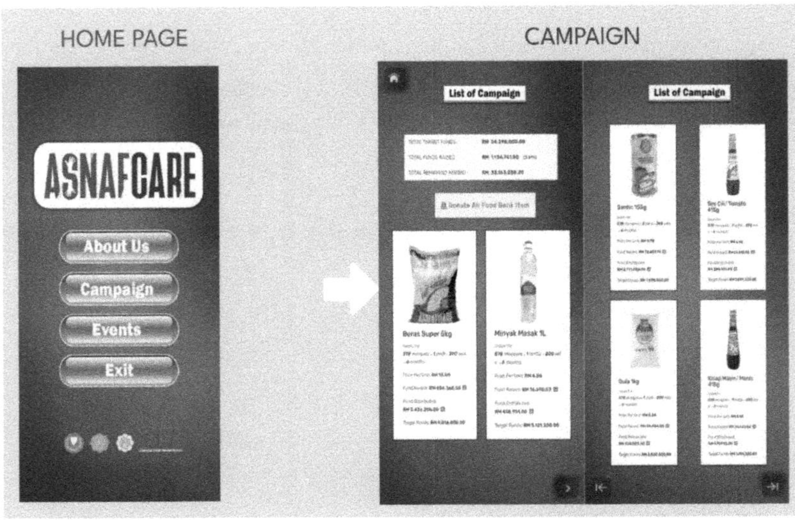

FIGURE 7.16
A "Campaign" page that allows users to select and donate from the list of campaigns.

housing. Users can navigate through pages using arrow buttons and return to the Home page at any time. Lastly, clicking the "Events" button takes users to LZNK's Facebook page, where they may need to log in to see the content.

7.5 Expert Evaluation of AsnafCare: Insights into Design, Content, and Interaction

A total of five experts (four males and one female) were interviewed, all of whom were involved in the evaluation phase of the AsnafCare mobile application prototype. Two of the male experts are content experts; one of them is the client of this project, while the other is a senior lecturer. Besides that, three experts are specialised in interface and interactive design, audio and database. The interview questions have been classified into design, content, and function, as stated in Table 7.4.

Table 7.4 presents a set of six questions addressed to a panel of experts, focusing on the aspects of design, content, and functionality of the AR4AsnafCare mobile application. In response to Question 1, "Is the AR4AsnafCare mobile application visually appealing in its design?", the majority of experts agreed that the application's design, particularly the main page, is visually appealing and engaging. For Question 2, which asked, "In your opinion, do you think the design of the AR mobile application can promote AsnafCare?", all experts concurred that the design

TABLE 7.4
Interview Question for Expert Review

No.	Questions	Focus
Q1	Is the AR4AsnafCare mobile application visually appealing in its design?	Design
Q2	In your opinion, do you think the design of the AR mobile application can promote AsnafCare?	Design
Q3	Does the information provided in the AR mobile application provide a comprehensive understanding of AsnafCare to the target user?	Content
Q4	Is the AR mobile application helpful for users to donate to Asnaf people?	Content
Q5	Are the font size and font type in the AR mobile application suitable for viewing and reading?	Function
Q6	Are all buttons in the AR mobile application functioning well?	Function

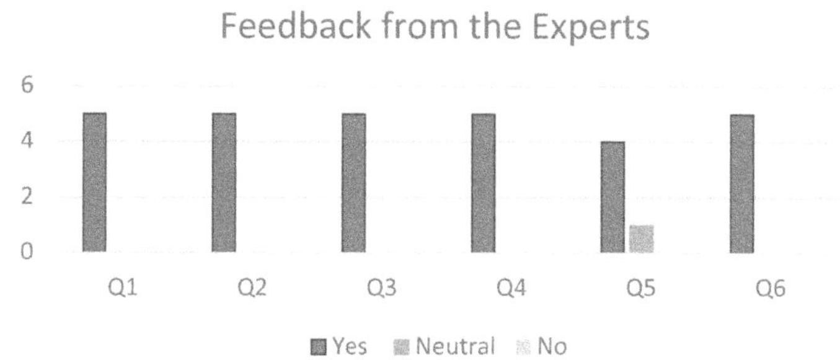

FIGURE 7.17
Feedback from the experts.

successfully supports the goal of promoting AsnafCare in a straightforward and aesthetically pleasing manner (Figure 7.17).

Regarding Question 3, most experts agreed that the AR4AsnafCare mobile application provides a comprehensive understanding of AsnafCare to its intended users. They noted that the app allows users to easily explore and gain meaningful insights into the purpose and initiatives of AsnafCare. In Question 4, all experts strongly agreed that the application effectively facilitates donations to Asnaf recipients. The straightforward item selection and donation process were cited as strengths that support ease of use for users wishing to contribute.

Meanwhile, Question 5 received slightly varied feedback. While most experts agreed that the font size and type used in the application are suitable for reading, one expert remained neutral, suggesting that improvements could be made to enhance text readability. Finally, in Question 6, all experts confirmed that the interactive buttons within the AR mobile application function correctly and support smooth navigation throughout the app. After conducting several interview sessions with the experts, they also provided their suggestions and valuable comments to improve the quality of the AR4AsnafCare mobile application, as shown in Table 7.5.

TABLE 7.5

Expert's Comments Based on Themes

Theme	Experts Comments
Design	The experts recommended that donation items be displayed individually on separate pages to improve clarity and navigation. Secondly, the inclusion of a "Home" button on each campaign page was advised to facilitate easier return to the main interface, thereby enhancing user convenience. Additionally, the experts proposed incorporating a Frequently Asked Questions (FAQ) section on the Home page. This feature would serve as a quick reference to provide users with essential information about AsnafCare, thereby supporting user understanding and engagement. Furthermore, it was suggested that auditory feedback, such as sound effects, be integrated when users interact with buttons. This would enhance interactivity and provide a more engaging experience. Lastly, the experts advised simplifying the overall interface by reducing the number of pages, aiming to streamline navigation and ensure a more intuitive user journey throughout the application.
Content	Several recommendations were proposed further to enhance the application's effectiveness and user engagement. Firstly, it was suggested that instead of incorporating a video component, the AR feature could be optimised by integrating an "INFO" function, allowing users to scan a QR code for relevant information. This modification would improve interactivity while maintaining informational clarity. Additionally, the inclusion of animated elements was recommended to create a more dynamic and engaging user experience. Experts also emphasised the importance of consistency in layout, suggesting that each page should feature a clearly visible title at the top to aid navigation and context comprehension. Moreover, it was proposed that the existing "WEBSITE" button be removed to streamline the interface. In place of this, the current "INFO" page could be redesigned as an AR-based feature, thereby maximising the core functionality of the application while enhancing the user's interaction with the content.
Function	The experts recommended redesigning the "CAMPAIGN" section as a navigation page rather than a button that redirects to a new page. This change is expected to provide a more engaging and intuitive user experience. Furthermore, the experts proposed consolidating all main functional buttons onto a single page. This would simplify navigation and reduce the number of steps required for users to access key features. Additionally, the experts advised exploring database integration methods that are compatible with both laptops and smartphones. This may involve revising the application's page architecture to ensure optimal performance across various devices. Finally, it was suggested that the label "ABOUT US" be changed to "INFO." This adjustment aims to improve accessibility and minimise the number of clicks required, allowing users to obtain information more efficiently.

Based on the opinion and recommendations provided by design and content experts during the expert review process, several enhancements were made to the content and interface design of the AsnafCare mobile application. These expert insights were instrumental in improving the overall quality of the application, particularly in ensuring that its interface is more

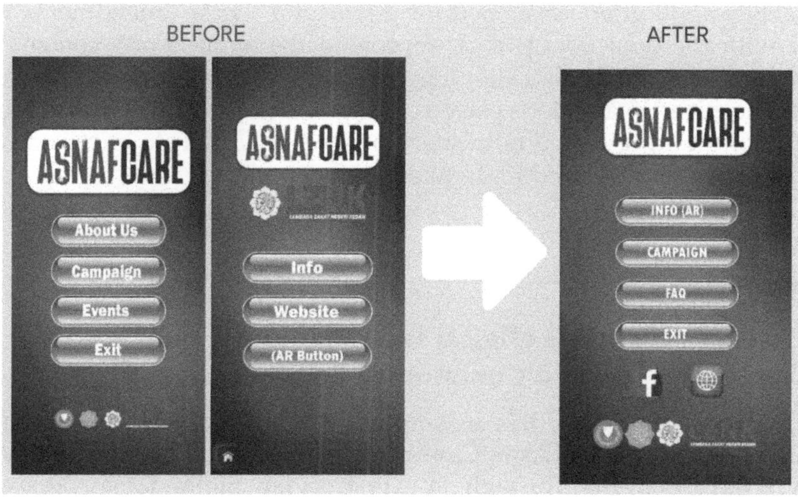

FIGURE 7.18
The changes to the interface by simplifying the pages from two pages to one page.

intuitive and enriched with relevant multimedia elements. As illustrated in Figure 7.18, the application interface underwent modifications in accordance with the recommendations of the experts. The layout was streamlined by eliminating unnecessary pages, thereby improving user navigation and efficiency. The "About Us" button was replaced with an "Info" button, which now prompts users to scan a QR code to access general information about AsnafCare. This modification aims to enhance user awareness of the fundraising initiative and its purpose.

Furthermore, the interface was consolidated by integrating two separate pages into a single page. The "Website" button was replaced with a clickable logo, relocated from the "About Us" section to the Home page. This logo now functions as a direct link to the official AsnafCare website, simplifying user access. While the "Campaign" button was retained, the "Events" button was replaced with a "Frequently Asked Questions (FAQ)" button. This new feature enables users to download a PDF document containing comprehensive information on the donation process, as well as additional details about AsnafCare. Additionally, the original "AR Button" was removed, and its functionalities were merged into the revised "Info" button, which now includes AR capabilities. To further improve accessibility, Facebook and Website buttons were added to the bottom of the application interface. These buttons provide users with direct access to the official AsnafCare website and social media page, thereby enhancing the application's connectivity and user engagement.

In response to the constructive feedback provided by subject matter experts, several modifications were implemented to enhance the overall quality of the

AR mobile application developed for AsnafCare. These amendments were made with the dual objective of improving the application's content and interface design, while also aligning with the identified needs of the target users. The expert evaluations played a critical role in guiding these enhancements, contributing to the refinement of the application to ensure a more effective, user-friendly, and high-quality AR experience.

7.6 Towards Inclusive Digital Interaction: AR for Social Welfare and Community Empowerment

In conclusion, this study has accomplished its primary objectives: (i) the development of the AR4AsnafCare mobile application and (ii) the evaluation of the application through an expert review methodology. However, it is significant to note that, at this stage, the study is limited to gathering preliminary feedback from experts concerning the design, content, and functionality of the proposed application. Although the expert feedback was systematically categorised and analysed, all comments were thoroughly considered to inform subsequent improvements to the application. Given that a more comprehensive evaluation is necessary, future work will focus on conducting a heuristic evaluation based on Nielsen and Molich's Design Guidelines, as well as performing user experience testing to refine the application further.

Acknowledgement

The researchers would like to express their sincere appreciation to the Research and Innovation Management Centre (RIMC) at Universiti Utara Malaysia (UUM), the Zakat and Innovation Research Institute (IPIZ UUM), and the Kedah State Zakat Board (LZNK) for their financial support of this study through the Public External Agency Scheme (SO Code 21318). Special thanks are also extended to the experts involved. A heartfelt thank you goes to our research assistants, Muhammad Aidil Fakhrullah Bin Mohd Khalid and Nurhanis Binti Hasim @ Hashim, for their invaluable contributions in designing and developing the AR mobile application to promote AsnafCare. We would also like to thank all the experts from the School of Multimedia Technology and Communication (SMMTC) and the Kedah State Zakat Board (LZNK) for their valuable insights and feedback on this study.

References

Abd Muin, M. A., Shuib, M. S., Omar, A. C., Abd Ghani, A. H, & Saidi, N. (2022). The challenges of the industrial revolution 4.0 in Islamic social entrepreneurship in the Covid-19 era. *Journal of Advanced Research in Applied Sciences and Engineering Technology, 28*(2), 235–246. https://doi.org/10.37934/araset.28.2.235246

Abdul Haniff, H. S. N., Long, M. N. H., & Ahmad, N. H. (2021). Inisiatif dan inovasi institusi zakat era pendemik Covid-19–Satu penelitian terhadap Lembaga Zakat Negeri Kedah (LZNK). *International Journal of Islamic Business (IJIB), 6*(2), 1–14. https://doi.org/10.32890/ijib2021.6.2

Abu Bakar, M. (2012). Hubungan antara agihan zakat dan kualiti hidup asnaf fakir dan miskin. *Tesis PhD.* Universiti Utara Malaysia.

Ahmad, K., & Yahaya, M. H. (2023). Islamic social financing and efficient zakat distribution: Impact of fintech adoption among the asnaf in Malaysia. *Journal of Islamic Marketing, 14*(9), 2253–2284. https://doi.org/10.1108/JIMA-04-2021-0102

Aircards. (2020, March 17). Alnwick Garden launch augmented reality brochure [Blog post]. *Aircards.* Retrieved September 2, 2025, from https://www.aircards.co/blog/alnwick-garden-augmented-reality-brochure

Akçayır, M., & Akçayır, G. (2017). Advantages and challenges associated with augmented reality for education: A systematic review of the literature. *Educational Research Review, 20,* 1–11. https://doi.org/10.1016/j.edurev.2016.11.002

Al Athar, M. D., & Al Arif, M. N. R. (2021). The intention of millennial generation in paying zakat through digital payments. *International Journal of Islamic Business and Economics (IJIBEC), 5*(1). https://doi.org/10.28918/ijibec.v5i1.3675

Al-Ansi, A. M., Jaboob, M., Garad, A., & Al-Ansi, A. (2023). Analysing augmented reality (AR) and virtual reality (VR) recent development in education. *Social Sciences & Humanities Open, 8*(1), 100532. https://doi.org/10.1016/j.ssaho.2023.100532

Alves, C., Machado, J., & Reis, J. L. (2024). Review for augmented reality shopping application for mobile systems. In *International Conference on Marketing and Technologies* (pp. 623–634). Singapore: Springer Nature Singapore. https://doi.org/10.1007/978-981-99-0333-7_45

Azarudin, A. (2021). Teknologi untuk insitusi zakat dan asnaf. Personal Communication, October 14, 2021.

Aziz, N., Omar, A. C., Mutalib, A. A., Ahmad, S. Z., & Muin, M. A. (2020). Uncovering the needs for a hybridised interaction design model for sign language learning through experts' feedback. *Journal of Physics: Conference, 1529,*(4), 1–10. https://doi.org/10.1088/1742-6596/1529/4/042102

Barta, S., Gurrea, R., & Flavián, C. (2023). How augmented reality increases engagement through its impact on risk and the decision process. *Cyberpsychology, Behavior, and Social Networking, 26*(3), 177–187. https://doi.org/10.1089/cyber.2022.0087

Bekele, M. K., Pierdicca, R., Frontoni, E., Malinverni, E. S., & Gain, J. (2018). A survey of augmented, virtual, and mixed reality for cultural heritage. *Journal on Computing and Cultural Heritage (JOCCH), 11*(2), 1–36. https://doi.org/10.1145/3145534

Chen, Y. P., & Ko, J. C. (2019). CryptoAR wallet: A blockchain cryptocurrency wallet application that uses augmented reality for on-chain user data display. In *Proceedings of the 21st International Conference on Human-Computer Interaction with Mobile Devices and Services* (pp. 1–5). https://doi.org/10.1145/3338286.3344386

Dieck, M. C. T., Jung, T., Lee, H., & Chung, N. (2024). Social presence and experience economy: The effects of augmented and virtual reality in museums. *International Journal of Mobile Communications, 23*(1), 85–109. https://doi.org/10.1504/IJMC.2024.135691

Egieya, Z. E., Ewuga, S. K., Adegbite, A. O., & Oke, T. T. (2023). The role of virtual and augmented reality in modern marketing: A critical review. *Computer Science & IT Research Journal, 4*(3), 244–272. https://doi.org/10.51594/csitrj.v4i3.660

El Filali, Y., & Krit, S. D. (2019). Augmented reality types and popular use cases. *International Journal of Engineering, Science and Mathematics, 8*(4), 91–97. https://doi.org/10.5220/0009776301070110

Fectar. (2020, December 10). Augmented reality charity donation card | AR print Christmas card [Video]. *YouTube.* https://www.youtube.com/watch?v=FGATsP5DSgY

Hairunnizam, W., Sanep, A., & Radiah, A. K. (2009). Pengagihan zakat oleh institusi zakat kepada lapan asnaf: Kajian di Malaysia. Seminar Kebangsaan Ekonomi Islam 2008/09, 10–11 February 2009, APIUM.

Hameed, H. (2020). Quantitative and qualitative research methods: Considerations and issues in qualitative research. *The Maldives National Journal of Research, 8*(1), 8–17. https://doi.org/10.62338/pw6mmp62

Hamzah, N. B., Masroom, M. N. B., Ruskam, A. B., & Saim, A. I. B. (2021). Penggunaan wang bantuan zakat dalam kalangan asnaf fisabilillah dan asnaf gharim di Universiti Teknologi Malaysia. *AZKA International Journal of Zakat & Social Finance*, 187–209. https://doi.org/10.51377/azjaf.vol1no2.37

Hassan, A., & Jung, T. (2018). Augmented reality as an emerging application in tourism marketing education. In Virtual and Augmented Reality: Concepts, Methodologies, Tools, and Applications, (pp. 1702–1720). IGI Global. https://doi.org/10.4018/978-1-4666-9837-6.ch008

Hidayat, R., & Wardat, Y. (2024). A systematic review of augmented reality in science, technology, engineering and mathematics education. *Education and Information Technologies, 29*(8), 9257–9282. https://doi.org/10.1007/s10639-023-12157-x

Huang, T. L., & Liao, S. (2015). A model of acceptance of augmented-reality interactive technology: The moderating role of cognitive innovativeness. *Electronic Commerce Research, 15*(2), 269–295. https://doi.org/10.1007/s10660-014-9163-2

Le, Q. T., Pedro, A. K. E. E. M., Lim, C. R., Park, H. T., Park, C. S., & Kim, H. K. (2015). A framework for using mobile based virtual reality and augmented reality for experiential construction safety education. *International Journal of Engineering Education, 31*(3), 713–725.

Lembaga Zakat Negeri Kedah (2020). AsnafCare. https://asnafcare.com.my/

Lembaga Zakat Negeri Kedah (2021). Zakat on Touch (Version 2.0.31) [Mobile Application Software]. https://play.google.com/store/apps/details?id=com.lznk.MyZakatKedah2&hl=en

Lembaga Zakat Selangor (2023). ZakatSelangor (Version 2.0.31) [Mobile Application Software]. https://play.google.com/store/apps/details?id=my.com.zakatselangor.zakatapp&hl=en-MY

Lokman, N. W. (2022). Perluasan tafsiran asnaf fakir dan miskin dalam konteks pandemik di Malaysia. *Journal of Fatwa Management and Research, 27*(4), 82–98. https://doi.org/10.33102/jfatwa.vol27no4.461

Majlis Agama Islam dan Adat Melayu Terengganu (MAIDAM). (2024, April 1). Sahabat MAIDAM (Version 1.2) [Mobile application]. Apple App Store. https://apps.apple.com/my/app/sahabat-maidam/id6479909636

Majlis Agama Islam Wilayah Persekutuan (2020). Mobile Jejak Asnaf MAIWP (Version 1.0.4) [Mobile Application Software]. https://play.google.com/store/apps/details?id=com.moja.mojaapp

Meerangani, K. A., Sharipp, M. T. M., Rosele, M. I., Hamid, M. F. A., & Razak, A. Q. A. (2021). Digitalisasi sistem pengurusan zakat di Malaysia: Potensi dan cabaran. *Journal of Business Innovation, 6*(1), 36.

Melo, G., Ravi, R., Jauer, L., & Schleifenbaum, J. H. (2023). Investigating the use of augmented reality head-mounted displays to teach design for additive manufacturing. In *International Conference on Additive Manufacturing in Products and Applications* (pp. 283–298). Cham: Springer International Publishing. https://doi.org/10.1007/978-3-031-42983-5_20

Mitsuhara, H., Tanimura, C., Nemoto, J., & Shishibori, M. (2021). Expressing disaster situations for evacuation training using markerless augmented reality. *Procedia Computer Science, 192*, 2105–2114. https://doi.org/10.1016/j.procs.2021.08.218

Mulyani, A., Kurniadi, D., & Akbar Musadad, M. (2021). Rancang bangun aplikasi pengenalan rukun Islam sebagai media pembelajaran menggunakan teknologi augmented reality. *Jarmal Algoritma, 18*(1), 50–61. https://doi.org/10.33364/algoritma/v.18-1.936

Nesterov, A., Kholodilin, I., Shishkov, A., & Vanin, P. (2017). Augmented reality in engineering education: Opportunities and advantages. *Communications-Scientific letters of the University of Zilina, 19*(4), 117–120. https://doi.org/10.26552/com.c.2017.4.117-120

NHS Blood and Transplant. (2016, May 17). NHS uses VR technology to attract new blood donors. NHS Blood and Transplant. https://www.blood.co.uk/news-and-campaigns/news-and-statements/nhs-uses-vr-technology-to-attract-new-blood-donors/

Nor, S. M., Yaacob, S. E., Rahman, A. A., & Zainal, H. (2024). Digitizing Zakat distribution in Malaysia: A case study on application process at Kedah State Zakat Board. *Samarah: Jurnal Hukum Keluarga dan Hukum Islam, 8*(3), 1901–1927.

Omar, A. C., Aziz, N., Muin, M. A. A., Annamalai, S. A., & Mahmad, M. A. (2021). Development and expert review of iZakat Kedah mobile application. *International Journal of Interactive Mobile Technologies, 16*(20), 34–49. https://doi.org/10.3991/ijim.v15i20.23715

Prodea, B. M., & Constantin, C. P. (2023). The role of augmented reality in digital marketing strategy. *Bulletin of the Transilvania University of Brasov.* Series V*: Economic Sciences*, 39–46. https://doi.org/10.31926/but.es.2023.16.65.1.5

Ramalho, F. R., Moreno, T., Soares, A. L., Almeida, A. H., & Oliveira, M. (2023, June). Application of Augmented Reality to Support Manufacturing Resilience. In *International Conference on Flexible Automation and Intelligent Manufacturing* (pp. 654–662). Cham: Springer Nature Switzerland. https://doi.org/10.1007/978-3-031-38165-2_76

Rodin, D. (2015). Pemberdayaan Ekonomi Fakir Miskin dalam Perspektif Al-Quran. *Economica: Jurnal Ekonomi Islam, 6*(1), 71–102. https://doi.org/10.21580/economica.2015.6.1.787

Rosele, M. I., Muneem, A., Rahman, N. N. B. A., & Ali, A. K. (2022). The digitalised zakat management system in Malaysia and the way forward. *AL-IHKAM: Jurnal Hukum & Pranata Sosial, 17*(1), 242–272. https://doi.org/10.19105/al-lhkam.v17i1.5365

Saidin, N. F., Halim, N. D. A., & Yahaya, N. (2015). A review of research on augmented reality in education: Advantages and applications. *International Education Studies, 8*(13), 1–8. https://doi.org/10.5539/ies.v8n13p1

Salleh, M. C. M., & Chowdhury, M. A. M. (2020). Technology adoption among zakat institutions in Malaysia. In *Indonesian Conference of Zakat-Proceedings* (pp. 1–14). https://doi.org/10.37706/iconz.2020.238

Saputra, M. A., Aji, P., & Utomo, H. P. (2015). Aplikasi Tuntunan Shalat Menggunakan Augmented Reality Berbasis Android. *eProceedings of Applied Science, 1*(3), 1662–1671.

Saro, N., Bhari, A., & Rani, A. M. (2023). The level of acceptance and intent to continue using digital zakat applications among the community: A preliminary study. *Perdana: International Journal of Academic Research, 16*(1), 89–96.

Sinha, M., & Srivastava, M. (2023). Augmented reality: New future of social media influencer marketing. *Vision*. https://doi.org/10.1177/09722629221147124

Spallone, R., Lamberti, F., Olivieri, L. M., Ronco, F., & Lombardi, L. (2023). Augmented reality and avatars for museum heritage storytelling. In A. Giordano, M. Russo, & R. Spallone (Eds.), *Beyond Digital Representation: Advanced Experiences in AR and AI for Cultural Heritage and Innovative Design* (pp. 241–258). Cham: Springer Nature Switzerland.

Suyuti, H., & Setyanto, A. (2023). The use of augmented reality technology in preserving cultural heritage: A case study of old Jami Mosque of Palopo. *Ceddi Journal of Information System and Technology, 2*(1), 28–37.

Tabung Baitulmal Sarawak (2021). Jejak Asnaf Versi 3.0 (Version 1.0.4) [Mobile Application Software]. https://play.google.com/store/apps/details?id=v3.jejak.asnaf

Thomas, D. J. (2016). Augmented reality in surgery: the computer-aided medicine revolution. *International Journal of Surgery, 36*(PA), 25. https://doi.org/10.1016/j.ijsu.2016.10.003

Umam, K., & Susandi, A. D. (2024). An exploration of students' anxiety in mathematics online learning using augmented reality at junior high school: A Rasch model construct. *Pegem Journal of Education and Instruction, 14*(1), 186–196. https://www.pegegog.net/index.php/pegegog/article/view/2254

Wanti, L. P., Prasetya, N. W. A., & Puspitasari, L. (2022). Implementation of marker-based tracking method on augmented reality–based applications to reduce the morbidity of pregnant women with preeclampsia. *International Conference on Computer Science and Engineering Technology Proceedings (ICCSET), 1*(1), 45–54.

Yawised, K., Apasrawirote, D., Chatrangsan, M., & Muneesawang, P. (2023). Travelling in the digital world: exploring the adoption of augmented reality (AR) through mobile application in hospitality business sector. *Journal of Advances in Management Research, 20*(4). https://doi.org/10.1108/JAMR-01-2023-0023

Section III

Building Immersive and Game-Driven Digital Worlds

8

From Play to Practice: Game-Based Waste-Sorting Education for Children

Hanhan Maulana, Herman Surdianto Soegoto, Irfan Dwiguna Sumitra, Rifki Aqila Zaidan, Noraziah ChePa, Nur Azzah Abu Bakar, and Azham Hussain

8.1 Introduction

Waste is the remains of human daily activities and/or natural processes in solid form. Waste producers are individuals who produce "unused material" through natural or non-natural processes (Gayatri, 2023). It means that waste is something that cannot be avoided in everyday life. The amount of waste generated is in line with the number of residents and the level of community consumption. The more residents in an area, the more waste is produced. Familiar sources of waste include plastic, cans, styrofoam, and food waste. Data from the National Waste Management Information System of Indonesia (SIPSN) revealed that the volume of waste generated in Indonesia in 2023 amounted to 19,281,377 tonnes.

Improper waste management can lead to environmental degradation and adversely affect public health. Maladies that can emerge due to inadequate waste management include diarrhoea, dengue fever, typhus, and various skin conditions. Environmental problems that also arise from waste are air pollution. Waste produces odours that interfere with breathing. Another problem is water pollution from leachate (liquid produced from exposure to rainwater in waste piles). It can seep into the soil and pollute both the soil and the surrounding water sources. These problems do not only occur around temporary disposal sites or final disposal sites, but can also occur in the residential environment.

In Indonesia, waste separation is commonly practised using five colour-coded bins: red for hazardous waste (B3), yellow for plastic waste, green for organic waste, blue for paper waste, and grey or black for residual waste. This system aligns with the government's comprehensive waste management policies. Waste Management emphasises the 3R principles—Reduce, Reuse, Recycle—and mandates that all parties, including individuals,

DOI: 10.1201/9781003662433-11

businesses, and governments, participate in waste reduction and handling. Building on this, Presidential Regulation No. 97/2017, known as Jakstranas, sets a national target to reduce waste by 30% and manage the remaining 70% by 2025, promoting integrated waste management strategies. Furthermore, Government Regulation No. 81/2012 requires waste segregation at the source into five categories, facilitating proper sorting and recycling. To address specific waste types, Government Regulation No. 27/2020 focuses on managing waste that requires special treatment due to its hazardous nature or volume. These regulations collectively support Indonesia's goal of a waste-free environment by 2025, encouraging responsible waste management practices nationwide.

The negative impact of waste can be managed through proper waste management. One effective approach is waste classification based on its type, as stated in government policy. Educating children about the hazards associated with waste can be an effective way to instil responsible waste disposal habits from a young age (Satria et al., 2021; Zolfaghary et al., 2021; Rahmayanti et al., 2020). In early childhood, they experience a golden age (the golden years). During this golden age, children will be more active, creative, and have a high level of curiosity. Previous research by Rahmayanti et al. (2020) developed an Android sorting waste game for early childhood, concluding that games can be used as an educational tool if implemented correctly. Educational games designed for children tend to be simple, making them easier to understand. Educational games can also display visuals and be equipped with sound. It will make it easier to convey material that is difficult for children to understand.

In this work, we conducted interviews with 28 elementary school children as the initialisation of the study. We found that children only understand two types of waste: organic and inorganic. After further observation, ten of them were still wrong in classifying the two types of waste. It also shows that the government's policy to classify waste into five categories is not yet feasible. Therefore, education about waste classification policies is necessary. The results of the initial questionnaire were reinforced by the findings of a survey conducted by the central statistics agency. The Central Statistics Agency of Indonesia surveyed 75,000 households in 2022. The survey results showed that as many as 47.59% of elementary school children were unaware of waste classification and did not classify waste in their daily lives. The survey results also showed that as many as 32.40% of elementary school children were aware of waste sorting but did not practice it.

This work aims to cultivate awareness of recycling towards better waste management through a game-based approach. We built a game related to waste classification based on applicable government regulations. We target elementary school students to learn with games as tools. We anticipate that this initiative will spark an interest in waste classification among elementary school students. This study also aims to educate students about waste classification. In this chapter, we explain the development and evaluation of educational games that can provide an understanding and knowledge of the concept of waste sorting. This game is designed to enhance children's understanding of waste selection. With games, children will be more interested in learning the concept. Furthermore, children can apply what they have learned about waste classification in everyday life after playing the game.

8.2 Game-Based Learning and Immersive Approaches to Waste Education

Over time, it has been noted that games can help improve a child's knowledge and skills in various areas of learning, including education. Educational games, as a fun approach, increase understanding of essential concepts, such as sorting waste. Recent evidence suggests that games, when applied alongside environmental education, enhance knowledge and encourage behaviour change towards more sustainable actions (Deterding et al., 2011). Games are designed to meet the developmental needs of children by facilitating ease of participation and learning through active and playful interactions, which help strengthen the retention of concepts such as sorting waste (Gee, 2003).

The creation of games has coincided with the development of various theories that focus on moderating the learning process and inciting pro-environmental actions. Estimates suggest that a game-centric approach, combined with features such as instant feedback and rewards, leads to improvements in children's participation in waste management activities, including sorting items for recycling. Evidence from numerous studies underscores the pivotal role of games in fostering environmental awareness. Castellano et al. (2021) empirically demonstrated that a serious game with a social robot interface enhanced children's attitudes towards recycling and their engagement. Similarly, Boncu et al. (2022) reviewed evidence indicating that games and gamification can have a positive influence on environmental attitudes and behaviours, including waste-sorting practices. Hoffmann and Pfeiffer (2022) examined two gameful strategies—repetition and elaboration—for strengthening learners' waste-sorting knowledge. More recently, Chen et al. (2024) investigated the underlying mechanisms, including self-efficacy and reduced psychological distance, through which interactive games influence pro-environmental behaviour.

Game-based educational tools are effective in promoting cognitive and behavioural changes in children. Hamari et al. (2016) found that immersion in games does not significantly influence learning outcomes; however, their study supports the view that game engagement positively contributes to learning. Children would better absorb waste separation information, for example, in a more stimulating and memorable way (Seaborn & Fels, 2015). Furthermore, the incorporation of educational information along with fun play ensures that children are not only learning, but also becoming aware of their responsibility in conserving the environment. In general, the studies above indicate that games have the potential to serve as a strong educational tool in raising children's awareness of waste-sorting and promoting long-term improvements in supporting environmental sustainability (Prensky, 2020).

8.3 Designing and Developing an Immersive Educational Game for Waste Sorting

This research comprises four distinct stages. The initial stage involves data collection. This work conducted an initial survey of 28 school children about the topic of waste classifications. Additionally, data were collected from the central statistics agency, which surveyed 75,000 families. The subsequent stage involves data analysis. It entails compiling, categorising, and identifying patterns or themes within the data to ascertain its underlying significance. Compiling data entails classifying it into themes, patterns, or categories based on the research objectives. The third stage is game development. We use the multimedia development life cycle method (Suryn, 2014; Pressman, 2005; Oshana & Kraeling, 2019). This method has six main stages, explained below:

a. Concept—Before the commencement of game development, a comprehensive analysis of the preceding game is conducted. This analysis encompasses various aspects, including the User Interface (UI), level layout, application targets, and the overall purpose of the application, to identify potential benefits and areas for improvement.
b. Design—After the concept analysis is complete, the next stage is the design stage. This stage involves compiling, depicting, and designing the UI for detailed game development. The application used for creating the UI design is Draw.io.
c. Material collecting—During the asset collection stage, the necessary resources for game development are gathered. Asset collection can take the form of downloading free assets from the internet, creating new assets, or modifying existing ones. Asset creation or modification is accomplished using the KRITA application.
d. Assembly—At the assembly stage, the existing assets are organised or modified until the educational game is complete. The existing

assets are organised according to the UI design created at the design stage. The application used at this stage is Unity.

e. Testing—Following the completion of the assembly and development stages of the educational game, the subsequent stage is the testing or application testing phase. This stage is conducted to determine whether the game that has been developed functions as intended.
f. Distribution—Once testing is completed and the educational game is functioning as intended, the application will be distributed to the intended user.

The last stage is evaluation. The research evaluation was conducted after the game was developed. We conduct a pre-test and a post-test. The test targets were sixth-grade elementary school students. The pre-test was conducted by giving a questionnaire about waste classification. The pre-test aims to determine the current level of students' understanding of waste classification. The post-test was conducted after students had undergone an educational experience facilitated by games. Following the game, students were given a questionnaire to assess their learning gains from the experience.

8.4 Evaluating the Impact of Game-Based Waste-Sorting Education

8.4.1 Data Gathering

This study gathers the challenges encountered by elementary school children. We conducted interviews with 28 elementary school children, and it can be concluded that all children can only distinguish between organic and inorganic waste. In fact, the Indonesian government, through the local government, has implemented a waste categorisation system into five categories. Based on the initial observations, it has been observed that 10 out of 28 children still lack knowledge about the waste disposal process and are unable to distinguish between organic and inorganic waste. Furthermore, we have also collected data from the Central Statistics Agency of the Republic of Indonesia. The statistics obtained from a survey of 75,000 households revealed that 47.59% of elementary school children were either unaware of waste sorting or did not engage in waste-sorting activities. Additionally, 32.40% of elementary school children were aware of waste sorting but did not actively participate in the process.

8.4.2 Data Analysis

This work analysed the waste categories agreed upon in Indonesia. In Indonesia itself, there are five waste categories that the government has officially recognised. The five types of waste are explained as follows:

a. Organic waste—Organic waste refers to material that readily decomposes in natural environments, characterised by its rapid rotting process. Examples of organic waste include leftover food, fallen leaves, and tree branches. This waste is typically segregated into green waste bins. By separating organic waste into distinct containers, its decomposition into compost becomes more manageable and efficient.
b. Inorganic waste—Inorganic waste refers to materials that are difficult to decompose, such as plastics, aluminium cans, and styrofoam. This waste is typically disposed of in yellow trash bins. The utilisation of inorganic waste can be facilitated through specialised trash bins, which enable its transformation into recycled crafts or its recycling in factories.
c. Hazardous and toxic waste (B3)—Biomedical waste (B3) is typically disposed of in red trash bins. B3 waste is waste that poses a risk to human health, animal welfare, or the surrounding environment. Examples of B3 waste include glass waste, detergent packaging, and other cleaning products, as well as insecticides and similar substances. To minimise potential impacts, B3 waste must be segregated into a specific container.
d. Paper waste—Paper waste is a specific type of waste that can be segregated into a blue trash container. Sorting paper waste facilitates the recycling process. Cardboard, paper scraps, pamphlets, paper packaging, and books are also included in the category of paper waste.
e. Residual waste—Residual waste refers to waste that falls outside the four primary categories of waste: solid waste, hazardous waste, medical waste, and electronic waste. Trash bins specifically designated for residual waste are typically grey in colour. Examples of residual waste include used diapers, used sanitary napkins, used chewing gum, and cigarette butts.

This study examines comparable games. The purpose of analysing similar applications is to assess the functionality and user experience of existing applications within the same domain as the software under investigation. The objective is to analyse the gameplay and user flow of the studied applications and identify the unique features of the software being developed in this study. The game analysed in this study is the Recycle game. The Recycle game is an Android-based educational game that focuses on waste sorting,

FIGURE 8.1
Recycle game.

featuring a straightforward gameplay mechanism. In this game, players slide the trash into the corresponding trash can based on its type. If a player incorrectly places the trash, the smartphone vibrates to indicate an error. This game incorporates a drag-and-drop concept. The Recycle game offers several advantages, particularly due to its simple gameplay concept, which makes it easily comprehensible to children. Users only need to select the appropriate trash type and drag it towards the intended trash can. However, the game does have a disadvantage, as its gameplay can become repetitive, leading to a sense of boredom among users quickly. Figure 8.1 presents the interface of the Recycle game.

8.4.3 Game Development

The game creation process begins with the creation of a concept. We start with a story about a fox. A fox is living in the forest. Because the forest inhabited by a fox is littered with garbage. The fox came out of his house to clean the area around his house of garbage. Then we compiled it into two gameplays. The first gameplay is a side-scrolling-based adventure game. The main character of the game must embark on an adventure to collect various types of garbage scattered throughout the game scene. The second gameplay is a time management game where players must put the trash found by the main character into the correct trash can. Based on this concept, we built the system functionality. The system has five main functionalities: playing an adventure, taking damage, picking up waste, activating checkpoints, and moving the character. The system's behaviour is explained using a use case diagram, as shown in Figure 8.2.

The main character in the game is a fox. This character can walk right, left and jump. The following image is a character design in the form of a sprite. We divide the game into five levels with different scenes. Then we provide a tutorial menu to make it easier for users to play the game. Each level is locked

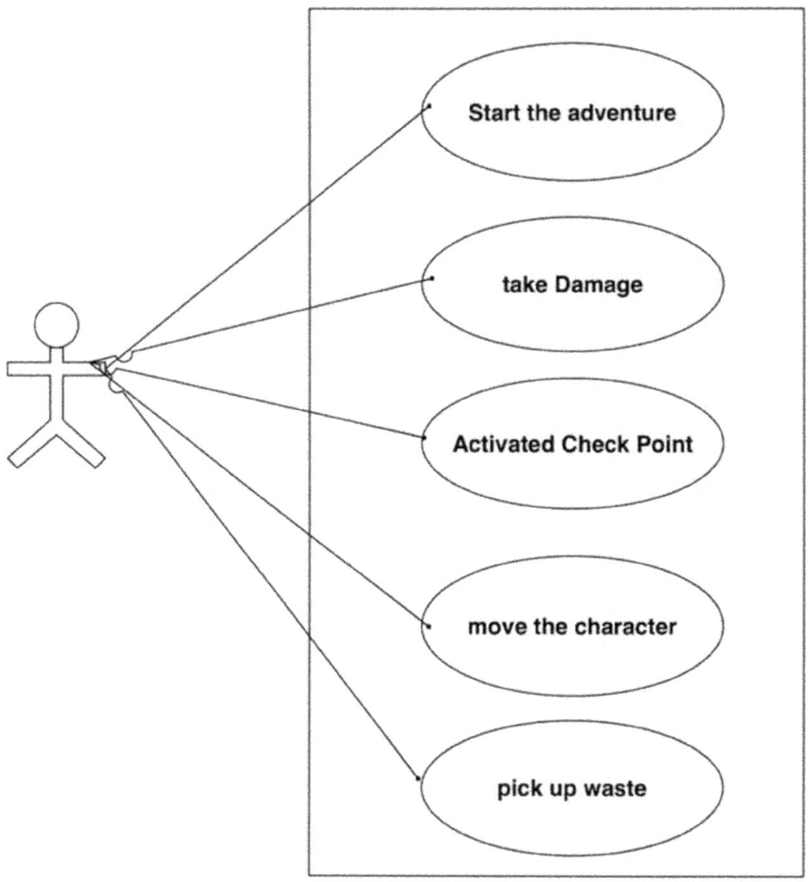

FIGURE 8.2
Use case diagram for the Recycle game.

and will only open after the player completes the previous level. Figure 8.3 explains all the levels in the game. The adventure scheme in the game is a side-scrolling game with a different environment at each level. Figure 8.4 illustrates an example of an environment at Level 1. Regarding the explanation of waste and its categories, we provide this information in the Info menu, as in Figure 8.5. In this menu, the definitions and examples of various types of waste are explained by their categories.

8.4.4 Evaluation

To evaluate the game's effectiveness, we engaged elementary school children in a socialisation exercise to introduce the concept of waste sorting. A total of 29 individuals participated in the evaluation phase. We used the pre-test method (administered before playing the game) and the post-test method

FIGURE 8.3
All levels in the game.

FIGURE 8.4
Example of game environment at level 1.

after playing the game. We gave the students questions, and then they had to categorise the waste on the evaluation sheet. Figure 8.6 illustrates the results of the pre-test and post-test.

Based on the findings presented in Figure 8.6, there is a notable disparity in the level of understanding among children regarding waste sorting. Approximately 90% of students demonstrated an improvement in their post-test scores compared to their pre-test scores. Only students numbered ten, 23, and 29, whose pre-test and post-test scores did not show a significant increase, were included in this analysis. The calculation of the N-gain value further supports this result. N-gain is computed by subtracting the post-test

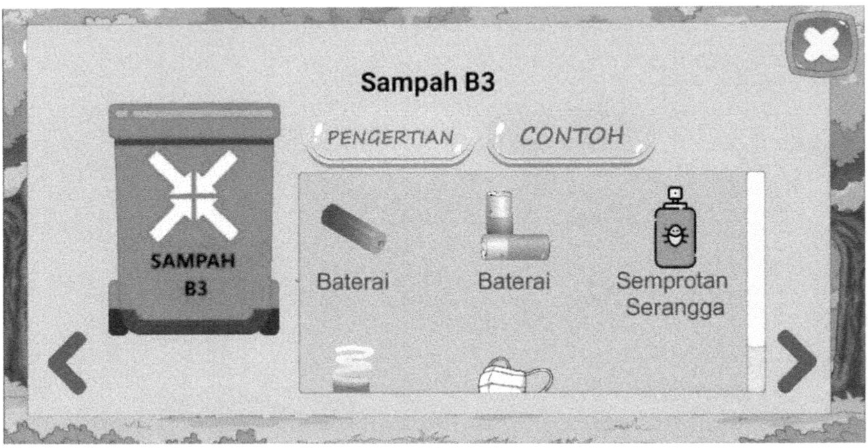

FIGURE 8.5
Information menu explains the waste categories.

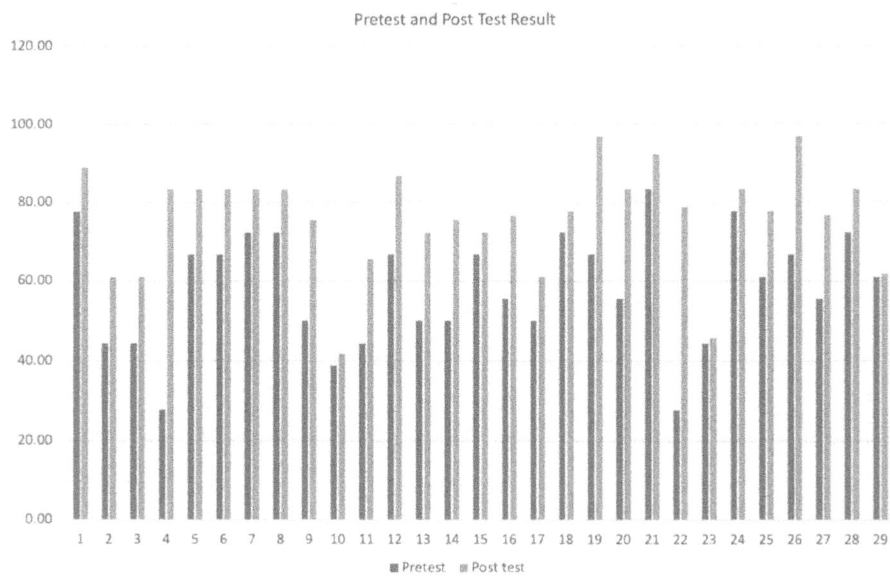

FIGURE 8.6
Pre-test and post-test results.

result from the pre-test score and dividing the result by the ideal value minus the pre-test score. The N-gain value obtained is 0.43, indicating a moderate level of gain (Meltzer, 2002).

This finding suggests that games are an effective medium for providing education to students. This finding aligns with other research, which suggests that game media is an effective learning medium (Gayatri, 2023; Dwisaputra et al., 2019; Florenza et al., 2021; Kidi et al., 2017; Metikaridis & Xinogalos, 2021; Rahmayanti et al., 2020; Sari et al., 2017; Satria et al., 2021; Sya'ban et al., 2021). Nevertheless, it is worth noting that 10% of children did not experience a substantial enhancement in their comprehension when utilising games as an educational tool. It can be attributed to their aversion to games, which warrants further consideration in the development of future games.

8.5 Towards Sustainability: Games as Tools for Eco-Awareness and Daily Practice

This study explains the process of developing an educational game that teaches elementary school children to sort waste. We analyse the types of waste, create a story concept, and then build a game application. We conducted pre-tests and post-tests to evaluate the effectiveness of the game media in providing waste-sorting education to elementary school children. Based on the test results, it can be concluded that this educational game can increase children's knowledge about the types of waste. Future research will analyse children's behaviour after playing the game. It is hoped that children will not only be able to sort waste but also apply the concept of sorting in their everyday lives.

Acknowledgement

This research is funded by Universiti Utara Malaysia and Universitas Komputer Indonesia (UNIKOM) through the International Matching Grant (SO Code 21531). The authors fully acknowledge UUM and UNIKOM for the approved funding, which made this research viable and effective.

References

Boncu, Ş., Candel, O. S., & Popa, N. L. (2022). Gameful green: A systematic review on the use of serious computer games and gamified mobile apps to foster pro-environmental information, attitudes and behaviors. *Sustainability*, *14*(16), 10400. https://doi.org/10.3390/su141610400

Castellano, G., De Carolis, B., D'Errico, F., Macchiarulo, N., & Rossano, V. (2021). PeppeRecycle: Improving children's attitude toward recycling by playing with a social robot. *International Journal of Social Robotics*, *13*(1), 97–111. https://doi.org/10.1007/s12369-021-00754-0

Chen, J., Wang, Y., & Zhang, Z. (2024). Exploring the role and mechanisms of environmental games in promoting pro-environmental behavior. *Frontiers in Psychology, 15*, 1331577. https://doi.org/10.3389/fpsyg.2024.1455005

Deterding, S., Dixon, D., Khaled, R., & Nacke, L. (2011). From game design elements to gamefulness: Defining "gamification". *Proceedings of the 15th International Academic MindTrek Conference: Envisioning Future Media Environments*, 9–15. https://doi.org/10.1145/2181037.2181040

Dwisaputra, A. S., Rokhmawati, R. I., & Akbar, M. A. (2019). Evaluasi user experience pada game augmented reality (sub projection mapping): Wall climbing menggunakan heuristic playbility (PLAY)(Studi kasus: Wahana Jawa Timur Park 3). *Jurnal Pengembangan Teknologi Informasi dan Ilmu Komputer, 3*(2), 2146–2153. https://j-ptiik.ub.ac.id/index.php/j-ptiik/article/view/4493

Florenza, F., Andreas, A., & Harnoko, I. (2021). Board game edukasi pengenalan fauna endemik Kalimantan untuk anak. *Rupaka, 4*(1). https://journal.untar.ac.id/index.php/Rupaka/article/view/16689

Gayatri, N. A. G. (2023). Design of an educational game design sorting waste Android based. *Ultima Infosys :Jurnal Ilmu Sistem Informasi, 14*(1), 11–18. https://doi.org/10.31937/si.v14i1.3113

Gee, J. P. (2003). What video games have to teach us about learning and literacy. *Computers in entertainment (CIE), 1*(1), 20–20. https://doi.org/10.1145/950566.950595

Hamari, J., Shernoff, D. J., Rowe, E., Coller, B., Asbell-Clarke, J., & Edwards, T. (2016). Challenging games help students learn: An empirical study on engagement, flow, and immersion in game-based learning. *Computers in Human Behavior, 54*, 170–179. https://doi.org/10.1016/j.chb.2015.07.045

Hoffmann, G., & Pfeiffer, J. (2022). Gameful learning for a more sustainable world: Measuring the effect of design elements on long-term learning outcomes in correct waste sorting. *Business & Information Systems Engineering, 64*(4), 459–482. https://doi.org/10.1007/s12599-021-00731-x

Kidi, N., Kanigoro, B., Salman, A. G., Prasetio, Y. L., Lokaadinugroho, I., & Sukmandhani, A. A. (2017). Android based Indonesian information culture education game. *Procedia Computer Science, 116*, 99–106. https://doi.org/10.1016/j.procs.2017.10.015

Meltzer, D. E. (2002). The relationship between mathematics preparation and conceptual learning gains in physics: A possible "hidden variable" in diagnostic pre-test scores. *American journal of physics, 70*(12), 1259–1268. https://doi.org/10.1119/1.1514215

Metikaridis, D., & Xinogalos, S. (2021). A comparative analysis of tools for developing location based games. *Entertainment Computing, 37*, 100403. https://doi.org/10.1016/j.entcom.2020.100403

Oshana, R., & Kraeling, M. (2019). *Software engineering for embedded systems: Methods, practical techniques, and applications*. Newnes.

Prensky, M. (2020). *The gamification of learning and instruction: Game-based methods and strategies for training and education*. John Wiley & Sons.

Pressman, R. S. (2005). *Software engineering: A practitioner's approach*. Palgrave Macmillan.

Rahmayanti, H., Oktaviani, V., & Syani, Y. (2020). Development of sorting waste game android based for early childhood in environmental education. *Journal of Physics: Conference Series, 1434*(1), 012029. https://doi.org/10.1088/1742-6596/1434/1/012029

Sari, S., Anjani, R., Farida, I., & Ramdhani, M. A. (2017). Using Android-based educational game for learning colloid material. *Journal of Physics: Conference Series, 895*(1), 012012. https://doi.org/10.1088/1742-6596/895/1/012012

Satria, E., Fitriani, L., Muhsin, Y. S., & Tresnawati, D. (2021). Development of educational games for learning waste management. *IOP Conference Series: Materials Science and Engineering, 1098*(3), 032064. https://doi.org/10.1088/1757-899X/1098/3/032064

Seaborn, K., & Fels, D. I. (2015). Gamification in theory and action: A survey. *International Journal of Human-Computer Studies, 74*, 14–31. https://doi.org/10.1016/j.ijhcs.2014.09.006

Suryn, W. (2014). *Software quality engineering: A practitioner's approach*. John Wiley & Sons.

Sya'ban, S. U., Baskoro, M. L., & Armayuda, E. (2021). Perancangan board game edukasi satwa endemik Pulau Jawa untuk anak usia 7 hingga 11 tahun. *AKSA: Jurnal Desain Komunikasi Visual, 4*(2), 600–611. https://doi.org/10.37505/aksa.v4i2.51

Zolfaghary, P., Zakerinia, M., & Kazemi, H. (2021). A model for the use of urban treated wastewater in agriculture using multiple criteria decision making (MCDM) and geographic information system (GIS). *Agricultural Water Management, 243*, 106490. https://doi.org/10.1016/j.agwat.2020.106490

9

Gamifying Eco-Awareness: Inspiring Sustainable Habits in Malaysian and Indonesian Schools

Noraziah ChePa, Nur Azzah Abu Bakar, Azham Hussain, Hanhan Maulana, Herman Surdianto Soegoto, Irfan Dwiguna Sumitra, and Laura Lim Sie-Yi

9.1 Introduction

Waste generation is a growing global concern, driven by rising populations and improved living standards. Its environmental impact is substantial, contributing to pollution and posing health risks (Odewabi et al., 2013). As public concern increases, governments are urged to address waste-related issues. Effective waste management has become vital to both national economies and public well-being. In response, the 2004 G8 Sea Island Summit launched the Global 3R initiative to promote reducing, reusing, and recycling as a means of establishing a sustainable, resource-efficient society (Sreenivasan et al., 2012). The recycling component of the 3R initiative supports environmental sustainability by reducing raw material use and diverting waste from landfills. Recyclable items include paper, metal, textiles, electronics, glass, batteries, and biodegradable waste. These materials are collected, sorted, and reprocessed into new products.

Top recycling countries such as Germany, Austria, South Korea, Wales, and Switzerland recycle between 49.7% and 56.1% of their waste due to strong policies and public engagement. In contrast, recycling awareness remains low in many developing and densely populated nations, where waste management is often seen as the government's responsibility (Wang et al., 2020; Vidanaarachchi et al., 2006). Demographics significantly influence recycling knowledge, attitudes, and practices (Xu et al., 2016; Oribe-Garcia et al., 2015; Mohamed & Abdul Rahman, 2014). Malaysia's 3R programme, launched in the 1980s, has had limited success; only 15% of waste is recycled despite campaigns and regulations (Bernama, 2016). In Russia, approximately 93% of waste is disposed of in landfills, with only 5% being recycled (Amelkina, 2020).

 DOI: 10.1201/9781003662433-12

Public awareness and education are vital for recycling success (Struk, 2017; Williams & Taylor, 2004). Studies emphasised the importance of incorporating sustainability education from early childhood (Buil et al., 2019; Davis, 2015; Iris, 2012), though its impact remains limited. Game-based learning (GBL) presents a promising approach to teaching children about recycling. It combines educational content with playful elements, enhancing motivation, emotional engagement, and spontaneous learning (Dickey, 2011; Hung et al., 2018; Nadolny et al., 2020; Plass et al., 2015; Walsh, 2020). GBL fosters creativity, resilience, and problem-solving and is increasingly integrated into digital learning environments (Oblinger, 2006; Isa et al., 2020; Chen et al., 2020). This chapter explores how GBL fosters eco-awareness among Malaysian and Indonesian students. By making recycling and waste management engaging, these games enhance understanding and encourage sustainable habits. Ultimately, they inspire the younger generation to contribute to a greener future.

9.2 Gamified Digital Interventions for Recycling Awareness

Since people nowadays lack a sufficient understanding of recycling, improper behaviours regarding waste management have arisen, highlighting the need for more education and recycling awareness (Konstantinidou et al., 2024). The trend of digital interventions using technology to increase awareness of recycling is on the rise. The advent of technology has facilitated the method of educating and motivating individuals to prioritise environmentally responsible waste management in their respective communities. By increasing recycling awareness, the dissemination of information has the power to induce a change in attitudes successfully.

Kamil and Ishak (2024) developed a mobile application for recycling awareness using Adobe Animate. By utilising animation, the application aims to raise awareness about the importance of recycling for the disposal of medications, packaging of skincare products, and textiles and fabrics, thereby improving the environment for the future (Kamil & Ishak, 2024). Despite the belief that recycling knowledge should begin at a young age, their intended audience consists of adults. One of the most important social responsibilities that needs to be nurtured in the community, particularly among the younger generation, is the education of recycling awareness (Ahmad et al., 2021).

Another animated comic on recycling has been presented by Ahmad at al. (2021) as an alternative learning and intervention application, namely i-Recycle. The purpose of this application is to support preschool children in learning and acquiring new knowledge. The i-Recycle system comprises a variety of narratives, including daily routines such as gathering recyclable items at home, assisting friends in cleaning up the park, and participating in educational activities at school. However, there is a lack of an interactive element that aids the learning of recycling knowledge.

Recycling is one way that younger generations are making a positive impact in the world and a force for social change. Social pressure, as well as intrinsic and extrinsic incentives, can be used to implement gamified learning and increase recycling intention. Game mechanics, such as leader boards, stages, points, and incentives, are crucial in creating a fun and meaningful activity that encourages recycling among young people (Cheng et al., 2021).

9.3 Designing and Implementing Game-Based Eco-Awareness Interventions

The overall methodology of the game-based eco-awareness intervention involved three main stages: preparation of eco-awareness games for both Malaysia and Indonesia, game-based eco-awareness sessions, and impact analysis. The flow of activities is illustrated in Figure 9.1.

9.3.1 Phase 1: Eco-Awareness Game Preparation

Before the intervention, two versions of eco-awareness games were successfully designed and developed by adapting our initial game to promote

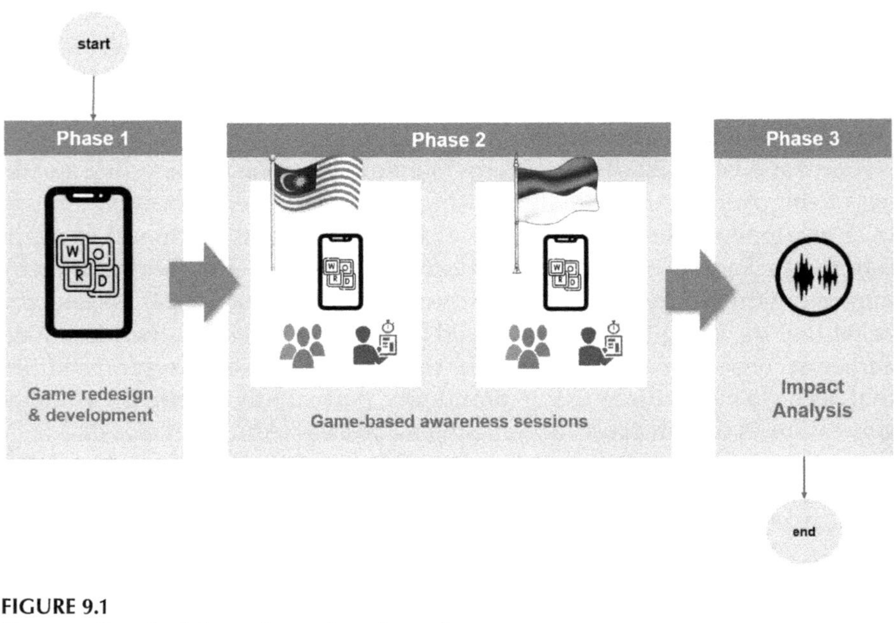

FIGURE 9.1
The overall methodology of game-based recycle awareness.

recycling awareness. Given that this study focuses on school children, both versions have been carefully redesigned to cater specifically to students in Malaysian and Indonesian schools. These adaptations ensure that the games align with the educational needs, language, locality, and environmental contexts of each country, making them more engaging and effective in fostering recycling awareness among young learners.

The Malaysian version of the eco-awareness game has been modified to better align with the study's objectives. While the original G-Ventures game featured five levels, the redesigned version now includes ten levels, with progressively increasing difficulty from level 1 to 10. However, the three types of recycling bins remain unchanged to reflect the current recycling practices implemented in Malaysia. The core gameplay of G-Ventures revolves around players repeatedly collecting and sorting different types of waste into designated recycling bins. This intentional repetition reinforces memory retention and deepens players' understanding of proper waste management. By consistently engaging with recycling codes and correct disposal methods, players develop familiarity with the process, making recycling an intuitive habit. Beyond education, the game transforms recycling into an enjoyable experience, fostering engagement and encouraging long-term behavioural change. Through interactive and immersive gameplay, G-Ventures aims to instil lifelong eco-conscious habits in players. The selected interfaces of the Malaysian version of the eco-awareness game are visually illustrated in Figure 9.2.

The Indonesian version of the eco-awareness game has undergone design modifications to align with the country's waste management system, which classifies waste into five main categories: organic waste, inorganic waste, hazardous and toxic waste (B3), paper waste, and residual waste. Waste categories are detailed in Table 9.1. To reinforce proper waste segregation practices, the game incorporates five distinct waste bins, each designated for a specific type of waste. These bins serve as visual aids to help players identify and categorise waste correctly, enhancing their understanding of waste disposal practices in Indonesia. By integrating these localised elements, the game ensures that children learn about their country's waste management policies in an engaging and interactive way.

The Indonesian version of the eco-awareness game is designed with a simplified structure, featuring only five levels compared to the Malaysian version, which consists of ten levels. Players are tasked with collecting different types of waste and placing them into the appropriate bins based on these categories. This focused approach ensures that players gradually build their understanding of proper waste segregation while maintaining engagement throughout the gameplay. By streamlining the levels, the Indonesian version provides a more accessible and manageable learning experience while still effectively promoting eco-awareness. Figure 9.3 shows the screenshots of the game.

Another key adjustment in the Indonesian version is the language adaptation. Unlike the Malaysian version, which is available in English, the

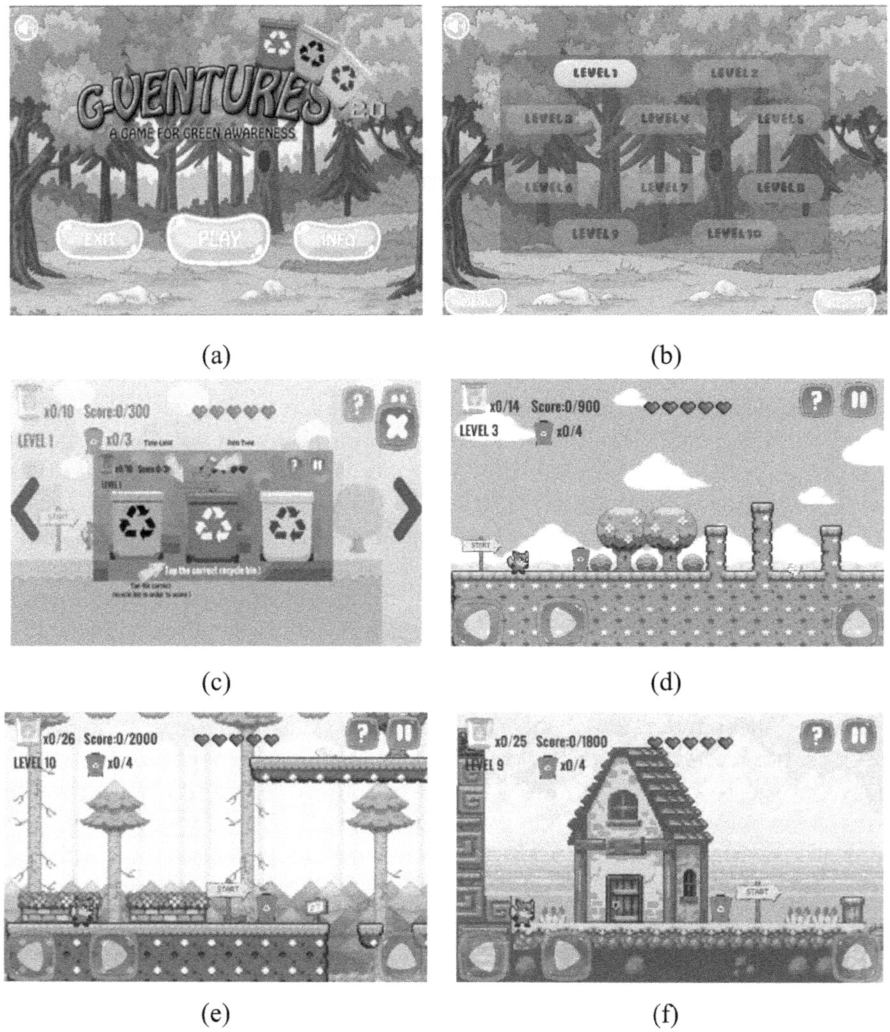

FIGURE 9.2
(a–f) The Malaysian version of the eco-awareness game.

Indonesian version is fully developed in the Indonesian language to improve accessibility and comprehension among local users. This linguistic adaptation enables players to understand game instructions, thereby enhancing their learning experience easily. Additionally, the use of familiar terminology and context-specific references ensures that the game resonates with Indonesian children, increasing their engagement and motivation to practice responsible waste disposal in their daily lives. These modifications help create a more meaningful and impactful educational experience tailored to Indonesia's environmental needs.

TABLE 9.1

Category of Waste for the Indonesian Eco-Awareness Game

Waste Category	Description
Organic	Organic waste decomposes naturally and quickly, including food scraps, leaves, and branches. It is typically placed in green waste bins, making composting more efficient.
Inorganic	Inorganic waste, like plastics, aluminium cans, and Styrofoam, decomposes slowly and is disposed of in yellow bins. Proper sorting enables recycling or repurposing for crafts.
Hazardous and Toxic (B3)	Biomedical waste (B3), disposed of in red bins, poses risks to health and the environment. It includes glass waste, detergent packaging, and insecticides, all of which require proper segregation to minimise harm.
Paper	Paper waste, including cardboard, pamphlets, and books, is sorted into blue bins to aid recycling.
Residual	Residual waste, disposed of in grey bins, includes items like diapers, sanitary napkins, chewing gum, and cigarette butts, which do not fit into primary waste categories.

9.3.2 Phase 2: Game-Based Eco-Awareness Sessions

The eco-awareness session in Malaysia engaged 30 students from Sekolah Kebangsaan Bandar Baru Sintok, specifically those in Standard 4 and 5. This selection was intentional, as children within this age group are at a crucial developmental stage where they begin forming lasting habits and attitudes. By focusing on these young learners, the session aimed to instil a strong foundation in eco-conscious behaviour, ensuring that the knowledge gained would have a lasting impact on their daily lives and future environmental practices. The diverse mix of participants further enriched the learning experience, fostering peer interaction and collaborative engagement in waste sorting and recycling awareness.

The first session began with a preliminary study to assess the students' initial awareness of recycling practices, establishing a baseline understanding before they were exposed to the game. Following this assessment, the students were introduced to the G-Ventures game through a detailed demonstration, which provided step-by-step guidance on its features, navigation, and objectives. This demonstration is essential in familiarising them with the game mechanics, ensuring they can engage effectively during the self-learning phase. For the remainder of the session, students explored the game independently, allowing them to interact with its content at their own pace and develop a personal understanding of recycling concepts. Figure 9.4 shows the photos of the session in Malaysia.

Session 2 focused on reinforcing and deepening the knowledge gained in the first session. The students continued to engage with the game through self-learning and guided activities, helping to solidify their understanding of recycling practices. This structured approach encouraged them to apply

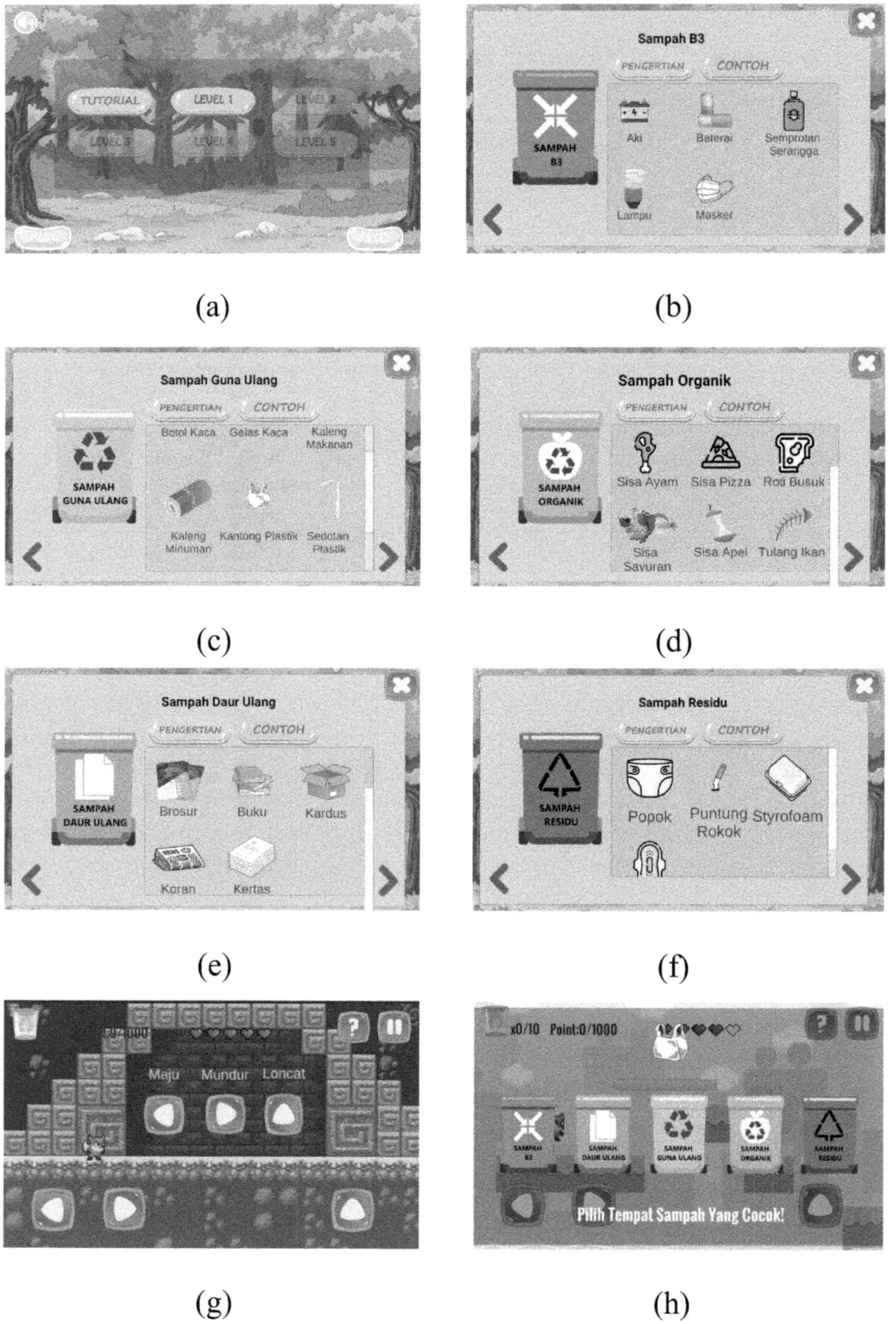

FIGURE 9.3
(a–h) The Indonesian version of the eco-awareness game.

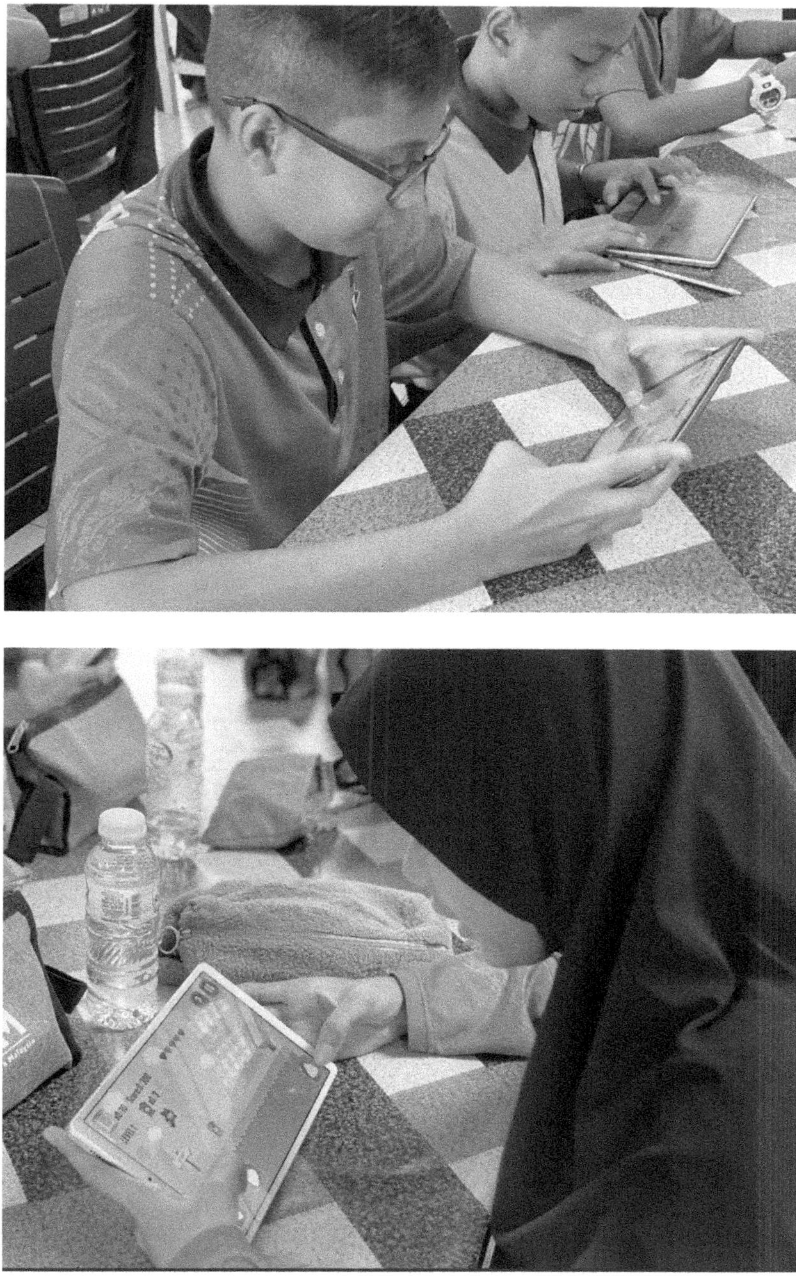

FIGURE 9.4
Game-based eco-awareness session at a Malaysian school.

their learning in a more interactive and meaningful way. After the gameplay session, an evaluation was conducted to measure their perceptions of the game and its impact on their awareness of recycling. This post-test assessment aimed to determine not only the effectiveness of the game in conveying the importance of recycling but also to measure the students' willingness to adopt recycling habits in their daily lives.

In Indonesia, game-based eco-awareness sessions were conducted as part of a socialisation exercise to introduce elementary school children to the concept of waste sorting. A total of 29 students participated in the evaluation phase, which utilised a pre-test and post-test approach. Before playing the game, students completed a pre-test to assess their initial understanding of waste categorisation. After engaging with the game, they took a post-test where they were required to categorise waste items on an evaluation sheet. This method enabled us to assess the game's effectiveness in enhancing students' knowledge and awareness of proper waste management practices.

9.3.3 Impact Analysis

The impact analysis phase examined several key aspects from a series of game-based eco-awareness sessions, including students' understanding of the importance of recycling, behavioural changes in their recycling practices, and the extent to which the eco-awareness game influenced their attitudes towards sustainability. The impacts are assessed using data collected from two game-based eco-awareness sessions, incorporating both direct observations and participant feedback. Additionally, a comparative analysis was also conducted to evaluate the differences in the game's impact between students in Malaysia and Indonesia. This cross-country comparison provides valuable insights into how cultural and environmental factors influence students' engagement and learning outcomes, offering a broader perspective on the effectiveness of game-based interventions in promoting recycling awareness.

9.4 How Games Inspire Recycling Awareness: Insights from Malaysia and Indonesia

This section discusses the findings on how GBL enhances eco-awareness among Malaysian and Indonesian students, inspiring the younger generation to contribute actively to a greener future.

9.4.1 Experiences from Malaysia

During the pre-test phase of the game-based awareness session, 67% of the participants demonstrated an understanding of the recycling concept.

Before the game-based session, 67% of participants demonstrated a basic understanding of recycling, indicating a level of awareness. This indicated that, although many students possessed some prior knowledge, there was still room for improvement. After engaging with the game, post-test results revealed a 10% increase, with 77% of participants now grasping the recycling concept. This improvement suggests that the interactive nature of the game reinforced learning more effectively than traditional methods. By making recycling education engaging and repetitive, the game successfully enhanced students' awareness, fostering a stronger understanding of proper waste management.

Before the game-based awareness sessions, 6.7% of participants had never engaged in recycling, indicating a small yet significant gap in awareness and motivation. This finding underscored the need for targeted educational efforts to encourage participation. However, the impact of the sessions became evident in the post-session assessment, where all participants, including those previously disengaged, had started practising recycling. This positive shift underscores the effectiveness of GBL in promoting recycling habits and enhancing environmental awareness among students, as illustrated in Figure 9.5.

This significant shift underscores the effectiveness of the game-based approach in educating students on the importance of recycling and inspiring them to incorporate these practices into their daily routines. The transition from a small percentage of non-participants to full engagement underscores the success of this intervention. It demonstrates how interactive educational tools can effectively transform awareness into action, even among those who were initially indifferent or resistant to the concept.

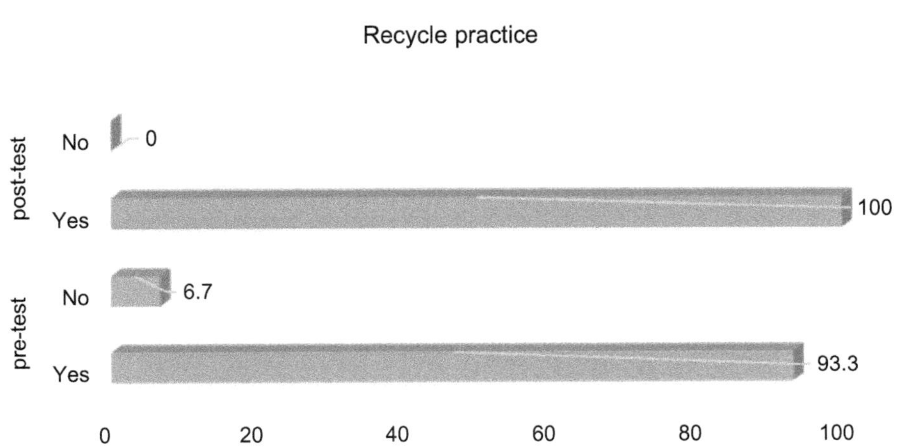

FIGURE 9.5
Recycle practice for the pre-test and post-test.

9.4.2 Experiences from Indonesia

The game-based eco-awareness session conducted in Indonesia involved 29 elementary school students and provided valuable insights into their understanding of waste sorting. The evaluation revealed a significant variation in the students' initial comprehension levels, highlighting the importance of interactive learning tools in reinforcing environmental awareness. Through a structured pre-test and post-test assessment, the study measured changes

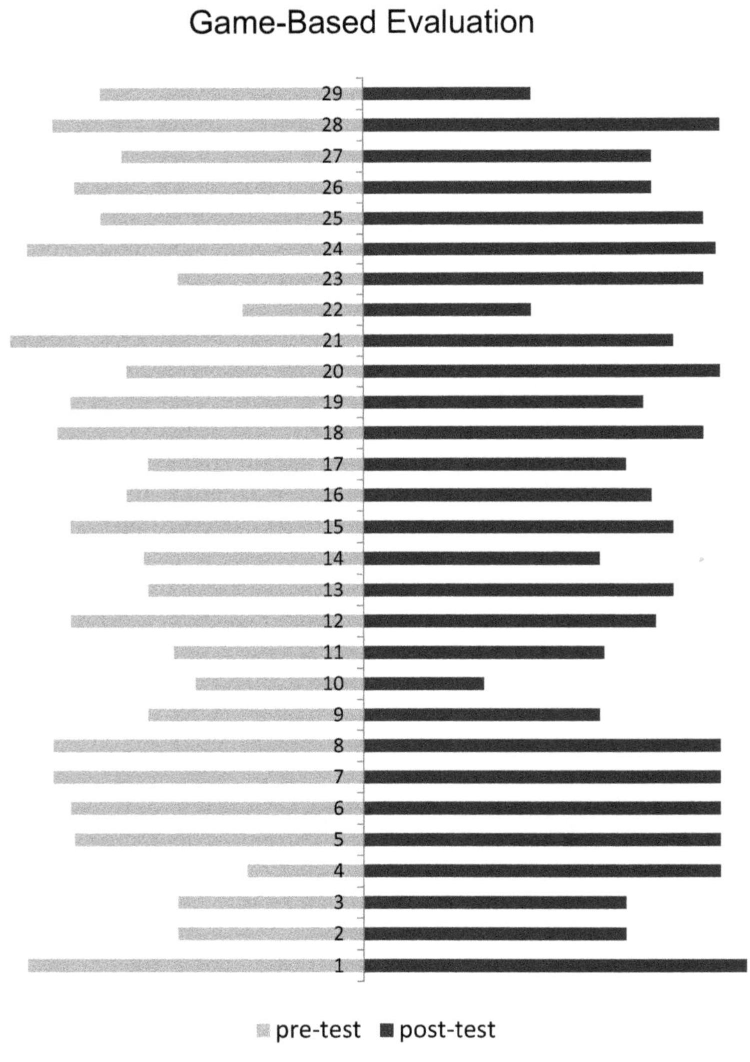

FIGURE 9.6
Pre-test and post-test findings for the game-based eco-awareness session at an Indonesian school.

in the students' ability to correctly categorise waste into designated bins after engaging with the game.

As shown in Figure 9.6, the results indicated that approximately 90% of students exhibited an overall improvement in their post-test scores, demonstrating the game's effectiveness in enhancing their knowledge of waste sorting. Specifically, 82.8% of students demonstrated a marked improvement in their ability to classify waste correctly, while 13.8% showed no improvement, suggesting that some students may require additional guidance or alternative instructional methods to grasp the concepts effectively. A small percentage (3.4%) maintained the same level of performance without any noticeable progress. These findings underscore the potential of GBL in promoting eco-awareness among young learners and emphasise the need for continuous refinement to ensure inclusivity and effectiveness in fostering sustainable habits.

9.5 Towards Sustainable Futures: GBL for Eco-Awareness

This study examines the effectiveness of GBL in promoting and inspiring eco-awareness among schoolchildren in Malaysia and Indonesia, with a specific focus on waste sorting and recycling habits. Two versions of an eco-awareness game were developed, tailored to the locality and waste management contexts of each country. Through interactive gameplay, students were introduced to proper waste disposal practices, reinforcing their understanding of responsible waste management. The study employed pre-test and post-test evaluations to measure improvements in students' knowledge and behavioural changes, revealing a significant positive impact in both countries. Findings suggest that digital educational tools can serve as effective interventions for instilling sustainable habits from an early age.

This study aligns with the Sustainable Development Goals (SDGs) introduced by the United Nations (UN), which promote a holistic approach to achieving sustainable development for all. Specifically, this research supports SDG 12 (Responsible Consumption and Production), which emphasises the importance of reducing waste through the principles of reduce, reuse, and recycle. By encouraging recycling, processed materials such as plastics, metals, and glass can be repurposed, reducing the need for new raw materials, conserving energy, and minimising environmental pollution.

Despite the growing emphasis on SDGs, research related to sustainable waste management remains limited, with most studies focusing on more prominent goals such as SDG 13 (Climate Action) and SDG 17 (Partnerships for the Goals) (Sweileh, 2020). This study contributes to bridging that gap by fostering recycling awareness and promoting responsible waste management practices among schoolchildren. By integrating GBL into eco-awareness education, this research not only supports SDG 12 but also highlights the importance of expanding sustainability research beyond traditionally prioritised areas. Ultimately, cultivating recycling habits through interactive and engaging methods can lay the foundation for a greener future, where younger generations actively contribute to environmental sustainability.

Acknowledgement

This research is funded by Universiti Utara Malaysia and Universitas Komputer Indonesia (UNIKOM) through the International Matching Grant (SO Code 21531). The authors fully acknowledge UUM and UNIKOM for the approved funding, which made this research viable and effective. We highly appreciate and acknowledge the cooperation and contributions of schools in Kedah and Bandung that participated in and assisted with this study.

References

Ahmad, S. Z., Kamarulzaman, N. A., & Mutalib, A. A. (2021). Cultivating recycling awareness in preschoolers using animated interactive comic. *2021 9th International Conference on Information and Communication Technology (ICoICT)*, 104–109. https://doi.org/10.1109/ICoICT52021.2021.9527465

Amelkina, O. (2020). The role of law for improving municipal solid waste management: Comparing Russia and Sweden (*Master's thesis*, Uppsala University).

Bernama. (2016, November 30). Only 15 per cent of Malaysians recycle: Minister. *Eco-Business*. https://www.eco-business.com/news/only-15-per-cent-of-malaysians-recycle-minister/

Buil, P., Roger-Loppacher, O., & Tintoré, M. (2019). Creating the habit of recycling in early childhood: A sustainable practice in Spain. *Sustainability, 11*(6393), 1–19. https://doi.org/10.3390/su11226393

Chen, M. B., Wang, S. G., Chen, Y. N., Chen, X. F., & Lin, Y. Z. (2020). A preliminary study of the influence of game types on the learning interests of primary school students in digital games. *Education Sciences, 10*(4). https://doi.org/10.3390/educsci10040096

Cheng, K. M., Koo, A. C., Mohd Nasir, J. S., & Wong, S. Y. (2021). Playing Edcraft at home: Gamified online learning for recycling intention during lockdown. *F1000Research, 10*, 1–17. https://doi.org/10.12688/f1000research.72761.2

Davis, J. M. (2015). *Young children and the environment: Early education for sustainability*. Cambridge University Press.

Dickey, M. D. (2011). Murder on Grimm Isle: The impact of game narrative design in an educational game-based learning environment. *British Journal of Educational Technology*, *42*(3), 456–469. https://doi.org/10.1111/j.1467-8535.2009.01032.x

Hung, H.-T., Yang, J. C., Hwang, G.-J., Chu, H.-C., & Wang, C.-C. (2018). A scoping review of research on digital game-based language learning. *Computers & Education*, *126*, 89–104. https://doi.org/10.1016/j.compedu.2018.07.001

Iris, D. (2012). Making 'place' for ecological sustainability in early childhood education. *Environmental Education Research*, *18*, 19–29. https://doi.org/10.1080/13504622.2011.572162

Isa, W. A. R. W. M., Suhaimi, A. I. H., Misron, M., Bohary, N. A. A., & Amin, I. M. (2020). Designing mobile-game based learning application for children on oral health education using Islamic culture. *International Journal of Advanced Science and Technology*, *29*(6), 1603–1611.

Kamil, M. H. F. M., & Ishak, A. (2024). Recycling awareness through mobile application: Selecting the categories of recyclable materials for environmental well-being. In *Board Diversity and Corporate Governance* (pp. 165–178). Springer. https://doi.org/10.1007/978-3-031-53877-3_14

Konstantinidou, A., Ioannou, K., Tsantopoulos, G., & Arabatzis, G. (2024). Citizens' attitudes and practices towards waste reduction, separation, and recycling: A systematic review. *Sustainability*, *16*(22), 1–36. https://doi.org/10.3390/su16229969

Mohamed, A., & Abdul Rahman, H. (2014). Study on public awareness towards recycling activity in Kota Bharu, Kelantan, Malaysia. *Advances in Environmental Biology*, *8*(15), 19–24.

Nadolny, L., Valai, A., Cherrez, N. J., Elrick, D., Lovett, A., & Nowatzke, M. (2020). Examining the characteristics of game-based learning: A content analysis and design framework. *Computers and Education*, *156*, 103936. https://doi.org/10.1016/j.compedu.2020.103936

Oblinger, D. G. (2006). Games and learning. *Educause Quarterly Magazine*, *29*(3), 5–7.

Odewabi, A. O., Ogundahunsi, O. A., & Ekor, M. (2013). Effects of exposure of solid wastes in relation to employment duration on some important markers of health and disease in waste management workers of Ogun state in Southwest Nigeria. *Human and Experimental Toxicology*, *32*(12), 1231–1244. https://doi.org/10.1177/0960327113488612

Oribe-Garcia, I., Kamara-Esteban, O., Martin, C., Macarulla-Arenaza, A. M., & Alonso-Vicarion, A. (2015). Identification of influencing municipal characteristics regarding household waste generation and their forecasting ability in Biscay. *Waste Management*, *39*, 26–34. https://doi.org/10.1016/j.wasman.2015.02.017

Plass, J. L., Homer, B. D., & Kinzer, C. K. (2015). Foundations of game-based learning. *Educational Psychologist*, *50*(4), 258–283. https://doi.org/10.1080/00461520.2015.1122533

Sreenivasan, J., Govindan, M., Chinnasami, M., & Kadiresu, I. (2012). Solid waste management in Malaysia – A move towards sustainability. In *Waste Management – An Integrated Vision*. IntechOpen. http://doi.org/10.5772/50870

Struk, M. (2017). Distance and incentives matter: The separation of recyclable municipal waste. *Resources, Conservation & Recycling*, *122*, 155–162. https://doi.org/10.1016/j.resconrec.2017.01.023

Sweileh, W. M. (2020). Bibliometric analysis of scientific publications on "sustainable development goals" with emphasis on "good health and well-being" goal (2015–2019). *Globalisation and Health*, *16*(1), 68. https://doi.org/10.1186/s12992-020-00602-2

Vidanaarachchi, C. K., Yuen, S. T. S., & Pilapitiya, S. (2006). Municipal solid waste management in the southern province of Sri Lanka: Problems, issues and challenges. *Waste Management*, *26*, 920–930. https://doi.org/10.1016/j.wasman.2005.09.013

Walsh, A. (2020). Playful learning for information literacy development. *IFLA Journal*, *46*(2), 143–150. https://doi.org/10.1177/0340035219874083

Wang, H., Liu, X., Wang, N., Zhang, K., Wang, F., Zhang, S., Wang, R., Zheng, P., & Matsushita, M. (2020). Key factors influencing public awareness of household solid waste recycling in urban areas of China: A case study. *Resources, Conservation & Recycling*, *158*, 104813. https://doi.org/10.1016/j.resconrec.2020.104813

Williams, I. D., & Taylor, C. (2004). Maximising household waste recycling at civic amenity sites in Lancashire, England. *Waste Management*, *24*(9), 861–874. https://doi.org/10.1016/j.wasman.2004.02.002

Xu, L., Lin, T., Xu, Y., Xiao, L., Ye, Z., & Cui, S. (2016). Path analysis of factors influencing household solid waste generation: A case study of Xiamen Island, China. *The Journal of Material Cycles and Waste Management*, *18*, 377–384. https://doi.org/10.1007/s10163-014-0340-0

10

Game-Based Interventions for Dyslexia: Usability Insights from DysPReX and MazeDyslexic

Nur Azzah Abu Bakar, Noraziah ChePa, and Mohd Adan Omar

10.1 Introduction

Reading skills open the door to all other learning. Children's reading ability impacts their success in other subjects and their ability to gain knowledge independently. However, some individuals are affected by phonological, speed naming, and/or comprehension deficits, leading to various difficulties in reading. Phonological deficit, as shown in Figure 10.1, is a distinctive criterion that distinguishes individuals with dyslexia from non-dyslexia.

As one of the most common learning disabilities, dyslexia affects an estimated 5%–10% of the population globally (Roongpraiwan et al., 2021; Knight,

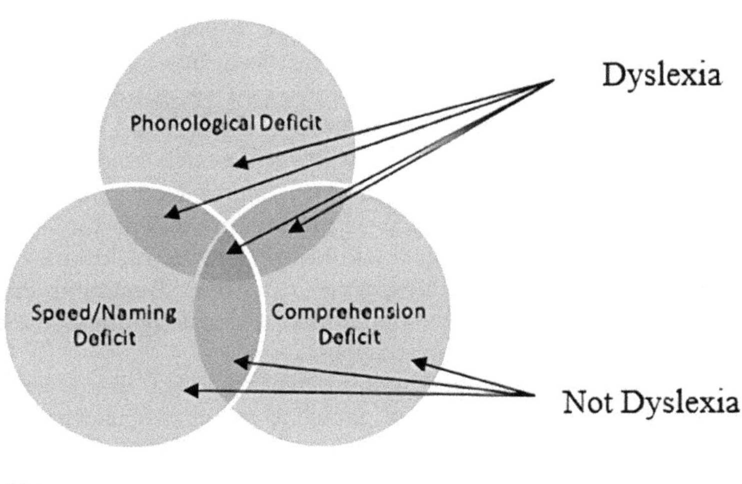

FIGURE 10.1
Types of deficits affecting an individual's reading skills.

DOI: 10.1201/9781003662433-13

2018). Despite being classified as a mental disorder by the International Classification of Mental Disorders and the Diagnostic and Statistical Manual of Mental Disorders (Schulte-Körne, 2010), dyslexia is not related to an individual's intelligence (Mohd Nor, 2021); the difference lies in how the brain interprets and processes language. Children with dyslexia have trouble connecting the sound made by a specific letter or deciphering the sounds of all the letters together that form a word. They often mix up similar-looking letters (Wan Mohammad et al., 2011; Hussin, 2012), have great difficulties in writing, poor spelling skills, and weak oral and written vocabulary, as well as difficulty in arranging the content of compositions (Ridzal et al., 2023). They are also significantly slower at naming things such as colours, numbers, and alphabets.

Traditional interventions for dyslexia have been well-established and widely used in educational settings. Trained educators or therapists typically deliver these interventions in a one-on-one or small-group setting; often, they involve direct, explicit instruction in the fundamental skills required for reading, such as phonological awareness, phonics, and decoding. Programmes like Orton-Gillingham, Lindamood-Bell, and Wilson Reading System have been extensively studied (Sayeski et al., 2019; Tomarong et al., 2023) and have proven effective for individuals with dyslexia. However, these programmes can be intensive and time-consuming, requiring significant commitment from both the learner and the instructor (Snowling & Hulme, 2021).

Besides, traditional dyslexia interventions emphasise structured literacy programmes that focus on phonemic awareness, phonics, fluency, vocabulary, and comprehension (Ehri, 2020). Unfortunately, the strategies do not work well for people with dyslexia, as they are unable to categorise the sounds of language or connect sounds to meaning in the same way as other students. Past studies (e.g., Orpi, 2019; Marshall, 2013; Swanson, 1999) have revealed that traditional methods have a limited impact on dyslexic children. Improvements through intensive reading interventions yield small to moderate effects over time, and there appears to be a subset of approximately 25% of problem readers who do not respond to special education interventions.

In the absence of satisfactory intervention through traditional special educational methods, several alternative treatments have been offered for dyslexia. These include biofeedback, hypnotherapy, music therapy, visual occlusion therapy, the Neural Organisation Chiropractic Technique, Primary Reflex Therapy, and dyslexia Dyspraxia Attention Treatment exercises. Researchers have also explored the potential of technology-assisted interventions to supplement traditional approaches.

Game-based interventions represent a newer approach that leverages the motivational and engaging nature of games to enhance learning. However, designing games for the needs of individuals with dyslexia requires careful consideration of their special needs to maximise their learning experience and overcome their difficulties; otherwise, game-based interventions will repeat the same mistakes as traditional interventions. For example, thousands of players with disabilities, including people with dyslexia, cannot enjoy the whole experience of video games because the games have limited accessibility features due to the complexity of commands and controls, texts which are difficult to understand because of their size, colour or font, complicated gameplay and non-modifiable controls (Fernández et al., 2019). Abu Bakar et al. (2023) and ChePa et al. (2022) investigated the specific needs of individuals with dyslexia and developed a comprehensive guideline for games to be used as intervention tools. This chapter discusses the evaluation of two games, named DysPReX and MazeDyslexic, that have been developed according to the specified guidelines.

10.2 From Traditional Interventions to Game-Based Solutions for Dyslexia

Over the last three decades, considerable research has focused on identifying the most effective methods for treating dyslexia. This body of knowledge is complex, in part because although all individuals with dyslexia have a similar problem, namely difficulty in reading, they have heterogeneous characteristics. Depending on the child's developmental level, the demands of reading and the required skills are quite different (Alexander & Slinger, 2004). To summarise, research on dyslexia has focused on three distinct stages: screening, assessment, and intervention. Various tools have been developed at each of these stages, traditionally or technologically, as solutions to issues surrounding dyslexia.

Several studies utilised games as an alternative to traditional intervention methods (e.g., Jaramillo-Alcázar et al., 2021; Cuschieri et al., 2014; Di Tore et al., 2014; Rello, Bayarri & Gorriz, 2012; Ahmad et al., 2012). Games add more fun and excitement to the teaching and learning process. Examples of off-the-shelf games for dyslexia include the board games (e.g., Zingo Sight Words, Scrabble Junior, Brainbox ABC, Monopoly Junior, and Alphabet Lotto) or digital games that run either on IOS or Android or both platforms (e.g., Draw Something, Hanging with Friends, Anagram Scramble, ABCya, Chicktionary, Boogle Bash, Knoword, Word Whomp, dyslexia Quest, Omoguru, Ostimo, and Reading Aids) or web-based (e.g., dyslexia Gold). Different strategies are used in these games such as draw out a given word, spell a complex word, create ambiguous word to puzzle others, make out words from a given set of letters, find word while beating the time allotted, use flashcards presented enjoyably, use visually comfortable font family and complete words by conjecture based on the word's definition and first letter. Some of these games still focus on building phoneme awareness, but more attractively and enjoyably; English is the sole language used in all of these games.

Advancements in artificial intelligence (AI) and digital tools have led to the development of technology-based interventions for dyslexia. AI-powered assistive tools, such as speech-to-text applications, predictive typing software, and audiobooks, have been integrated into classrooms to support learners with dyslexia. AI has been identified as a powerful tool that enables students with dyslexia to keep pace with their peers. However, some educators have expressed concerns that students may become overly dependent on AI, potentially reducing their engagement in active learning (Associated Press, 2023).

In addition to AI-based tools, mobile applications and interactive e-learning platforms designed for dyslexic learners have gained popularity. Findings from Wai et al. (2023) indicated that the interventions focused on assistive technology tools and mobile learning applications became the favourite choice in Malaysia to assist students with dyslexia in ameliorating their learning difficulties. Game-based learning (GBL) has emerged as an effective method for dyslexia intervention, leveraging interactive and motivational elements to enhance reading skills. Recent studies suggest that educational games can aid dyslexic students in improving phonological processing, working memory, and reading fluency (Bakar et al., 2022).

A notable study conducted by Franceschini et al. (2021) investigated the effect of action video game training on the reading abilities of dyslexic children. The randomised controlled trial revealed significant improvements in reading accuracy, speed, and comprehension after game-based training sessions (Franceschini et al., 2021). A longitudinal study by Rodríguez-Ferrer et al. (2023) compared gamification-based interventions to traditional methods among Spanish adolescents with dyslexia. The experimental group, which used gamified learning strategies, demonstrated statistically significant improvements in reading comprehension and academic performance compared to the control group. These findings suggest that game-based interventions may be a viable alternative to traditional literacy instruction for individuals with dyslexia.

Furthermore, a study by Alizadeh et al. (2023) compared the effectiveness of computer game-based executive function training and sensory integration exercises on dyslexia symptoms. Results indicated that both interventions reduced symptoms of dyslexia, although sensory integration exercises had more lasting effects. This suggests that combining game-based interventions with sensory-based therapy may enhance long-term learning outcomes. While traditional literacy interventions remain the gold standard, research suggests that technology- and game-based interventions can complement these methods. According to a meta-analysis by Alsuwat and Young (2016), hybrid approaches that integrate structured literacy instruction with interactive digital tools yield the highest success rates in improving the reading skills of students with dyslexia. The integration of these approaches, tailored to individual needs, holds promise for enhancing reading skills and academic performance in individuals with dyslexia. However, most existing dyslexia intervention tools are predominantly designed in English, reflecting Western linguistic and orthographic systems. This creates a significant gap in the Malaysian context, where many children, especially in rural and Malay-speaking communities, learn to read and write in Bahasa Melayu as their first language. Bahasa Melayu has different phonological, morphological, and syntactic structures compared to English, meaning that English-based tools may not be effective in identifying or supporting dyslexic learners in this linguistic context.

Without culturally and linguistically appropriate tools, many Malay-speaking children with dyslexia may go undetected or receive interventions that are not optimised for their language of instruction. This not only delays support but can also affect their confidence, academic performance, and long-term literacy outcomes.

Therefore, there is an urgent need to develop localised, research-informed dyslexia intervention tools in Bahasa Melayu, tailored to the phonological and linguistic features of the language, to ensure early and accurate support for Malay-speaking children at risk of dyslexia.

10.3 Designing and Evaluating Dyslexia-Friendly Immersive Games

The methodology is structured into four main phases, as illustrated in Figure 10.2.

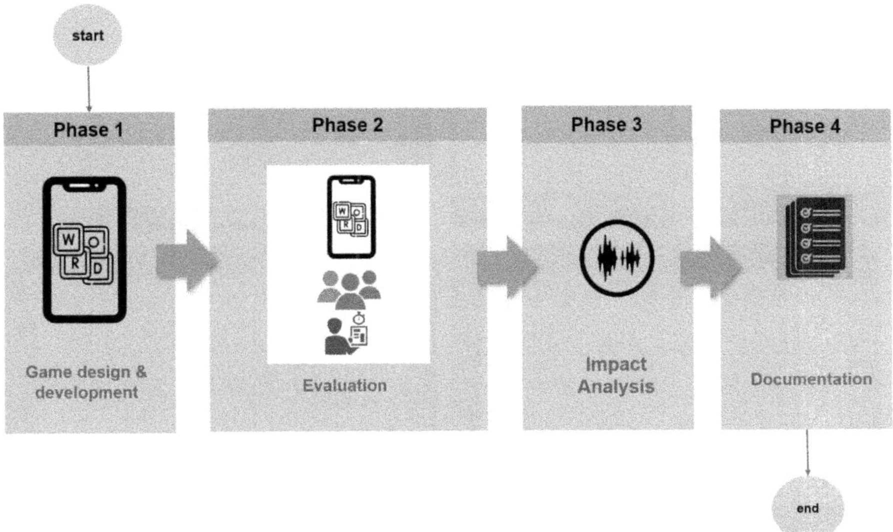

FIGURE 10.2
The research methodology.

10.3.1 Game Design and Development

As mentioned earlier, a comprehensive guideline for designing dyslexia-friendly games has been successfully developed and evaluated in our previous research (Abu Bakar et al., 2023; ChePa et al., 2022). This guideline serves as a structured framework to enhance the accessibility and effectiveness of educational games for individuals with dyslexia. It focuses on four key elements: device and platform compatibility, essential game features, game-play mechanics, and user interface design. Each of these elements plays a crucial role in ensuring that the games are engaging, user-friendly, and supportive of the needs of dyslexic learners. A visual representation of the existing guideline is provided in Figure 10.3, offering a clear overview of its components and structure.

In accordance with the existing guideline, two educational games specifically designed for children with dyslexia have been developed: DysPReX and MazeDyslexic. These games are tailored to enhance literacy skills through interactive and engaging gameplay. Both games are designed to run on the Android platform, ensuring accessibility and ease of use across a wide range of devices. To provide a clearer visualisation of their design and functionality, selected user interfaces from DysPReX and MazeDyslexic are illustrated in Figures 10.4 and 10.5, respectively.

The main functions of the DysPReX game include "Kenal Huruf", "Bina Perkataan", "Teka Perkataan", "Teka Huruf", "Eja", and "Isi Sebutan", as

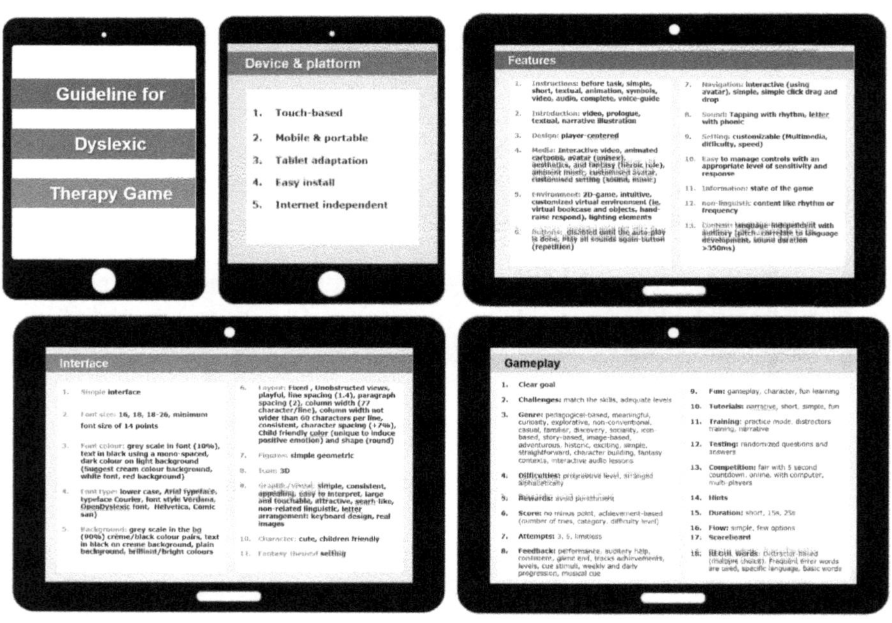

FIGURE 10.3
Guidelines for the Dyslexic games.

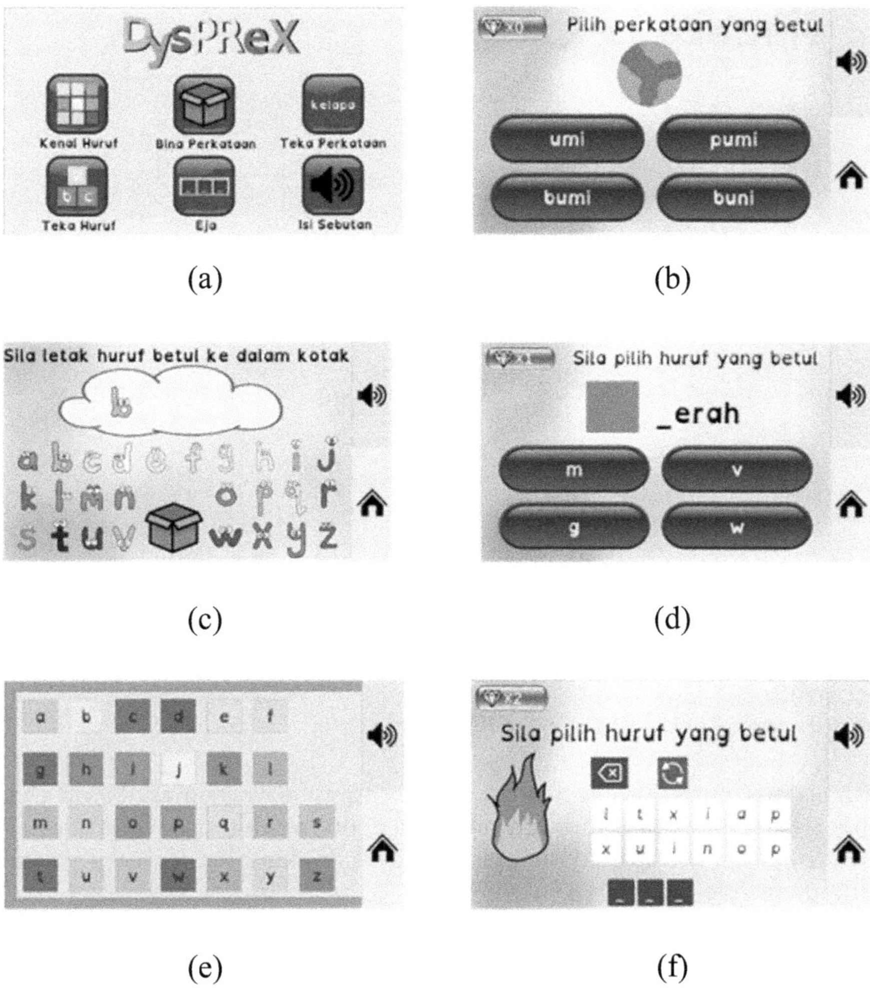

FIGURE 10.4
(a–f) Selected interfaces of DysPReX.

illustrated in Figure 10.4a. Each of these functions plays a crucial role in enhancing language and literacy skills through interactive learning experiences. A detailed visual representation of each function is provided in Figure 10.4b–f, respectively, showcasing their individual interfaces and features.

Our second game is MazeDyslexic, an interactive, game-based intervention tool designed to support Malaysian children with dyslexia aged 3–10 in developing essential literacy skills, including reading, spelling, and word decoding. Addressing the shortage of Malay-language educational resources, the game provides an engaging learning experience through clear audio-visual

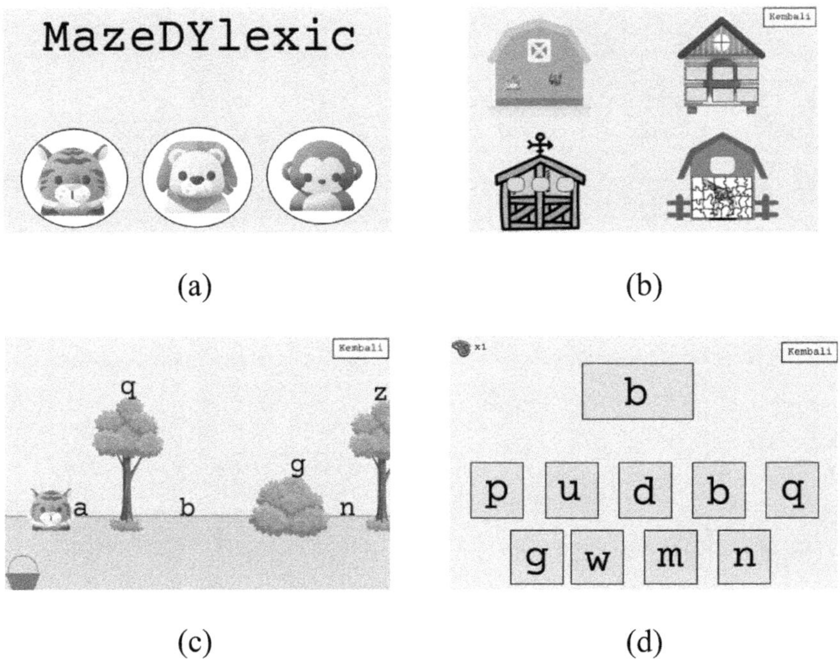

FIGURE 10.5
Selected interfaces of MazeDyslexic.

instructions, customisable avatars, and a variety of vocabulary-based challenges. Players navigate through gates and doors, receive visual and auditory cues, and earn rewards for completing tasks, making the learning process both interactive and enjoyable.

Developed using Unity, the game is optimised for Android devices, ensuring accessibility and convenience for users anytime, anywhere. To enhance the learning experience, MazeDyslexic includes a built-in hints system that assists players in overcoming challenges and a reward system that encourages progress and motivation through various incentives. The game is designed with offline functionality, allowing children to continue learning without requiring an internet connection. Selected interfaces and key features of MazeDyslexic are shown in Figure 10.5.

The user interface is designed for ease of navigation, featuring audio-assisted instructions to support young learners. Players can personalise their experience by selecting avatars and exploring different game sections, such as Word Hunt and Alphabetic Puzzle, which reinforce literacy skills through interactive gameplay. The application also features a scalable difficulty system, allowing for smooth progression tailored to the child's learning needs. Additionally, a progress-tracking chart helps monitor improvements over time, providing valuable insights into the child's literacy development.

By combining engagement and education, MazeDyslexic empowers dyslexic children to overcome literacy challenges in a fun, interactive, and supportive environment, fostering confidence and enhancing their reading abilities.

10.3.2 Evaluation

The evaluation of MazeDyslexic involved 11 Dyslexic students and focused on four key aspects: visual appeal and design, functionality and performance, audio clarity, and educational value and engagement. These criteria were assessed to ensure the software provides an effective, engaging, and user-friendly experience for children with dyslexia. The visual appeal and design evaluation examined the aesthetic quality of the software, including the clarity and attractiveness of avatars, colours, animal images, screen layouts, and animations. It also assessed the readability of fonts and the overall engagement level of the visual elements to determine their suitability for the target audience. Functionality and performance focused on the technical aspects of the game, such as the smoothness of avatar movements, responsiveness of buttons, system stability, and ease of navigation, ensuring that users could interact seamlessly with the software.

The audio clarity component assessed the effectiveness of voice instructions and the comprehensibility of in-game questions. This included evaluating the clarity and audibility of spoken instructions to ensure children could follow along without confusion. The educational value and engagement analysis examined whether the software effectively supports dyslexic children in learning to read. It considered the relevance and sufficiency of exercises, the appropriateness of the instructional content, and whether the games were engaging enough to maintain user interest. By evaluating these factors, MazeDyslexic was assessed for its ability to provide an enjoyable and effective learning experience tailored to children with dyslexia.

The evaluation of DysPReX was conducted with 30 respondents. The assessment was conducted through an online meeting, during which the developer demonstrated the game's flow and features and then collected feedback from the participants. Based on the evaluation results, the majority of respondents expressed satisfaction with the game while also providing constructive suggestions for improvement. In response, the developer implemented several enhancements to address key feedback points, refining the overall gameplay experience.

10.3.3 Impact Analysis

The impact analysis phase plays a crucial role in evaluating the effectiveness of the DysPReX and MazeDyslexic games in improving literacy skills among children with dyslexia. This phase focuses on assessing how these game-based interventions influence the children's reading, spelling, and word decoding abilities through a structured evaluation process. Our initial plan was to measure the impact on dyslexic children at dyslexia Incubator in Universiti Utara Malaysia (UUM). Based on the initial plan, a pre-test and post-test experimental design is implemented, where dyslexic children participate in game-play sessions over a specific period. Before engaging with the games, the participants undergo an initial assessment (pre-test) to establish a baseline of their literacy skills. Following the intervention period, a post-test is conducted to evaluate improvements in reading accuracy, spelling proficiency, and cognitive engagement.

The plan involved collecting quantitative data through performance metrics embedded in the games, such as completion rates, accuracy levels, and response times. Additionally, qualitative insights are gathered through structured observations, teacher feedback, and parental interviews to assess behavioural changes, motivation levels, and overall user experience. By conducting a comprehensive impact analysis, this phase provides valuable evidence on the effectiveness of DysPReX and MazeDyslexic in supporting literacy development among children with dyslexia. The findings provide a foundation for further improvements and the broader adoption of these digital interventions in educational settings.

However, due to unforeseen circumstances, there were no longer any dyslexic children enrolled at the dyslexia Incubator in UUM, making it impossible to conduct the planned experiment. As an alternative, the study was conducted at the dyslexia Association Malaysia in Sungai Petani, Kedah, involving 11 students diagnosed with dyslexia. The participants were recruited by a teacher from the association, who played an essential role in facilitating the experiment. We experienced difficulties in recruiting a large number of participants, as not many dyslexic students were affiliated with the association.

To ensure a diverse range of participants, students aged 5–13 were selected to test the application. The study utilised a combination of digital and physical resources to experiment effectively. The teacher was provided with the APK file of the application, a demo video, and the necessary assessment forms, which were made available both online via Google Forms and offline as printed PDF documents. These materials enabled the teacher to guide the students through the testing process while collecting valuable feedback.

This approach enabled a structured and systematic evaluation of the games' usability, effectiveness, and impact on the literacy skills of dyslexic children. Despite the initial setback, relocating the study to the dyslexia Association Malaysia in Sungai Petani ensured that the research could proceed with an appropriate group of participants, ultimately contributing to the assessment and refinement of the developed dyslexic learning tools.

10.3.4 Documentation

The documentation phase focuses on systematically recording all aspects of the research, ensuring that the development, implementation, and evaluation of DysPReX and MazeDyslexic are well-documented. This includes compiling literature reviews, game design specifications, testing procedures, participant feedback, and experimental results. The goal is to provide a clear and structured account of the research process for future reference and improvement.

Both qualitative and quantitative data are carefully organised and analysed. Qualitative insights, such as teacher and student feedback, are analysed, while quantitative data, including pre-test and post-test scores, completion rates, and error logs, are statistically examined. Additionally, modifications made to the games based on usability testing are systematically recorded to track improvements. The final stage of this phase involves preparing comprehensive research reports, academic papers, and presentation materials to communicate findings to educators and researchers. This ensures that the study's contributions to dyslexic education and GBL are well-documented, reproducible, and useful for future advancements in the field.

10.4 Usability Outcomes of DysPRex and MazeDyslexic

DysPReX and MazeDyslexic were carefully designed to provide an engaging and interactive learning experience, incorporating elements tailored to the unique needs of individuals with dyslexia. Both games are fully compatible with the Android platform, ensuring accessibility and ease of use for a wide range of users. To assess their effectiveness, both DysPReX and MazeDyslexic underwent a comprehensive usability evaluation, where their functionality, user interface, and overall user experience were analysed. The evaluation aimed to determine how well the games aligned with the intended learning objectives and whether they provided an intuitive and engaging environment for children with dyslexia. Feedback from participants and educators played a crucial role in refining the games and enhancing their usability.

The successful design, development, and usability assessment of these two mobile games signify the achievement of the research objectives, which focus on the development of effective digital interventions for dyslexic children based on existing guidelines. These findings provide valuable insights into GBL approaches and underscore the importance of incorporating well-structured, dyslexia-friendly elements into educational game design.

10.4.1 The Acceptance of a Mobile Game-Based Application for Dyslexic Children

Both games have undergone a comprehensive evaluation to assess their acceptance among users. The assessment focused on four key measures: usability, functionality, learnability, and satisfaction. These factors were carefully analysed to determine how effectively the games meet user expectations, ensuring they are intuitive, engaging, and fully functional for their intended audience.

For usability (see Figure 10.6), the majority of respondents strongly agreed with the aspect "Images are easy to understand" for DysPReX, with an average rating of 4.83. This indicates that the images used in the game are clear and straightforward, making it easier for respondents to interpret and engage with the content. The high rating reflects the effectiveness of the game's visual elements in supporting user comprehension, particularly for dyslexic learners who benefit from clear and intuitive imagery. Additionally, the results for other aspects within this section were also consistently high, with all ratings exceeding the average threshold of 2.5. This suggests that the overall visual design of the DysPReX game is well-received and meets user expectations. The positive feedback highlights the importance of well-structured, easily recognisable images in enhancing the user experience and ensuring that the game remains accessible and engaging for its intended audience.

For functionality (see Figure 10.7), respondents expressed high levels of satisfaction across all five key measures, with results consistently exceeding the average benchmark. The evaluation indicates that the game meets user expectations in terms of performance, responsiveness, and overall usability. The majority of respondents also strongly agreed that all game features function effectively, resulting in an impressive average rating of 4.8. This positive feedback highlights the game's smooth performance and reliability, reinforcing its effectiveness as an engaging and well-executed tool for individuals with dyslexia.

The evaluation of the game's learnability (see Figure 10.8) revealed that the highest-rated aspect was respondents' confidence in using the game, with the majority strongly agreeing, resulting in an average score of 4.67. This indicates that users found the game intuitive and easy to navigate, fostering a sense of confidence in its use. Additionally, the other learnability measures

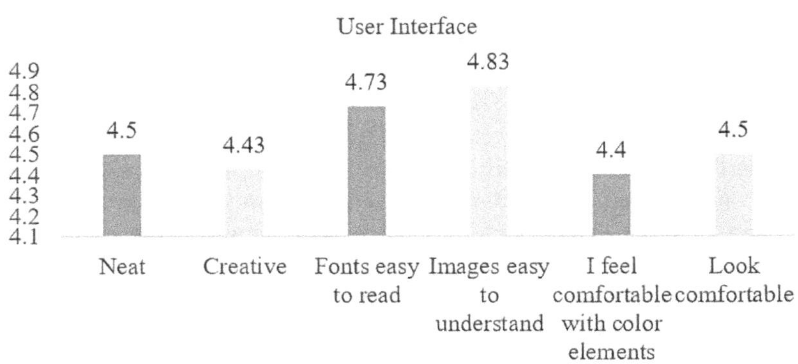

FIGURE 10.6
Response to usability of the game.

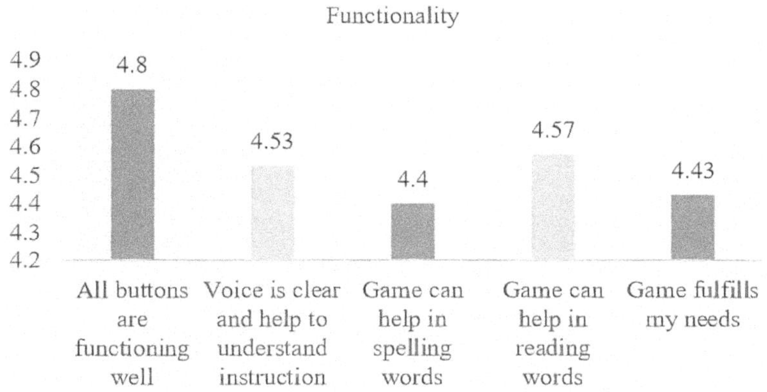

FIGURE 10.7
Response to functionality of the game.

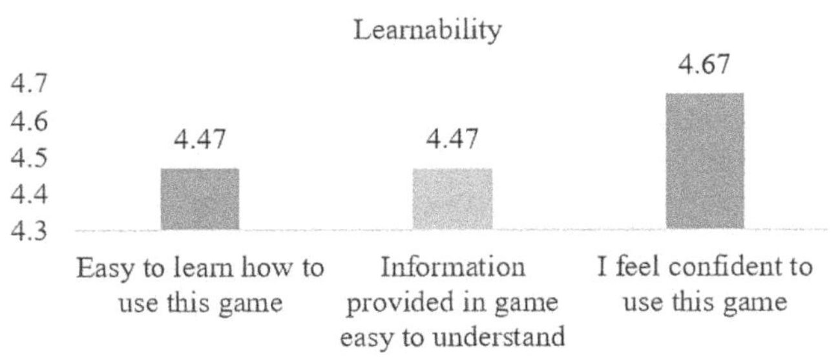

FIGURE 10.8
Response to learnability of the game.

received consistently high ratings, each averaging 4.47, further affirming the game's user-friendly design. Overall, all three measures of learnability exceeded the average benchmark, demonstrating that the game effectively supports ease of use and enhances the learning experience for its intended audience.

In terms of satisfaction (see Figure 10.9), the majority of respondents expressed a high level of approval, with the overall average rating reaching 4.7. This indicates that users found the game enjoyable, engaging, and well-designed, meeting their expectations. The lowest-rated aspect, "The game included all functions I expected it to have", received an average score of 4.47, suggesting that while most users were satisfied, some felt there was room for additional features or improvements. However, all satisfaction-related aspects scored well above average, reinforcing the game's positive reception and its ability to deliver a rewarding user experience.

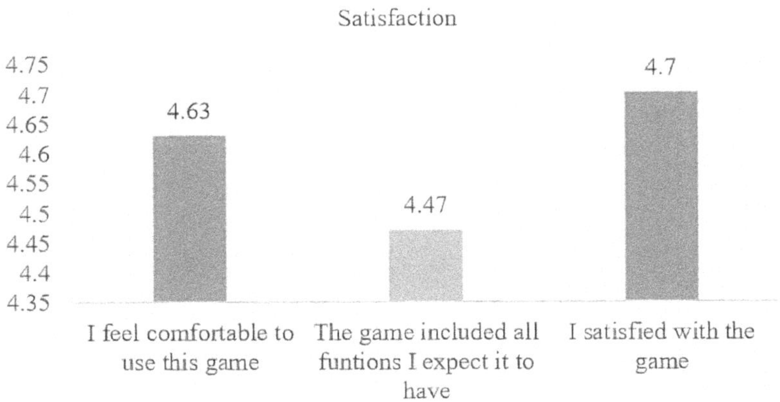

FIGURE 10.9
Response to satisfaction with the game.

For the MazeDyslexic game, the majority of respondents (90.9%) agreed that the layout of elements is visually appealing and well-structured. Specifically, 45.5% of respondents agreed, while an equal 45.5% strongly agreed, demonstrating a significant level of satisfaction with the game's design. This overwhelming positive perception suggests that the software successfully incorporates an engaging and dyslexia-friendly layout that enhances user experience. Only a small minority (9.1%) of respondents disagreed with the statement, indicating that while the design was well-received overall, some users had reservations or personal preferences that differed from the majority.

The results suggest that the visual design of MazeDyslexic plays a crucial role in engaging users, particularly children with dyslexia, by providing an aesthetically pleasing and user-friendly interface. The strong approval ratings affirm that the game's layout successfully captures users' attention and enhances the overall gaming experience, making it a valuable tool for dyslexic learners. However, the minority feedback also indicates room for further refinement to accommodate a broader range of user preferences.

10.4.2 The Impact of a Mobile Game-Based Application for Dyslexic Children

The evaluation findings highlight the positive impact of both DysPReX and MazeDyslexic in supporting children with dyslexia through an engaging, interactive, and well-structured learning experience. The results indicate high levels of acceptance, with strong ratings across key areas, including usability, functionality, learnability, and satisfaction. The majority of respondents found the games visually appealing, with clear and easily understandable images that enhance the learning process. Additionally, the functionality of the games was highly rated, demonstrating their reliability and smooth performance.

Furthermore, the evaluation results emphasise the games' effectiveness in fostering confidence and ease of use among players, as reflected in the strong learnability ratings. Respondents also expressed high satisfaction, confirming that the games successfully deliver an enjoyable and educational experience. Although minor suggestions for improvement were noted, such as enhancing expected features, the overall feedback indicates that the games provide a valuable digital intervention for children with dyslexia. The positive reception of these games reinforces their potential as effective learning tools, bridging the gap in dyslexia-friendly educational resources while promoting literacy development in a fun and accessible manner.

10.5 Towards Inclusive Digital Interaction: Games for Dyslexia Intervention

The past few years have seen significant advancements in dyslexia interventions, with both traditional and technology-based methods demonstrating effectiveness. Structured literacy programmes continue to be foundational in addressing dyslexia, while AI-driven and game-based interventions offer engaging and personalised learning experiences. The integration of these approaches, tailored to individual needs, holds promise for enhancing reading skills and academic performance in individuals with dyslexia. Continuous improvement to these intervention tools is necessary and significant, considering that dyslexia often accompanies people through many stages of life. Past studies (Wilmot et al., 2023; Xiao et al., 2022) established that dyslexia is also associated with various health issues, including mental health. The persistence of these symptoms can lead to long-term mental health challenges if not adequately addressed. Beyond academic challenges, dyslexia affects a person's ability to comprehend information, communicate in writing, and even set goals for the future. As people with dyslexia struggle to adapt to a setting that does not always fit their unique cognitive traits, practical intervention tools must not ignore their special needs, which many have been included in the guidelines. DysPReX and MazeDyslexic incorporate these needs into features such as dyslexia-friendly fonts, colour-coded letters, and auditory feedback, which we believe have a positive influence on users' evaluation of the games. Future work should focus on incorporating more features suggested by the guideline to improve the effectiveness of game-based dyslexia intervention tools.

Acknowledgement

This work was supported by the *Geran Penjanaan* Research Scheme (SO Code: 21120) provided by UUM. The authors fully acknowledge UUM for the approved funding, which makes this important research viable and effective.

References

Abu Bakar, N.A., ChePa, N. & Lim, L.S. (2023). Criteria for the dyslexic games: A systematic literature review. *Journal of Human Centered Technology, 2*(1), 3242. https://doi.org/10.11113/humentech.v2n1.35

Ahmad, S.Z., Nik Ludin, N.N.A.A, Mohd Ekhsan, H., Rosmani, A.F., & Ismail, M.H. (2012). Bijak Membaca - Applying phonic reading technique and multisensory approach with interactive multimedia for dyslexia children. In *IEEE Colloquium on Humanities, Science & Engineering Research (CHUSER 2012)*, December 3–4, Kota Kinabalu, Sabah, Malaysia. https://doi.org/10.1109/CHUSER.2012.6504375

Alexander, A.W. & Slinger, A. (2004). Current status of treatments for dyslexia: Critical review. *Journal of Child Neurology I, 19*(10). https://doi.org/10.1177/08830738040190100401

Alizadeh, P., Shafie, H., & Moghimi, R. (2023). Comparative analysis of computer game-based executive function training and sensory integration exercises in dyslexia intervention. *Journal of Pediatric Education, 15*(3), 112–127.

Alsuwat, S. & Young, J. (2016). Meta-analysis of the effects of traditional versus technology-based instruction on reading comprehension of EFL Students. *EFL Journal, 1*(3). https://doi.org/10.21462/eflj.v1i3.18

Associated Press. (2023). *AI is a game changer for students with disabilities*. https://apnews.com

Bakar, S., Mahamarowi, N. & Mustapha, S. (2022). Game-based learning as a teaching and learning tool for dyslexic children. In *2022 IEEE 10th Conference on Systems, Process & Control (ICSPC)* (pp. 50–55). IEEE. https://doi.org/10.1109/ICSPC55597.2022.10001824

ChePa, N., Abu Bakar, N.A. & Lim, L.S. (2022). Criteria and guidelines for dyslexic intervention games. *International Journal of Advanced Computer Science and Application (IJACSA), 13*(9), 162–172.

Cuschieri, T., Khaled, R., Farrugia, V.E., Martinez, H.P., & Yannakakis, G.N. (2014, September). The iLearnRW game: Support for students with dyslexia in class and at home. In *2014 6th International Conference on Games and Virtual Worlds for Serious Applications (VS-GAMES)* (pp. 1–2). IEEE. https://doi.org/10.1109/VS-Games.2014.7012167

Di Tore, P.A., Di Tore, S. & Mangione, G.R. (2014). Madrigale: A multimedia application for dyslexia and reading improvement gamifying learning experience. *IEEE Computer Society*, pp. 486–491. https://doi.org/10.1109/INCoS.2014.48

Ehri, L.C. (2020). The science of reading and why it matters. *Reading Research Quarterly, 55*(S1), S45–S60. https://doi.org/10.1002/rrq.334

Fernández, M., Jaramillo-Alcázar, A., Galarza-Castillo, M., and Luján-Mora, S. (2019). A serious game to learn basic English for people with hearing impairments. In *Proceedings of the International Conference on Information Technology & Systems*, Munich, Germany, 18–20 December 2019. https://doi.org/10.1007/978-3-030-11890-7_63

Franceschini, S., Bertoni, S., & Ronconi, L. (2021). Action video game training improves text reading accuracy, rate, and comprehension in children with dyslexia: A randomised controlled trial. *Journal of Learning Disabilities, 54*(6), 589–602. https://doi.org/10.1038/s41598-021-98146-x

Hussin, H. (2012). Mobile dyslexic specialised digital game-based learning object for learning letters (DOLL) [*Project Dissertation*] – Universiti Teknologi Petronas.

Jaramillo-Alcázar, A., Venegas, E., Criollo -C, S. & Luján-Mora, S. (2021). An approach to accessible serious games for people with dyslexia. *Sustainability, 13*, 2507. https://doi.org/10.3390/su13052507

Knight, C. (2018). What is dyslexia? An exploration of the relationship between teachers' understandings of dyslexia and their training experience. *dyslexia, 24*(3), 207–219. https://doi.org/10.1002/dys.1593

Marshall, A. (2013). When phonics doesn't work. *dyslexia the Gift*. https://www.dyslexia.com/

Mohd Nor, M.F. (2021). *Disleksia bukan bodoh*. https://www.sinarharian.com.my/article/135326/KHAS/Pendapat/Disleksia-bukan-bodoh

Orpi, D. (2019). Why systematic synthetic phonics is best for dyslexic students. *Thrive Literacy Corner.* https://thriveedservices.com/why-systematic-synthetic-phonics-is-best-for-dyslexic-students/

Rello, L., Bayarri, C. & Gorriz, A. (2012). What is wrong with this word? Dyseggxia: A game for children with dyslexia. In the *Proceedings of ASSETS'12*, October 22–24, 2012, Boulder, Colorado, USA. https://doi.org/10.1145/2384916.2384962

Ridzal, D.F.S., Mu'alimin, M., & Usriyah, L. (2023). The influence of dyslexia on children's psychological development. *Journal of Social Research, 2*(8), 2453–2457. https://doi.org/10.55324/josr.v2i8.1247

Rodríguez-Ferrer, J.M, Manzano-León, A., Aguilar-Parra, J.M. & Cangas, A. (2023). Effectiveness of gamification and game-based learning in Spanish adolescents with dyslexia: A longitudinal quasi-experimental research. *Research in Developmental Disabilities, 141*. https://doi.org/ 10.1016/j.ridd.2023.104603

Roongpraiwan, R., Ruangdaraganon, N., Visudhiphan, P., & Santikul, K. (2021). Prevalence and characteristics of psoriasis patients in a primary care area in Thailand. *Journal of the Medical Association of Thailand, 104*(4), 610–614. https://doi.org/10.35755/jmedassocthai.2021.04.11913

Sayeski, K.L., Earle, G.A., Davis, R., & Calamari, J. (2019). Orton Gillingham: Who, what, and how. *Teaching Exceptional Children, 51*(3), 240–249. https://doi.org/10.1177/0040059918816996

Schulte-Körne, G. (2010). The prevention, diagnosis, and treatment of dyslexia. *Deutsches Ärzteblatt International, 107*(41), pp. 718–27. https://doi.org/10.3238/arztebl.2010.0718.

Snowling, M.J., & Hulme, C. (2021). Learning to read: What we know and what we need to understand better. *Child Development Perspectives, 15*(1), 1–7. https://doi.org/10.1111/cdep.12005

Swanson, H.L. (1999). *Interventions for Students with Learning Disabilities: A Meta-analysis of Treatment Outcomes*. New York: Guilford Press.

Tomarong, L., Abendan, C.F., Kilag, O.K., Apas, M., Undalok, V., & Alcorcon, J.J. (2023). The lindamood-bell reading intervention: A pathway to enhanced reading skills in pupils. *Excellencia: International Multi-disciplinary Journal of Education (2994–9521), 1*(5), 322–332.

Wai, L., Jiar, Y., & Handayani, L. (2023). A systematic review on interventions for children with dyslexia. *International Journal of Evaluation and Research in Education (IJERE), 12*(3), 1674. https://doi.org/10.11591/ijere.v12i3.25099

Wan Mohammad, W.M.R., Subramaniam, V., Abd Aziz, A.Y. & Abdul Rahim, N. (2011). dyslexia in the aspect of Malay language spelling. *International Journal of Humanities and Social Science, 1*(21), 266–268.

Wilmot, A., Hasking, P., Leitão, S., Hill, E., & Boyes, M. (2023). Understanding mental health in developmental dyslexia: A scoping review. *International Journal of Environmental Research and Public Health, 20*(2), 1653. https://doi.org/10.3390/ijerph20021653

Xiao, P., Zhu, K., Liu, Q., Xie, X., Jiang, Q., Feng, Y., Wu, X., Tan, J. & Song, R. (2022). Association between developmental dyslexia and anxiety/depressive symptoms among children in China: The chain mediating of time spent on homework and stress. *Journal of Affective Disorders, 297*, 495–501. https://doi.org/10.1016/j.jad.2021.10.120

Section IV

Society and the Human Experience in Immersive Worlds

11

Avatars and Digital Identity in the Metaverse

Lee Kai Lun

11.1 Introduction

Metaverse is a virtual shared platform where people connect seamlessly through augmented reality (AR) and the internet. It offers a radically different experience from traditional social media like Instagram, Facebook, X, or Snapchat. In the metaverse, identity, representation, expression, and presence are reimagined through customisable avatars that go far beyond static profile pictures, unlike social media. Moreover, users can express themselves as idealised, fantastical, anonymous, or entirely fictional beings, unrestricted by real-world limitations. Unlike social media, avatars enable a greater flexibility in appearance and behaviour, fostering immersive, interactive experiences in rich digital environments.

The concept of "avatar" originates from deep-rooted religious and cultural traditions. In Hindu theology, an avatar is derived from the Sanskrit word meaning "incarnation" which originally referred to divine manifestations, particularly of the god Vishnu, who is believed to descend to Earth in human form to restore cosmic order (Jones, 2015; Sharma, 2020). Over time, this concept has been adapted into modern contexts, especially in the digital age. An avatar is now commonly described as a character or digital figure created by individuals to represent themselves in a virtual environment that allows users to engage or interact in the virtual worlds by acting as a graphical proxy (Evallyo, 2019; Szolin et al., 2023). They play a crucial role in fulfilling the users' needs in constructing their digital identities across various sectors of the digital world.

In the early development of the avatar, avatars were displayed as a 2D view as 2D images, icons, or even pixel-based characters. These were often used in early chatrooms, forums, and 2D video games such as in Neopets, Habbo Hotel, MSN Messenger, Yahoo! Chat, and Club Penguin. This was the earliest form of digital self-representation. Despite the limited and simple expression, they functioned well for establishing a basic online identity. As the development of technology progresses, 3D avatars are introduced as a more realistic, customisable, and more intriguing representation. Compared to a 2D avatar,

DOI: 10.1201/9781003662433-15

a 3D avatar allows to perform more complex interactions, such as complex gestures, more realistic emotions, and even interaction using full-body 3D interaction (Gillies et al., 2015). Moreover, with the introduction of AR and virtual reality (VR), 3D avatars are now the norm and implemented in various sectors including gaming, education, and social interaction such as in Fortnite, VRChat, Second Life, Spatial, and Microsoft Mesh.

In both the digital and physical worlds, individuals require a recognisable identity to participate meaningfully in social interactions. Just as a person in real life holds an identity, their presence in the digital world also demands a form of identification that makes them visible and distinguishable in online spaces. Identity is defined as a person's name and other facts that prove who they are (Cambridge University Press, n.d.). It is the state of being that differentiates an individual, group, or organisation from others. Identity includes various factors that could help in defining individuals and communities such as nationality, race, culture, gender, age, and family background (Blue et al., 2018). It plays an essential role in shaping behaviour, interactions, and outcomes. Furthermore, it also impacts broader fields like politics, economics, and even religion.

When society started shifting into the digital age, social behaviours and interactions increasingly took place not just in the real world but also in digital spaces. Identity verification also evolved from traditional paper documentation to cyber-based authentication methods which are a vital element of the digital economy and society as they grant individuals access to various online services and transactions (Blue et al., 2018; Robles-Carrillo, 2024). Hence, this transformation introduces the concept of digital identity that can be defined as a digital reference to a person with attributes that can be revoked, deleted, transferred, or exchanged, such as citizenship, institutional affiliations, and ownership records (Sedlmeir et al., 2021; Preukschat & Reed, 2021). This enables individuals to prove who they are through digital identification, authentication, or authorisation processes.

Both avatars and digital identity are key components of the virtual world. They are deeply interconnected similar to the relationship between a person and their real-world identity. In the metaverse, digital identity works as an overall representation of a user that encompasses personal information, login credentials, privacy data, and attributes which help define the individual's access, roles, and authority in digital spaces. Digital identity forms the foundation of how users are recognised and authenticated in the metaverse. Meanwhile, for avatar, it serves as the visual representation of the digital identity, a customisable 3D or graphical character that is perceived by others in virtual environments (Kim et al., 2023). Through avatars, it assists users to navigate digital spaces, interact with others, engage in activities, express emotions, and use body language. Therefore, with the combination of digital identity and avatar, it completes the online version of the user.

11.2 Avatar Design and Personal Expression

In order to own an avatar in the metaverse, users must first design and create one. Designing an avatar is a crucial process that allows user to express personal expression, shape their social identity, and interact with others in virtual environments (Noisri et al., 2024). Compared to the traditional online profiles, avatars in the metaverse offer a more dynamic and customisable experience. Users can design their avatar from playful, cartoon-style characters to realistic, human-like figures that reflect facial expressions and movements using cutting-edge VR and AR technologies. Various platforms allow users to design avatars and use them across different metaverse platforms. For instance, Ready Player Me, VRoid Studio, Genies, and Tafi Avatars support not only in metaverse platforms like Meta Horizon Worlds, Meta Horizon Workrooms, VRChat, and Rec Room that require VR equipment, but also various cross-platform metaverses such as Spatial.io, Zepeto, The Sandbox, and Roblox that do not require a VR headset.

11.2.1 Avatar Customisation

Realism of human interaction is the main component of the metaverse and this is achieved not only through emotional expression but also through broader forms of personal expression that reflect the user's identity and individuality (Spadoni et al., 2023). Hence, avatar personalisation plays a crucial role in creating or customising the avatar as it helps the users to experience being themselves or even someone else in the virtual world, incorporating their desired characteristics and abilities (Ribeiro et al., 2024).

Users are generally provided with a comprehensive range of customisation options, including gender presentation, clothing styles, hairstyles, makeup, facial features, body types, and wardrobe selections. Each of these categories contains numerous detailed sub-options that allow a high degree of personalisation. Furthermore, the diversity of customisation allows users to upload their designs or incorporate indigenous cultural elements into their avatars. For example, Rochman (2023) explores the use of Punakawan *wayang kulit* characters to create culturally rooted avatars to preserve and promote Nusantara heritage. This includes integrating traditional features such as batik patterns within the metaverse environment. Such practices contribute to inclusivity by representing diverse cultural identities, religious practices, disabilities, and individual traits.

Such customisation features allow users to construct avatars that align with how they wish to be perceived within virtual environments. In addition to representing personal identity, avatars also function as cultural and social signifiers, providing users with the opportunity to express their heritage, beliefs, and presence in shared digital spaces. Figure 11.1 illustrates the custom avatar creator SDK available on the Ready Player Me (2023) platform.

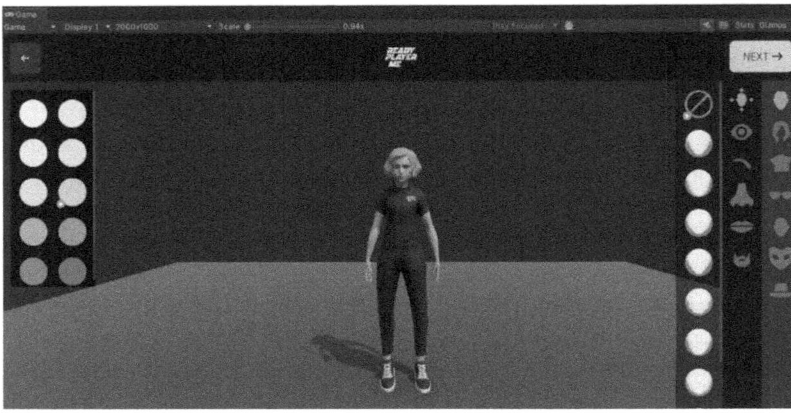

FIGURE 11.1
Customisation of avatar in Unity SDK.

Additionally, platforms such as Ready Player Me, Luma AI, and Banuba allow users to generate avatars directly from selfies. By using facial recognition and rendering technology, these platforms can create realistic 3D avatars that closely resemble the user. When compared to those cartoon-like characters, these lifelike avatars with personalised facial features and expressions could represent the individual identity and enhance user relatability. Users tend to have greater trust, affinity, and preference when their avatar looks more human-like (Seymour et al., 2021). Thus, this underlined the importance of making highly realistic and personalised avatars in digital environments especially in professional settings such as virtual meetings, business networking, and digital events. These are the environments where user expression and responsiveness are highly valued.

Avatar customisation is also not limited to representing as human-like avatars in the metaverse. Users can design their avatars in various non-human forms, such as animals, mythical creatures like dragons, aliens, robots, cyborgs, anime characters, or even creations that they created by themselves. These avatars not only allow users to show their creativity and stand out in virtual environments, but also serve as a medium to express their feelings or even escape real-world limitations. Non-human avatars provide highly enjoyment than humanoid avatars as they contribute to the feeling of excitement and curiosity of body transformation during virtual experiences (Lee et al., 2018).

11.2.2 Avatar Customisation Limitations

Despite the avatar design in the metaverse empowering personal expression, there are still several weaknesses and limitations. One of the main factors is monetisation. While many platforms provide various inclusive design options and advanced customisation features such as specific outfits, hairstyles, or accessories, they often put a paywall to restrict these designs. As a result, only the premium users could afford these customisations. This reduces the equal opportunities to avatar expression among the users. Another major limitation is the technical constraint. Metaverse platforms still have issues like poor scalability, end-to-end latency, limited computational capacity on user devices, low visual quality in avatar embodiment, high resource cost for realism, and high resource demands to achieve realism (Cheng et al., 2022). These challenges indicate that current metaverse platforms are not yet capable of supporting a large number of high-quality, realistic avatars at the same time as this would burden on both the network and user devices. Consequently, these issues hinder users' ability to represent their identities and emotions through avatars in the metaverse.

11.3 Psychology of Avatars and Influence on Self-Perception and Behaviour

As digital representations of users within the metaverse, avatars are often presumed to reflect the user's actions and decisions in the virtual world. However, research has shown that avatars, particularly those created by the users themselves, can also exert a psychological influence on users' self-perception and behaviour. An experimental study conducted by Yee and Bailenson (2007) on individuals' behaviour and their digital self-representation introduced the Proteus Effect.

The Proteus Effect is a psychological phenomenon that describes the user's behaviour changes according to the characteristics of their avatar in a digital environment. Through the study, it has been shown that avatars can significantly influence users' self-perception. According to Bem's (1972) self-perception theory, individuals tend to understand or infer their attitudes, emotions, and beliefs by observing their behaviour. The research conducted a t-test on avatar attractiveness revealed a conclusion where users who designed their avatars more attractively tended to be more social and open in manner, where users were more willing to move closer and share personal information compared to those with less attractive avatars. This reflects the theory that perceiving oneself as attractive can increase confidence and sociability due to altered self-perception even in a virtual place.

Not only that, but the Proteus Effect also found that the avatar could influence the behaviour of the user. Study from Snyder and Swann (1978) discovered a phenomenon called behavioural confirmation. It is a process that describes how a perceiver's expectations can influence the target's behaviour which potentially reinforces the original expectations. In their seminal study, the male participants who believed they were speaking to a female participant that is attractive on the telephone tended to behave softly and friendlier. This led the female participants to behave in a more friendly and engaging manner regardless of their actual appearance. Yee and Bailenson (2007) argue that similar effects are increasingly prevalent in virtual environments as the perceiver user interacting with the target user that has an attractive or distinctive avatar may unconsciously influence others to behave more positively and socially. These showcase the importance of how the avatars affect human interaction and cognition in the virtual environment.

In a creative and limitless virtual environment, the creation of an avatar often leads users to delve into their inner selves, inspiring themselves the identity they wish to be not only in a virtual environment, but in real life too. The process of designing an avatar enables individuals to explore a wide range of identities, including gender, race, age, or even some fantasies that do not exist in the real world. These digital representations allow users to not only express who they are but also embody their ideal selves or some alternative selves which they hope to explore or become. Coble et al. (2024) highlight a generational gap in avatar creation between the younger and the adults. They found that younger users often view avatars as playful extensions of their interests, whereas adult users are more likely to create avatars that represent the idealised versions of themselves. This difference lies in how self-perception influences the way individuals wish to present in virtual space and real life too. Moreover, the identity exploration through avatars contributes to a self-perception feedback loop among the users. For instance, when users observe their avatars exhibiting traits such as confidence, shyness, rudeness, power, or selfishness, they may internalise or improvise their behaviours. Over time, this process can potentially lead to real changes in the users' attitudes and behaviours.

In addition, the use of avatars not only extends to improvising behaviour but could also potentially enhance mental health outcomes. One notable application is the Virtual Reality Exposure Therapy that aims to provide virtual stimulations for user to overcome their fear or disorder by gradually exposing them towards the fear that is stimulated through a virtual world (Freeman et al., 2017). This approach has gained widespread adoption globally. Avatar embodiment has shown promising results in treating phobias and other anxiety-related disorders where users who embody avatars with dissimilar avatars reduced social anxiety and social phobia compared to users who embody avatars with their face (Aymerich-Franch, 2020). This effect could be explained as the user's distorted image could be corrected by providing them a "new self." Hence, avatars play a significant role in psychological development by shaping identity and fostering personal growth by enhancing users' self-esteem and improving their mental health.

However, despite numerous studies and treatments showing psychological benefits among users, there are also potential negative psychological impacts. While using avatars as their idealised representations can boost user self-esteem, excessive identification towards these idealised versions could create an illusion among themselves that leads to distorted self-perceptions, body image dissatisfaction, and unrealistic self-expectations. Ferrer-García et al. (2018) research extends the assumption as its findings revealed that women with larger body sizes who own virtual avatars are more likely to experience body size overestimation and increased dissatisfaction with their real-life appearance, due to the comparison effect. This dissonance between virtual and real selves can make them feel worse about their body image and even decrease their self-acceptance. Additionally, as the limitless customisation towards avatars, certain avatar appearance also becomes the target of cyber-harassment. Behm-Morawitz and Schipper (2016) revealed a harsh truth where sexualised female avatars are more frequently subjected to cyberbullying and harassment compared to male avatars. This showcases the gendered risks associated with avatar representation. Moreover, the fantasy and freedom of avatars in virtual environments can be appealing to the user especially for those who are experiencing mental health challenges or real-life difficulties. In such cases, users may turn to the virtual world as an escape, increasing the risk of overuse or addiction compared to reality.

As a result, these findings underscore that the avatar is like a double-edged sword in shaping user identity, where it could promote psychological well-being but may also lead to psychological strain when being misused or overly idealised. As virtual environments and avatars become increasingly realistic and advanced, both positive and negative psychological impacts will likely intensify. Hence, without the implementation of proper safeguards or interventions to mitigate these negative effects, such influence may become increasingly problematic, potentially undermining the intended purpose of the metaverse as a space for empowerment, creativity, and personal growth.

11.4 Social Identity and Interaction through Avatars

Social identity refers to an individual's self-concept derived from their membership in one or more social groups. It can sometimes conflict with personal identity, as it emphasises a collective sense of "us" and "we" over an individual sense of "I" and "me." Social identity is both a product of social interactions and a factor that shapes those interactions which serves as a foundation for group-based social connections (Tajfel & Turner, 2004; Haslam et al., 2022). This fosters a shared sense of identity, thereby reinforcing social identity within the group. Despite facilitating easier interactions, such communities still often lack of lack physical co-presence, which leads to a diminished "we-mode" mindset and weaker social bonding (Riva et al., 2024). However, the metaverse through virtual and AR technologies has the potential to activate cognitive "we-mode" thinking and cultivate social identity in ways comparable to real-world environments.

In society, human communication, whether verbal or nonverbal, emits feelings, attitudes, conflicts, and interests. This exchange of cues is often known as social signals. They serve as indicators that help individuals to understand and respond to one another (Vinciarelli, 2016). These social signals play a crucial role in shaping social identity such as the way we speak, dress, behave, or gesture. Looking into the avatar perspective, avatars function like a social signal in the physical world where they play a crucial role in communicating the unspoken message. The way users customise or interact with avatars reflects their affiliation with particular communities or social groups. For instance, avatars equipped with premium customisations, NFTs, or luxury items often signal higher socioeconomic status while avatars with basic customisation typically indicate newcomers or starters in the metaverse. These visual elements showcase the hierarchies within the digital communities similar to how luxurious items function in the real world.

Besides representing socioeconomic status, an avatar could also serve as a different membership or identity according to its particular communities. To make it more precise, avatar customisation may vary across different contexts such as in professional settings, users may choose formal attire, whereas in gaming or fandom communities, they might adopt science-fiction-inspired designs or even their favourite anime characters.

Avatars also enable users to embody a variety of personas or roles within the metaverse, such as heroes, villains, mentors, students, teachers, or workers. By replicating real-world scenarios, such customisation actually enhances the sense of realism and fosters a sense of belonging within metaverse communities. Consequently, users' behaviours may adapt to the norms and expectations of the community as they see themselves as part of the member in the group (Teng et al., 2023). This sense of belonging within the metaverse team or community could lead to increasing loyalty towards the group.

The avatar serves as a powerful language that enables users to express emotion and social signals through body movements, gestures, and real-time interaction. With the engagement of immersive technologies, body language such as nodding, waving, hugging, or any posture movement in the avatar plays as an expression in a certain communication context. These small engagements such as a brief, spontaneous hug with another avatar during the interaction in the VRChat platform, embodied an expression of friendship and mutual understanding that they shared in their relationship with each other (Zhou et al., 2025). Hence, these body-to-body interactions, despite happening just in the metaverse realm, still give a social disclosure in the group's interaction. Not only that, the real-life interaction such as voice chat gives more sense of acceptance such that in the online gaming platform where they could coordinate strategies, interpret intentions and build social relationships (Wadley et al., 2015).

While avatars can foster social identity and community formation, they can also reinforce divisions through in-group and out-group dynamics. The in-group consists of those with whom a user identifies, while the out-group comprises individuals perceived as different or outside the community (Bernstein, 2015). For instance, avatars representing disabilities, non-binary identities, unconventional forms, or different skin tones and genders may be ignored or even discriminated against in certain communities. Although customisation offers creative freedom, it does not guarantee acceptance. Bartlett and Krogmeier (2025) found that the metaverse often lacks acceptance and inclusion for dark-skinned avatars in addressing racial bias. This pattern suggests that light-skinned avatars are frequently treated as the default "in-group," while dark-skinned avatars are positioned as the "out-group."

In essence, an avatar is not merely a digital representation of a user within the metaverse; it also shapes how others perceive the user and how the user perceives themselves within a digital group or society, much like in the physical world. Features such as language, avatar mobility, and embodied sensory elements are key components that facilitate a person's integration into social discourse within the metaverse.

11.5 The Future of Avatars and Evolving Digital Identity in Virtual Economies

With the rapid evolution of immersive technologies, the metaverse is poised to become the central hub for economic, social, and cultural activities. As the representation of users within this environment, avatars will play an increasingly important role in it. They will evolve from simple graphical representations into more sophisticated, diverse, and fully integrated digital identities in the metaverse. Therefore, the future generations of avatars are expected to be more advanced, versatile, and powerful than those available today.

Nevertheless, despite the technological advancements that help in building a lifelike and realistic virtual environment, the presence of realistic avatars in the metaverse is still uncommon. These issues reduced the user interest, social interaction experience, and even constrained their personal expression and body gesture (Talapuru et al., 2024). Moreover, the current technologies in creating realistic avatars have yet to fully convince users of their photo-realistic custom-made avatars due to the lack of their characteristic features (Puri et al., 2017). Hence, given this trajectory, the development of realistic avatars is likely to be the main progress in the coming years. It can be anticipated that, shortly, realistic avatars will become a standard feature across both social and professional metaverse platforms.

In addition, as a virtual platform that encourages body motion and gesture, full-body motion tracking is likely to become a key feature for future avatars as current consumer-grade VR systems often lack lower-body tracking, which results in incomplete gesture representation in virtual environments (Jiang et al., 2022). Even when full-body motion tracking is available, the sensors often encounter issues such as calibration errors, spacing inconsistencies, nonlinearity, and displacement (Kim et al., 2019; Park et al., 2025). However, the most significant barrier is still the high cost of full-body motion tracking suits, which is not affordable for most standard users. Although the adoption of full-body motion may still be some distance away, there are several emerging studies that have found that the combination of artificial intelligence with motion-tracking suits could substantially enhance movement precision and gesture from the users. For example, Zhang et al. (2025) demonstrated that combining AI algorithms with smart clothing achieves ultra-accurate dynamic 3D avatars. This shows the effectiveness in improving user engagement in VR activities. Such advancements could deliver highly realistic, lifelike avatar experiences which enable seamless embodiment within the metaverse.

As avatars continue to evolve and become a crucial part of the metaverse, their role will not only be limited to a visual representation for expression or interaction. Avatars are expected to have greater significance on digital identity, economic assets, and personal profiles. Similar to how influencers and content creators monetise their identity on social media, avatars could also cultivate and commercialise their identities in digital communities. With a greater influence across the community such as gaming environments, virtual workplaces, and social hubs, users could use avatars to generate revenue through sponsorships, public appearances, digital branding, collaborations, and awareness campaigns. This development could create business opportunities, corporate strategies, and even avatar-related professions.

The influence of avatars on economic, social, and personal significance in the metaverse communities could potentially lead to some new issues and challenges particularly in the realm of identity governance. As avatars are tied to economic assets or reputational value, they may become the prime targets for cybercrime and identity theft which could lead to hacking, fraud, and other malicious activities. Besides, without adequate regulation and security measures, sensitive personal information such as real names, addresses, and bank account details could also be leaked which could potentially damage a user's real-life reputation and safety. Therefore, a robust digital identity management system is essential to safeguard every user in the metaverse. The use of technologies such as blockchain and privacy filters can be adopted to reform governance frameworks and address privacy concerns (Wang & Wang, 2023). Nevertheless, technological safeguards alone are insufficient. Users must also be equipped with proper awareness and education to protect their data and privacy in the metaverse.

Given the previously mentioned issues, the growing impact of avatars in the future metaverse is likely to raise significant concerns. The extent to which these challenges can be addressed will depend on how effectively both users and developers balance technological advancements in enhancing avatar capabilities and improving user experiences, while also safeguarding privacy, regulating data collection, and preventing the misuse of avatars within virtual environments.

References

Aymerich-Franch, L. (2020). Avatar embodiment experiences to enhance mental health. *Technology and Health*. Academic Press. https://doi.org/10.1016/B978-0-12-816958-2.00003-4

Bartlett, K. A., & Krogmeier, C. (2025). Observations on virtual reality avatar alignment with research participants' skin tone and gender. *IEEE Conference Virtual Reality and 3D User Interfaces (VR)*, 288–295. https://doi.org/10.1109/VR59515.2025.00053

Behm-Morawitz, E., & Schipper, S. (2016). Sexing the avatar. *Journal of Media Psychology, 28*(4), 161–174. https://doi.org/10.1027/1864-1105/a000152

Bem, D. J. (1972). Self-perception theory. *Advances in Experimental Social Psychology, 6*, 1–62. Academic Press. https://doi.org/10.1016/S0065-2601(08)60024-6

Bernstein, M. J. (2015). Ingroups and outgroups. The Wiley Blackwell Encyclopedia of Race, Ethnicity, and Nationalism (pp. 1–3). Wiley. https://doi.org/10.1002/9781118663202.wberen482

Blue, J., Condell, J., & Lunney, T. F. (2018). A review of identity, identification and authentication. *International Journal for Information Security Research*. https://api.semanticscholar.org/CorpusID:88500772

Cambridge University Press. (n.d.). Identity. *Cambridge Dictionary*. https://dictionary.cambridge.org/dictionary/english/identity

Cheng, R., Wu, N., Varvello, M., Chen, S., & Han, B. (2022). Are we ready for metaverse? a measurement study of social virtual reality platforms. *ACM Internet Measurement Conference*, 504–518. https://doi.org/10.1145/3517745.3561417

Coble, K., Ratican, J., & Hutson, J. (2024). Beyond the pixelated mirror: Understanding avatar identity and its impact on in-game advertising and consumer behavior. *Metaverse, 4*(2). https://doi.org/10.54517/m.v4i2.2377

Evallyo, V. D. (2019). The avatar's nature and its modern modifications. *International Conference on Art Studies: Science, Experience, Education (ICASSEE)*, 384–389. https://doi.org/10.2991/icassee-19.2019.79

Ferrer-García, M., Porras Garcia, B., Moreno, M., Bertomeu, P., & Gutiérrez-Maldonado, J. (2018). Embodiment in different size virtual bodies produces changes in women's body image distortion and dissatisfaction. *Annual Review of CyberTherapy and Telemedicine, 16*(1), 111–117.

Freeman, D., Reeve, S., Robinson, A., Ehlers, A., Clark, D., Spanlang, B., & Slater, M. (2017). Virtual reality in the assessment, understanding, and treatment of mental health disorders. *Psychological Medicine, 47*(14), 2393–2400. https://doi.org/10.1017/S003329171700040X

Gillies, M., Brenton, H., & Kleinsmith, A. (2015). Embodied design of full bodied interaction with virtual humans. *International Workshop on Movement and Computing*, 1–8. https://doi.org/10.1145/2790994.2790996

Haslam, S. A., Haslam, C., Cruwys, T., Jetten, J., Bentley, S. V, Fong, P., & Steffens, N. K. (2022). Social identity makes group-based social connection possible: Implications for loneliness and mental health. *Current Opinion in Psychology, 43*, 161–165. https://doi.org/10.1016/j.copsyc.2021.07.013

Jiang, J., Streli, P., Qiu, H., Fender, A., Laich, L., Snape, P., & Holz, C. (2022). AvatarPoser: Articulated full-body pose tracking from sparse motion sensing. *European Conference on Computer Vision*, 443–460. Springer Nature Switzerland. https://doi.org/10.1007/978-3-031-20065-6_26

Jones, N. F. (2015). From gods to gamers: The manifestation of the avatar throughout religious history and postmodern culture. *Berkeley Undergraduate Journal, 28*. https://api.semanticscholar.org/CorpusID:148172652

Kim, D., Kwon, J., Han, S., Park, Y.-L., & Jo, S. (2019). Deep full-body motion network for a soft wearable motion sensing suit. *IEEE/ASME Transactions on Mechatronics, 24*(1), 56–66. https://doi.org/10.1109/TMECH.2018.2874647

Kim, D. Y., Lee, H. K., & Chung, K. (2023). Avatar-mediated experience in the metaverse: The impact of avatar realism on user-avatar relationship. *Journal of Retailing and Consumer Services, 73*, 103382. https://doi.org/10.1016/j.jretconser.2023.103382

Lee, D.-Y., Cho, Y.-H., & Lee, I.-K. (2018). Being them. *ACM Symposium on Virtual Reality Software and Technology*, 1–2. https://doi.org/10.1145/3281505.3283384

Noisri, S., Wisessing, P., Srisupakwong, K., Santoso, H. B., & Wittisittikulkij, L. (2024). Designing avatar system and integrate to the Metaverse. *International Technical Conference on Circuits/Systems, Computers, and Communications (ITC-CSCC)*, 1–6. https://doi.org/10.1109/ITC-CSCC62988.2024.10628399

Park, M., Lee, J., Yang, H., & Kim, J. (2025). Designing and analyzing virtual avatar based on rigid-body tracking in immersive virtual environments. *IEEE Access, 13*, 5522–5533. https://doi.org/10.1109/ACCESS.2025.3525630

Preukschat, A., & Reed, D. (2021). *Self-sovereign identity*. Manning Publications.

Puri, A., Baker, S., Hoang, T. N., & Zuffi, R. C. (2017). To be (me) or not to be? *Australian Conference on Computer-Human Interaction*, 503–507. https://doi.org/10.1145/3152771.3156166

Ready Player Me Team. (2023). Build your Custom Ready Player Me Avatar Creator in Unity SDK. *Ready Player ME*. https://readyplayer.me/blog/introducing-ready-player-me-custom-avatar-creator-sdk-in-unity

Ribeiro, A., Vieira, V., Alves, L., & Maciel, C. (2024). VISHnu: An approach to support the personalization of self-expressive avatars using context-awareness. *International Journal of Human-Computer Studies, 185*, 103243. https://doi.org/https://doi.org/10.1016/j.ijhcs.2024.103243

Riva, G., Wiederhold, B. K., & Mantovani, F. (2024). Searching for the Metaverse: Neuroscience of physical and digital communities. *Cyberpsychology, Behavior, and Social Networking, 27*(1), 9–18. https://doi.org/10.1089/cyber.2023.0040

Robles-Carrillo, M. (2024). Digital identity: An approach to its nature, concept, and functionalities. *International Journal of Law and Information Technology, 32*, eaae019. https://doi.org/10.1093/ijlit/eaae019

Rochman, M. F. (2023). Adaptasi budaya nusantara sebagai tema pembuatan karakter avatar 3D untuk Metaverse. *DeKaVe, 16*(2), 154–167. https://doi.org/10.24821/dkv.v16i2.11121

Sedlmeir, J., Smethurst, R., Rieger, A., & Fridgen, G. (2021). Digital identities and verifiable credentials. *Business & Information Systems Engineering, 63*(5), 603–613. https://doi.org/10.1007/s12599-021-00722-y

Seymour, M., Yuan, L. (Ivy), Dennis, A. R., & Riemer, K. (2021). Have we crossed the uncanny valley? Understanding affinity, trustworthiness, and preference for realistic digital humans in immersive environments. *Journal of the Association for Information Systems, 22*(3), 591–617. https://doi.org/10.17705/1jais.00674

Sharma, S. (2020). Hindu Diaspora in James Cameron's Avatar. *Migration, Diaspora and Nation Building*. https://www.academia.edu/45668011/Hindu_Diaspora_in_James_Camerons_Avatar

Snyder, M., & Swann, W. B. (1978). Behavioral confirmation in social interaction: From social perception to social reality. *Journal of Experimental Social Psychology, 14*(2), 148–162. https://doi.org/10.1016/0022-1031(78)90021-5

Spadoni, E., Carulli, M., Mengoni, M., Luciani, M., & Bordegoni, M. (2023). Empowering virtual humans' emotional expression in the Metaverse. *International Conference on Human-Computer Interaction*, 133–143. Springer Nature Switzerland. https://doi.org/10.1007/978-3-031-35897-5_10

Szolin, K., Kuss, D. J., Nuyens, F. M., & Griffiths, M. D. (2023). Exploring the user-avatar relationship in videogames: A systematic review of the Proteus effect. *Human–Computer Interaction, 38*(5–6), 374–399. https://doi.org/10.1080/07370024.2022.2103419

Tajfel, H., & Turner, J. C. (2004). The social identity theory of intergroup behavior. *Political Psychology* (pp. 276–293). Psychology Press. https://doi.org/10.4324/9780203505984-16

Talapuru, S., Dantu, R., Zaman, S., Quach, V., & Pokharel, A. (2024). Fostering the Metaverse immersion: Unraveling personalized dynamic human avatars. *IEEE International Conference on Metaverse Computing, Networking, and Applications (MetaCom)*, 143–150. https://doi.org/10.1109/MetaCom62920.2024.00016

Teng, C.-I., Dennis, A. R., & Dennis, A. S. (2023). Avatar-mediated communication and social identification. *Journal of Management Information Systems, 40*(4), 1171–1201. https://doi.org/10.1080/07421222.2023.2267320

Vinciarelli, A. (2016). Computing technologies for social signals. *Emotions and Personality in Personalized Services: Models, Evaluation and Applications* (pp. 101–118). Springer International Publishing. https://doi.org/10.1007/978-3-319-31413-6_6

Wadley, G., Carter, M., & Gibbs, M. (2015). Voice in virtual worlds: The design, use, and influence of voice chat in online play. *Human–Computer Interaction, 30*(3–4), 336–365. https://doi.org/10.1080/07370024.2014.987346

Wang, S., & Wang, W. (2023). A review of the application of digital identity in the Metaverse. *Security and Safety, 2*, 2023009. https://doi.org/10.1051/sands/2023009

Yee, N., & Bailenson, J. (2007). The Proteus Effect: The effect of transformed self-representation on behavior. *Human Communication Research, 33*(3), 271–290. https://doi.org/10.1111/j.1468-2958.2007.00299.x

Zhang, C., Zhang, L., Tian, Y., An, Z., Li, B., & Li, D. (2025). AI-enabled full-body dynamic avatar reconstruction using triboelectric smart clothing for metaverse applications. *EScience, 5*(4), 100373. https://doi.org/10.1016/j.esci.2025.100373

Zhou, S., Zamani, E., & Toth, Z. (2025). Embodied communication via virtual reality devices: The visual-body language of avatar in Metaverse. *UK Academy for Information Systems Conference Proceedings 2025*, 39. https://aisel.aisnet.org/ukais2025/39

12

Virtual Reality and the Elderly: Immersive Experiences for Quality of Life

Hafizan Mat Som and Amzari Ghazali

12.1 Immersive Technologies and the Elderly: Opportunities for Enhanced Quality of Life

Immersive technology, an evolving domain within the broader field of information technology, aims to blur the line between the physical world and the digital or simulated world, thus creating a sense of immersion. This sense of "being there" allows users to interact with the three-dimensional world in ways that feel intuitive and natural. In doing so, it offers the potential for a range of applications far beyond traditional computing interfaces. The most recognised types of immersive technologies include virtual reality (VR), augmented reality (AR), and mixed reality (MR). VR is a fully immersive environment that can either simulate the real world or create a completely fictitious one. Users wear headsets and often use hand-held controllers to interact with this environment. Meanwhile, AR, unlike VR, overlays digital elements onto the real world through devices like smartphones or AR glasses. This creates an enhanced version of reality to add information or improve life in real time. Finally, MR is a hybrid of VR and AR, offering a real-world and digital overlay where physical and digital objects coexist and interact in real time.

The general functions of immersive technologies can be categorised into various types of human-computer interaction, such as simulation, entertainment, and telepresence. These technologies offer users new ways to visualise data, interact with complex systems, and collaborate in real-time settings. From training pilots in simulated cockpits to providing new dimensions in gaming, the application spectrum is broad and continually expanding. Immersive technology can also significantly enhance the quality of life (QoL) by offering innovative solutions for healthcare, education, and social interaction. These technologies provide engaging environments for physical

DOI: 10.1201/9781003662433-16

rehabilitation, cognitive training, and emotional well-being. They also combat isolation by enabling virtual social interactions, making them especially beneficial for populations such as older people who may face mobility and social constraints.

The elderly population in Malaysia, as well as globally, has been increasing year by year. To address the rise in this demographic, preserving and enhancing the QoL for these seniors is of the utmost importance. One of the most pressing issues that many elderly individuals face is emotional isolation and loneliness, often exacerbated by the loss of a spouse or lifelong friends. Loneliness not only affects emotional well-being but also has tangible effects on physical health, such as increased risks of heart disease, depression, and cognitive decline. The lack of social engagement can contribute to a decreasing QoL as one ages, and traditional support networks or social services often fall short of addressing these emotional needs fully.

Another significant concern for older people is the decline in physical health and mobility. Chronic conditions like arthritis, diabetes, and heart disease become more prevalent with age, often limiting the ability to engage in physical activities or even perform basic daily tasks. This loss of independence can be psychologically distressing and further deteriorate the QoL. Cognitive issues such as dementia and Alzheimer's disease also play a role in diminishing QoL. These conditions not only impair memory and reasoning but often lead to behavioural changes that can strain relationships and further isolate the individual. Furthermore, the rapid advancement of technology often leaves many older adults behind. The technological divide not only limits their access to services but also makes it challenging to engage in an increasingly digital society, exacerbating feelings of isolation and inadequacy.

Thus, the primary aim of this first VR research was to explore the impact of VR technology on older people. The participants were residents of Rumah Seri Kenangan Seri Iskandar. This session was part of a broader study that seeks to understand how immersive technologies can positively impact the emotional and physical well-being of the elderly, particularly for those with limited mobility or declining mental faculties. Participants, aged between 65 and 77, engaged with VR experiences designed to stimulate cognitive function and physical activity. The focus of the study was to measure key aspects of mood, mobility, and overall well-being, both before and after exposure to VR, with the hypothesis that VR could serve as a therapeutic tool to improve the QoL in older adults.

The primary aim of this research is to comprehensively investigate the role and impact of VR technology on the elderly population in Malaysia. Specifically, the study intends to achieve three key objectives. First, it aims to explore the current perspectives of elderly individuals in Malaysia regarding VR Technology. Second, the research aims to assess the tangible impact of VR technology on physical, cognitive, and psychological aspects among the elderly, addressing the question of how these technologies may affect overall well-being. Lastly, the study aims to identify the prerequisites for and barriers to the adoption of VR technology among the elderly population in Malaysia. By understanding these facilitators and challenges, stakeholders can develop more effective strategies to boost technology acceptance and integration within this age group, ensuring that the benefits of such advancements are maximised for an older demographic.

This work focused on the application of VR among older people. The choice of VR is based on its immersive nature, which allows older people to experience a wholly digital environment, thereby potentially mitigating specific issues they face, such as mobility restrictions or a lack of exposure to novel experiences. The primary issues that this work addressed include:

a. Loneliness – Many elderly individuals face social isolation, which can lead to feelings of loneliness. VR can potentially bridge this gap by allowing them to interact in virtual social environments or partake in group activities they might otherwise be unable to join.
b. Impairment – Mobility and sensory impairments can limit the activities and experiences available to older individuals. VR can provide simulations of experiences that are physically challenging or otherwise inaccessible. On the other hand, by attracting older people to visit the Elderly Activity Centre (in Malay, Pusat Aktiviti Warga Emas – PAWE) to experience this VR technology, they can improve their physical movement instead of just sitting at home and doing nothing.
c. Emotional Stress – VR can offer therapeutic and relaxing experiences, such as virtual nature walks, meditation sessions, or exposure to calming environments, thereby reducing stress.

Thus, this work intends to investigate (i) What is the potential of older adults in Malaysia regarding VR technology usage?, (ii) How does VR application impact the physical, cognitive, and psychological well-being of older adults?, and (iii) What are the facilitators and challenges faced by older people in Malaysia when adopting VR technology?

12.2 VR for Health, Social Connection, and Engagement in Aging Populations

According to an article on the Tangram Insurance Services website, an insurance company based in the US, VR can also contribute to improved health. In a study published in the US National Library of Medicine, stroke patients are reported to recover faster when they use VR to practice movements that they are still learning to perform in real life (Tangram Insurance Services, 2023). VR can also be used to help people with dementia remember things they have seen or heard, things they have done, and even things that they have learned (Tabbaa et al., 2019). VR for seniors can serve as a tool for enhancing motivation by increasing patient engagement. Syed-Abdul et al. (2019) demonstrate that VR has been utilised in several studies, where patients participating in interactive games involving VR exhibit increased motivation and better performance on tasks compared to those who do not use VR.

Lee et al. (2019) discovered that applications of AR and VR for older people primarily fall into four categories: health, social, fun, and convenience. According to Seifert and Schlomann (2021), AR and VR hold considerable promise in five key aspects of life for older adults, starting with real-world orientation. Applications in this domain include virtual tourism and shopping experiences, offering relaxation options for older people. In the realm of education, these MR technologies can revolutionise learning methodologies and enrich intergenerational educational experiences, particularly those centred on personal interests and social interactions (Baker et al., 2020; Corregidor-Sánchez et al., 2020; Seifert & Schlomann, 2021). Health is another crucial area where VR and AR are being used for purposes such as psychotherapy and physical rehabilitation (Lee et al., 2019; Syed-Abdul et al., 2019). In terms of entertainment, MR games have gained traction, especially after the success of phenomena like Pokémon GO, leading to the development of more age-appropriate games, such as roller coaster simulations and car racing (García-Betances et al., 2015; Khazanchi, 2018; Piech & Czernicki, 2021). Lastly, AR and VR are creating new avenues for social engagement for older people, through interactions with avatars or embodied agents, making them feel less isolated and more connected through shared emotions and stories (Falconer et al., 2016; Mapplewood Senior Living, 2023; Optale et al., 2010).

According to some local research articles on this issue, older people in Malaysia face issues with isolation, which negatively impacts the cognitive, physical, and psychological quality of their lives (Azila Salleh et al., 2022; Ibrahim et al., 2016; Ibrahim & Ahmad, 2022; Ismail, 2021). PAWE, an activity centre for senior individuals managed by the Community Welfare Department (*Jabatan Kebajikan Masyarakat*), offers various activities, including religious gatherings, cooking, and socialising. Introducing VR applications could serve as an appealing content addition, potentially attracting more seniors to engage with PAWE. This work builds upon a few frameworks developed by previous researchers, including Lee et al. (2019) and Baragash et al. (2022). The former proposed a design framework for an AR/VR application targeting older people, while the latter had developed a VR and AR application framework aimed at improving the QoL for older adults. The term QoL refers to the overall well-being of individuals and societies, encompassing both the negative and positive aspects of life. It measures life satisfaction, encompassing aspects such as physical health, family, education, employment, wealth, safety, security, freedom, religious beliefs, and the environment. QoL is a highly subjective and multidimensional concept, often differing from person to person based on individual needs, goals, and cultural background. QoL encompasses various domains, including, but not limited to, physical health, psychological state, economic stability, social interactions, environment, and beliefs.

12.3 Designing and Conducting VR Interventions for Elderly Care

This project employed a qualitative approach, including post- and pre-interview sessions during the intervention, which utilised a VR application within a specific timeframe and setup. An observation was also conducted during the use of VR technology at the target centre, Rumah Seri Kenangan, Seri Iskandar. Three sessions were conducted with the same participants to see the effect and passion. The data collection involved qualitative methods, including interview sessions and an observational deck. This approach leveraged data and findings obtained from semi-structured interviews with the participants. A pre- and post-interview survey was conducted with the target respondents to gather their responses regarding knowledge, experience, and feedback related to immersive technology and IT-based applications used in daily life. Figure 12.1 illustrates the research activities undertaken to achieve the research aims and objectives.

The study included a diverse group of ten participants (six men and four women), each with distinct health conditions, such as hypertension,

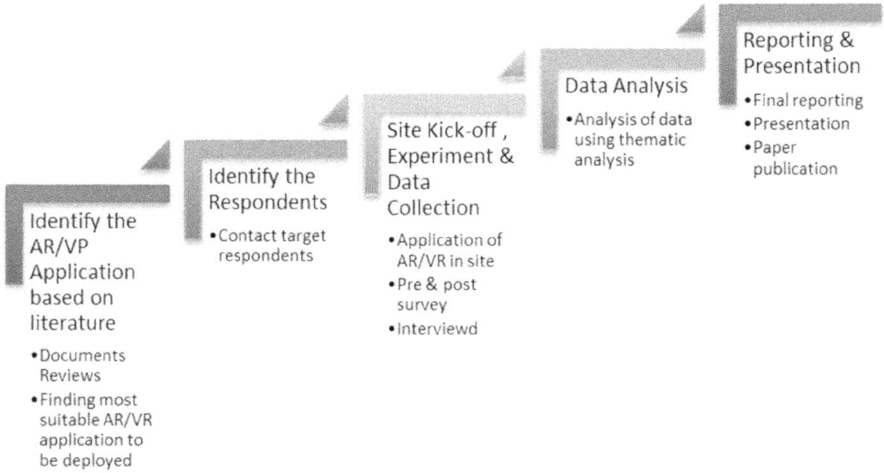

FIGURE 12.1
Research activities.

schizophrenia, and liver disease. This diversity of health issues reflects the varied nature of physical and mental health challenges often encountered in an ageing population. The fact that some participants were taking medications for conditions like schizophrenia and hepatitis adds another layer of complexity to the study, as medication can influence both cognitive and physical responses to VR. Therefore, understanding how these conditions interact with the VR experience is crucial for interpreting the results. The inclusion of participants with these conditions also underscores the potential of VR to be applied across a broad spectrum of health scenarios in elderly populations.

12.4 Impact of VR on Mood, Mobility, and Cognitive Focus

12.4.1 Data Collection via Observation – Pre-session Procedure

12.4.1.1 Effect on Blood Pressure and Heart Rate

Vital signs, including blood pressure and heart rate, were recorded before and after the VR session to gauge the physiological impact of the experience. For instance, Participant 1's blood pressure increased from 103/67 to 124/77, suggesting a rise in physical engagement or excitement during the session. This slight increase could suggest that VR stimulates mild physical activity, even in individuals who are otherwise sedentary. On the other hand, Participant 2's blood pressure decreased from 151/96 to 130/73, a significant drop that might suggest a calming or stress-relieving effect for him. These contrasting responses underscore the varied ways in which VR can impact physiological states in elderly individuals, depending on their initial condition and their level of engagement with the technology.

12.4.1.2 Mood and Mobility before the VR Session

Before the session began, most participants reported feeling neutral, neither excited nor distressed, and a majority were capable of walking unassisted, reflecting a baseline level of independence. However, the variation in initial mood, with some participants feeling excited, could be due to the novelty of the technology. For elderly individuals, the anticipation of engaging with something new and unfamiliar can trigger positive emotional states, suggesting that the very prospect of a VR session can stimulate enthusiasm and mental alertness. Meanwhile, the ability of most participants to walk unassisted suggests the potential for VR to augment mobility in relatively active elderly individuals, potentially preventing or delaying the onset of more severe physical decline.

12.4.2 Data Collection via Observation – During VR Session

12.4.2.1 Activity and Duration of VR Use

During the session, participants interacted with VR environments for 10–15 minutes, a relatively short but impactful duration. They engaged in cognitive and movement-based games specifically designed to challenge their mental focus and motor coordination. The 10- to 15-minute window was long enough to observe meaningful reactions without overwhelming the participants, many of whom are not accustomed to sustained engagement with digital environments. These cognitive and movement-based activities allowed the researchers to assess both mental agility and physical dexterity. The positive feedback, with an average well-being score of 4 out of 5 before VR use, suggests that participants were generally open to new experiences and possibly expected beneficial outcomes from the session.

12.4.2.2 Engagement and Ease of Use

The study measured engagement using a scale of 1–5, with most participants rating their engagement at 4. It suggests that, despite their age and potential unfamiliarity with technology, most participants were able to immerse themselves effectively in the VR experience. However, some participants reported difficulties with the technology, rating ease of use as low as 2. This discrepancy highlights a critical challenge in applying VR technology to elderly populations: while the potential for engagement is high, user-friendly interfaces are essential. Cognitive impairments or a lack of prior exposure to modern technology can hinder the ability of some elderly individuals to fully benefit from VR, suggesting that future applications must prioritise intuitive design and gradual onboarding processes.

12.4.3 Data Collection via Observation – Post-VR Session

12.4.3.1 Mood after the VR Session

Post-session mood reports indicated that most participants felt neutral or happy, with no significant physical discomfort apart from one individual who experienced anxiety. This mood shift points to the psychological benefits of VR, where even neutral mood maintenance can be considered a success, especially in populations prone to depression, anxiety, or social isolation. The outlier who felt anxious may reflect a common concern among elderly users: the disorienting or overwhelming nature of immersive experiences. For future sessions, it would be beneficial to calibrate the intensity of the VR content more effectively, possibly by offering more familiar or calming environments for first-time users.

12.4.3.2 Improved Focus and Mobility

VR's effect on cognitive focus and physical mobility was evaluated positively across participants, with many reporting marked improvements. For example, tasks involving object interaction, such as shooting games or throwing cubes, require fine motor skills and hand-eye coordination, which are often diminished in elderly individuals. The fact that some participants reported better mobility afterwards suggests that VR can stimulate physical movements that they may not normally engage in, even in a safe and low-risk environment. The increased focus observed after the session suggests that VR may serve as a tool to re-engage cognitive functions, potentially offering therapeutic benefits for elderly individuals experiencing cognitive decline.

12.4.3.3 General Well-Being and Enjoyment

Most participants reported a positive impact on their overall well-being after the session, describing the experience as enjoyable. One participant, however, noted difficulty using the VR system, which impacted his enjoyment. Another participant expressed fear during the session, reporting a sensation of isolation from reality. It underscores the importance of carefully selecting VR content for elderly users, ensuring that the experiences are engaging without being disorienting or overwhelming. This feedback reveals that while most participants enjoyed the session, more attention should be paid to designing or selecting VR environments that cater to the unique psychological needs of elderly individuals, especially those who may be prone to anxiety or confusion.

12.4.4 Data Collection via Interview Session – Post VR Session

12.4.4.1 Themes Based on Research Objectives

The interview data from the VR tryout sessions were collected in two phases. In addition to the elderly participants, six caretakers and one director of the Elderly Care Centre were also interviewed to provide a comprehensive perspective on the use of VR technology in this context. The collected data were transcribed and analysed using NVivo software, a qualitative data analysis tool, to categorise and identify key themes. Keywords such as *potential, impact, mood, movement, difficulties, worries, technical, and behaviour* were used to guide the initial coding process. Following the initial analysis, the data were re-clustered and organised according to the research objectives, which focused on three main areas: (i) the potential and impact of VR technology on elderly users, (ii) the challenges faced by elderly individuals when using VR, and (iii) the facilitation needed to support the adoption of VR technology among older people in Malaysia. This structured approach allowed for a deeper understanding of the opportunities and barriers associated with integrating VR into elderly care, providing valuable insights for future implementation and refinement of VR-based interventions.

12.4.4.2 Theme 1: Potential and Impact

Most participants expressed interest in participating in future VR sessions, indicating that the initial session successfully sparked curiosity and enthusiasm. However, two participants declined further participation – one citing difficulties with the technology and the other expressing fear of potential harm from VR. These remarks highlight the importance of adopting personalised approaches to VR integration in elderly care. While most elderly individuals may respond positively, a subset may require more gradual exposure, additional reassurance, or simplified VR interfaces to ensure comfort and usability. Some participants suggested trying different games, such as netball and shooting games, indicating that physical and competitive elements within VR experiences resonate well with this demographic. Such activities could offer both physical and mental stimulation, making them particularly appealing. Based on the VR sessions conducted at RSK, participants were asked about the potential of VR applications for elderly residents in the care centre. The potential and impact of VR can be grouped into several key points:

a. Enhancement of cognitive abilities
    - Memory improvement – VR-based cognitive games, such as puzzles and memory recall activities, can stimulate brain functions and potentially slow cognitive decline in elderly individuals.

b. Promotion of emotional well-being
    - Stress reduction and relaxation – Virtual environments, such as serene beaches, fishing ponds, or tranquil forests, can offer therapeutic effects, reducing anxiety, depression, and stress.

c. Improvement in physical activities
    - Interactive VR games – Games like VR shooting, bowling, or virtual tennis can encourage movement and enhance coordination, making physical activity enjoyable.
    - Sports simulations – Elderly users can engage in low-impact VR sports simulations, promoting mobility, strength, and overall physical health in a safe environment.
    - VR meditation applications – Participants can learn to breathe calmly and engage in self-reflection, promoting relaxation and mindfulness.

d. Stimulating creativity and interests
    - Music therapy – VR applications can enable elderly individuals to play musical instruments in virtual environments, stimulating creativity and enjoyment.

e. Positive impact on mental health
   - Alleviating boredom – Immersive VR activities offer a break from monotonous daily routines at the care centre, providing a stimulating and engaging alternative.
   - Encouraging optimism – Virtual environments can create a sense of wonder and curiosity, boosting mood and fostering a positive outlook on life.

12.4.4.3 Theme 2: Challenges and Barriers

Some challenges identified from the session were as follows:

a. Good eyesight requirement – One major challenge encountered was the need for participants to have adequate eyesight to engage with VR activities fully. Several participants struggled to see or react to certain aspects of the VR games, which hindered their ability to immerse themselves in the experience fully. It highlights the need for visual accessibility features or larger, clearer graphics for elderly users with declining eyesight. Male-3 annotated that using the glasses support together with the VR headset can improve the eyesight to see through the apps.
b. Grip strength – The ability to properly hold and operate the VR joystick was another issue, as some participants struggled to maintain a steady grip. Many elderly individuals experience reduced hand strength or dexterity, which affects their ability to control and navigate the VR environment effectively. The majority of participants have difficulty gripping and using the VR joystick. In future sessions, alternative control mechanisms or adapted joysticks may be necessary.
c. Language barriers – Language posed a significant barrier for some participants. As many elderly individuals in the study did not understand English, it became necessary to offer briefings and instructions in their native language before each game. This extra step ensured that participants understood how to engage with the VR content, but it also slowed down the session and required more facilitation from the staff. Offering more localised content or multilingual support in the future could alleviate these challenges.
d. Unsuitability for individuals with hearing impairments – Some VR applications rely heavily on audio cues, such as music or sound effects, to guide user movements and interactions. However, these features pose significant challenges for elderly individuals with hearing impairments, as they may struggle to perceive or respond to auditory prompts. This limitation not only hinders their ability to engage with the VR experience fully but also excludes them from

benefiting from applications designed to enhance cognitive and physical functions. Addressing this issue requires the development of VR applications that incorporate visual or haptic feedback as alternative cues, ensuring inclusivity for users with hearing difficulties.

12.4.4.4 Theme 3: Facilitation Factors to Address Challenges

Based on the interview with the participants, the caretaker and director of the Elderly Care Centre, this facilitation is needed to improve engagement and usage of VR among older people.

a. Good eyesight requirement:
   - Implement large and high-contrast graphics – Ensure VR content utilises bold, high-contrast visuals with larger fonts and simpler elements that elderly users can perceive more easily.
   - Adjustable visual settings – Provide customisable options, such as brightness, font size, and magnification, to cater to individual visual needs.
   - Audio cues and feedback – Integrate auditory guidance to complement visual cues, allowing participants to rely less on sight.
   - Specialised VR headsets – Offer VR headsets designed for users with visual impairments, including built-in magnifiers or adjustable lenses.

b. Grip strength
   - Ergonomic and lightweight controllers – Use controllers with larger, easier-to-grip handles designed for users with reduced strength or dexterity.
   - Hand-free interaction options – Incorporate motion-sensing or hand-tracking technology to allow users to navigate the VR environment without holding a device.
   - Controller straps or holders – Add straps or grips that stabilise the controller in the participant's hand to reduce strain and slippage.
   - Adjustable sensitivity – Enable adjustable sensitivity settings in the controls to accommodate users with a limited range of motion.

c. Language barriers
   - Localised content – Develop VR applications with content available in the local languages spoken by the participants.
   - Multilingual interface and instructions – Include options to select preferred languages for menus, subtitles, and voice prompts.
   - Cultural adaptation – Design content that incorporates culturally relevant themes and experiences to enhance relatability and engagement.

- Pre-session orientation – Provide detailed, language-specific briefings and guides before VR sessions to ensure all participants understand the objectives and navigation.

d. Hearing impairments

- Visual feedback integration – Replace or supplement audio cues with visual indicators, such as on-screen prompts, flashing lights, or colour changes, to guide user interactions effectively.
- Haptic feedback – Incorporate vibration or tactile feedback through VR controllers or wearable devices to provide physical cues for actions or alerts.
- Subtitles and captions – Include customisable subtitles or captions for any spoken instructions, dialogues, or sound effects within the VR environment.
- Sign language support – Integrate sign language avatars or interpreters within the VR experience to assist with instructions or content delivery.

By integrating these facilitation factors, VR sessions can become more inclusive, accessible, and effective for elderly participants, ultimately improving their overall experience and engagement.

12.5 Towards Inclusive Immersive Care: VR as a Tool for Aging Well

The first and second VR sessions yielded generally positive outcomes, with noticeable improvements in participants' mood, cognitive focus, and mobility. These results highlight the potential of VR technology as a valuable therapeutic tool for elderly care, offering a unique combination of cognitive stimulation, physical engagement, and emotional well-being in a fun and interactive manner. However, the sessions also revealed critical challenges related to ease of use, visual accessibility, and overall user experience. For instance, some participants struggled with navigating the VR interface, while others faced difficulties due to visual impairments or initial anxiety about using the technology.

Despite these challenges, the majority of participants expressed enthusiasm for continuing with future VR sessions, underscoring the technology's appeal and potential benefits. To ensure broader adoption and inclusivity, it will be essential to refine VR experiences by making them more intuitive, visually accessible, and anxiety-free. It includes incorporating user-friendly designs, providing clear instructions, and tailoring content to accommodate the diverse needs of elderly users, such as those with hearing or visual impairments.

Looking ahead, future sessions should focus on addressing these barriers while exploring additional applications of VR in elderly care, such as social interaction, memory enhancement, and physical rehabilitation. By doing so, VR can become a more inclusive and effective tool for improving the QoL for the ageing population, fostering both mental and physical well-being in a meaningful way.

Acknowledgement

We would like to acknowledge the grant funder, the Murata Science Foundation International Grant (UTP 015ME0–388), for funding this research paper and its publication.

References

Azila Salleh, N., Masayu Rosliah Abdul Rashid, S., & Norliati Fitri Md Nor, N. (2022). Kesejahteraan hidup warga emas: persepsi warga emas terhadap penubuhan pusat aktiviti warga emas (PAWE) di Marang, Terengganu. *Journal of Social Sciences and Humanities, 19*(4), 210–228.

Baker, S., Waycott, J., Robertson, E., Carrasco, R., Neves, B. B., Hampson, R., & Vetere, F. (2020). Evaluating the use of interactive virtual reality technology with older adults living in residential aged care. *Information Processing and Management, 57*(3). https://doi.org/10.1016/j.ipm.2019.102105

Baragash, R. S., Aldowah, H., & Ghazal, S. (2022). Virtual and augmented reality applications to improve older adults' quality of life: A systematic mapping review and future directions. In *Digital Health* (Vol. 8). SAGE Publications Inc. https://doi.org/10.1177/20552076221132099

Corregidor-Sánchez, A. I., Segura-Fragoso, A., Criado-álvarez, J. J., Rodríguez-Hernández, M., Mohedano-Moriano, A., & Polonio-López, B. (2020). Effectiveness of virtual reality systems to improve the activities of daily life in older people. *International Journal of Environmental Research and Public Health, 17*(17), 1–24. https://doi.org/10.3390/ijerph17176283

Falconer, C. J., Rovira, A., King, J. A., Gilbert, P., Antley, A., Fearon, P., Ralph, N., Slater, M., & Brewin, C. R. (2016). Embodying self-compassion within virtual reality and its effects on patients with depression. *BJPsych Open, 2*(1), 74–80. https://doi.org/10.1192/bjpo.bp.115.002147

García-Betances, R. I., Jiménez-Mixco, V., Arredondo, M. T., & Cabrera-Umpiérrez, M. F. (2015). Using virtual reality for cognitive training of the elderly. *American Journal of Alzheimer's Disease and other Dementias, 30*(1), 49–54. https://doi.org/10.1177/1533317514545866

Ibrahim, N., & Ahmad, N. A. (2022). Peminggiran sosial dalam kalangan warga emas: Intervensi ke arah penuaan sihat. In N. Che Mohd Nasir, M. R. Kamaluddin, & M. A. Jasni, (Eds.), *Penyisihan Sosial Kumpulan Marginal* (pp. 44–70). UUM Press.

Ibrahim, N., Mat Saad, Z., & Ahmad Ramly, F. Z. (2016). Keberkesanan Pusat Aktiviti Warga Emas (PAWE) di bawah Dasar Warga Emas Negara. *Jurnal Pembangunan Sosial, 19*. https://doi.org/10.32890/jps.19.2016.11531

Ismail, R. (2021). Program dan aktiviti warga emas: Satu kajian di Pusat Aktiviti Warga Emas (PAWE) Negeri Kedah. *International Journal for Studies on Children, Women, Elderly and Disabled, 14*, 1–7.

Khazanchi, A. (2018). How virtual reality benefits seniors shattering assumptions to meet unique needs. *Microsoft Design*. https://medium.com/microsoft-design/how-virtual-reality-benefits-seniors-a1896aa41e7e

Lee, L. N., Kim, M. J., & Hwang, W. J. (2019). Potential of augmented reality and virtual reality technologies to promotewellbeing in older adults. *Applied Sciences (Switzerland), 9*(17). https://doi.org/10.3390/app9173556

Mapplewood Senior Living. (2023). Benefits of virtual reality for older adults. *Maplewood Senior Living*. https://www.maplewoodseniorliving.com/blog/benefits-of-virtual-reality-for-older-adults/

Optale, G., Urgesi, C., Busato, V., Marin, S., Piron, L., Priftis, K., Gamberini, L., Capodieci, S., & Bordin, A. (2010). Controlling memory impairment in elderly adults using virtual reality memory training: A randomised controlled pilot study. *Neurorehabilitation and Neural Repair, 24*(4), 348–357. https://doi.org/10.1177/1545968309353328

Piech, J., & Czernicki, K. (2021). Virtual reality rehabilitation and exergames-physical and psychological impact on fall prevention among the elderly-a literature review. *Applied Sciences (Switzerland), 11*(9). https://doi.org/10.3390/app11094098

Seifert, A., & Schlomann, A. (2021). The use of virtual and augmented reality by older adults: Potentials and challenges. *Frontiers in Virtual Reality, 2*. https://doi.org/10.3389/frvir.2021.639718

Syed-Abdul, S., Malwade, S., Nursetyo, A. A., Sood, M., Bhatia, M., Barsasella, D., Liu, M. F., Chang, C. C., Srinivasan, K., Raja, M., & Li, Y. C. J. (2019). Virtual reality among the elderly: A usefulness and acceptance study from Taiwan. *BMC Geriatrics, 19*(1). https://doi.org/10.1186/s12877-019-1218-8

Tabbaa, L., Ang, C. S., Rose, V., Siriaraya, P., Stewart, I., Jenkins, K. G., & Matsangidou, M. (2019, May 2). Bring the outside in: Providing accessible experiences through VR for people with dementia in locked psychiatric hospitals. *Conference on Human Factors in Computing Systems – Proceedings*. https://doi.org/10.1145/3290605.3300466

Tangram Insurance Services. (2023). The benefits of virtual reality for seniors. https://www.tangramins.com/news-insights/the-benefits-of-virtual-reality-for-seniors/

13

AI vs Human Judgement: A Comparative Analysis of MyBuddy Application and Manual Assessment in Predicting At-Risk Students

Noraziah ChePa, Ahmad Hanis Mohd Shabli, Azizi Ab Aziz, Wan Hussain Wan Ishak, and Laura Lim Sie-Yi

13.1 Introduction

School dropout is often linked to disengagement, which can stem from various factors such as academic difficulties, behavioural issues, and personal hardships (Szabó et al., 2024; Washor & Mojkowski, 2014). Some students, while remaining enrolled, may still experience disengagement, which can eventually lead to their withdrawal from school. As a result, their future is put at risk, highlighting not only inadequate preparation for postsecondary education but also the broader negative consequences that follow (Bóbó et al., 2022; Marlow & Rehman, 2021; Robison et al., 2017; Sagatun et al., 2014). Previous studies have explored various methods and models to detect student disengagement and school dropout (Fredricks et al., 2019; Garrett-Peters et al., 2019; Järvinen & Tikkanen, 2019; Soland et al., 2019; Sumardi et al., 2023). However, these approaches often lack comprehensiveness due to the complex and multifaceted nature of student disengagement, which is influenced by a wide range of factors (Bills & Howard, 2021).

The complexity of school disengagement, driven by multiple interrelated factors, has made it challenging to develop a robust computational model for early prediction. To address this gap, this study introduces a heterogeneous adaptive computational model designed to identify students at risk of dropping out. This model has been integrated into the *MyBuddy* application and has undergone a comprehensive technical assessment (Chepa et al., 2023). However, its effectiveness depends on the precise calibration of key parameters to ensure that its predictions align with real-world data. The model's

 DOI: 10.1201/9781003662433-17

practical impact lies in its ability to link observable behavioural patterns with decision-making processes, enhancing early intervention efforts.

Model calibration aims to align predicted outcomes with actual results by refining parameter estimates. Unlike merely matching structure or behaviour, calibration establishes a direct link between them, ensuring that the model accurately represents real-world dynamics. A well-calibrated model enhances confidence in its validity, provided the parameter values are appropriately set (Oliva, 2003). Therefore, this chapter focuses on calibrating the proposed computational model (which is the engine of the *MyBuddy* application) to improve early prediction of school disengagement among at-risk students. This can be accomplished by comparing the risk levels assessed by humans with the predicted risk levels generated by the *MyBuddy* application.

13.2 Understanding Student Disengagement: Challenges in Education

A complex interpretation of attitudes towards the school and its community, together with its behavioural, emotional, and cognitive components, collectively constitutes school engagement as a multi-dimensional meta-construct (Martins et al., 2022). In other words, school disengagement has an adverse impact on participation in the educational process, encompassing interactions with individuals, activities, objectives, beliefs, and the overall school environment, thereby hindering favourable educational outcomes and connections to both school and community, ultimately leading to student dropout (Szabó et al., 2024).

The phenomenon of school dropout among students remains a pervasive global issue, preventing them from accessing educational opportunities and hindering their prospects. Previous research indicates that the global dropout rate for middle and upper secondary school students ranges from 17% to 50%, with emerging countries exhibiting a higher prevalence (Cui et al., 2018). One major cause for concern is the high rate of school dropouts, which will have far-reaching consequences for the next generation, not only globally but also for the Malaysian cohort (Mikkay Ei Leen et al., 2022).

This problem is a significant concern in Malaysia, as it adversely affects future generations, according to data from the Department of Statistics, Malaysia. In 2018, 15.1 million children were born, accounting for around 46.6% of Malaysia's total population. By 2030, this predicts an exponential rise in the number of children (Syaiful et al., 2023). At that point, those dropping out of school will ultimately make up more than half of the nation's entire population. Based on this estimate, every child, except one, is not attending school.

These children are predisposed to encounter economic hardships, social stigma, restricted employment opportunities, and diminished income levels (Roslan et al., 2025). Beyond the immediate impact on the adolescent's life, dropping out of school may have far-reaching effects for their families, communities, and society as a whole. These include disruptions to the adolescent's social life, early entry into the illegal labour market, continued poverty, and involvement in criminal activities (Vázquez-Nava et al., 2019).

The phenomenon of school disengagement has been identified as a significant indicator of dropout rates. It is a consequence of complex, multifaceted processes that are non-linear in nature. Although numerous of studies have been conducted on school dropout (Dupéré et al., 2021; González-Rodríguez et al., 2019; Hoff et al., 2015; Peguero et al., 2019; Syaiful et al., 2023), academic (dis)engagement (Anderson et al., 2019; Helal et al., 2018; Quin et al., 2018) and behavioural engagement in school (Cristea et al., 2024; Fredricks et al., 2019; Hawkins et al., 2013; Pengpid & Peltzer, 2020), and taking into account the association between school disengagement and dropout, previous studies have not yet solved the challenging problem of predicting disengagement in at-risk students by combining trustworthy information from many sources or factors that influence the risk into a comprehensive understanding of the relationship between them.

The difficulty of mitigating school dropout rates endures despite the use of numerous strategies throughout time. Despite employing several tactics, achieving conclusive results remains challenging. Given the persistent challenges, there is a pressing need to investigate creative solutions, with the integration of information technology, especially artificial intelligence, being a potential approach.

13.3 From Traditional Models to AI-Driven Prediction of Disengagement

This section discusses previous research on engagement studies that used various approaches in predicting disengagement on academic (dis)engagement, behavioural (dis)engagement, and emotional (dis)engagement. Subramainan et al. (2016) developed an emotion-based model for classroom engagement using agent-based simulations. Students' emotional well-being affects their academic engagement and achievement. This work presented a student engagement paradigm that enhances emotions, boosting engagement and academic success (Subramainan et al., 2016). However, this research focuses solely on classroom engagement in improving academic achievement, excluding other elements that may also affect student engagement.

Soland et al. (2019) criticised current methods for measuring disengagement in standardised testing environments and suggested more sophisticated methods that distinguish between test disengagement and general academic disengagement. The author believes that understanding academic disengagement is crucial for assessing student performance and designing effective remedies for disengagement. Soland's theoretical model focuses on social-emotional competencies, growth mindset, self-efficacy, and self-management engagement indicators (Soland et al., 2019). Nonetheless, due to measurement overlap, student disengagement may be misinterpreted.

Anderson et al. (2019) developed a model linking students' self-efficacy and perceived control to school engagement, emphasising the importance of student agency, personalised learning, and supportive environments. However, reliance on self-reports limits the generalisability of the findings.

Bjugstad et al. (2023) investigated the impact of social and environmental factors on school engagement among Latino youth, focusing on cognitive, behavioural, and relational dimensions. Yet, the study's sampling method and reliance on self-reporting limit its ability to track long-term changes or establish causality. Katsantonis et al. (2024) proposed a longitudinal model on post-compulsory education persistence in the United Kingdom, identifying parental education, self-regulation, and engagement as key predictors. The study is statistically robust, but limited engagement measures and the omission of factors such as cognitive ability and social class constrain its findings.

Existing models for addressing school disengagement have several key limitations. They often focus too narrowly on individual aspects of engagement, neglecting the issue's complexity. Additionally, many models fail to consider the diversity of student populations, limiting their applicability to heterogeneous groups. Most are not adaptable to digital platforms, reducing their practical use in modern education. Furthermore, reliance on predictive analytics without a strong theoretical foundation and incomplete factor selection can result in inaccurate assessments of student disengagement. Thus, this study proposes a comprehensive computational model for predicting school disengagement, which has been integrated into the *MyBuddy* intelligent system as an engine.

13.4 *MyBuddy*: AI-Powered Prediction for At-Risk Students

MyBuddy is an intelligent predictive system designed to assist in identifying students at risk of disengaging from school. *MyBuddy* presents intricate technology that provides a distinctive potential to revolutionise the strategy for managing school disengagement. *MyBuddy* enables the prompt identification of at-risk students, enabling immediate and targeted interventions (Chepa et al., 2023). *MyBuddy* was developed based on the requirements gathered from several sessions of requirement gathering with all target user groups, including school counsellors, the District Education Offices (PPD), and the Kedah State Education Department (JPNK).

MyBuddy is a translation of an intelligent model that involves 14 predictive factors attributed to the four main entities of student dropout: student-related factors, family factors, and environmental factors. Family size, family income, marital status, and educational level are four attributes of the family entity, while teacher, schoolmates, distance to school, school atmosphere, and involvement of the Parent-Teacher Association are five key attributes of the environmental factor. For the student entity, the five main attributes influencing student engagement are the student's physical condition, academic performance, disciplinary record, attendance record, and employment opportunities in the surrounding area.

All 14 predictive factors were identified through a systematic literature review and subsequently validated through an expert review. This multilevel perspective acknowledges that elements at both the individual and societal levels, including, but not limited to, a student's intrinsic drive, academic success, and psychological well-being, are crucial in determining the extent to which students actively participate in school. *MyBuddy* prediction system is available on both websites and mobile platforms. The interfaces of *the MyBuddy* website and application are visually illustrated in Figures 13.1 and 13.2, respectively. The primary function of MyBuddy is to identify students' risk of disengaging from school as early as possible and subsequently suggest appropriate interventions at the right time for these students.

The levels of risk are categorised using a three-colour coding system to ensure clear and intuitive identification. Green signifies low risk, indicating that the student is not currently at significant risk of disengagement. Yellow represents medium risk, suggesting that the student may be exhibiting early warning signs and requires monitoring or intervention. Red denotes high risk, highlighting students who are in urgent need of support due to a substantial likelihood of disengagement. This standardised colour-coding system is consistently applied across both web and mobile platforms, ensuring a seamless and user-friendly experience for educators, counsellors, and stakeholders accessing the data.

The primary users of MyBuddy are educational stakeholders in Kedah, including the Kedah State Education Department (JPNK), District Education Offices (PPD), and school counsellors. Nevertheless, prior to the implementation of the system, the model must be calibrated, and its parameters must be adjusted to maximise the model's performance and improve prediction precision (Sung & Tuo, 2024). In general, the procedure involved comparing the model's outputs to human assessment data, subsequently modifying the model's parameters to reduce apparent disparities. The following section provides a detailed discussion of the methodology for model calibration used in this chapter.

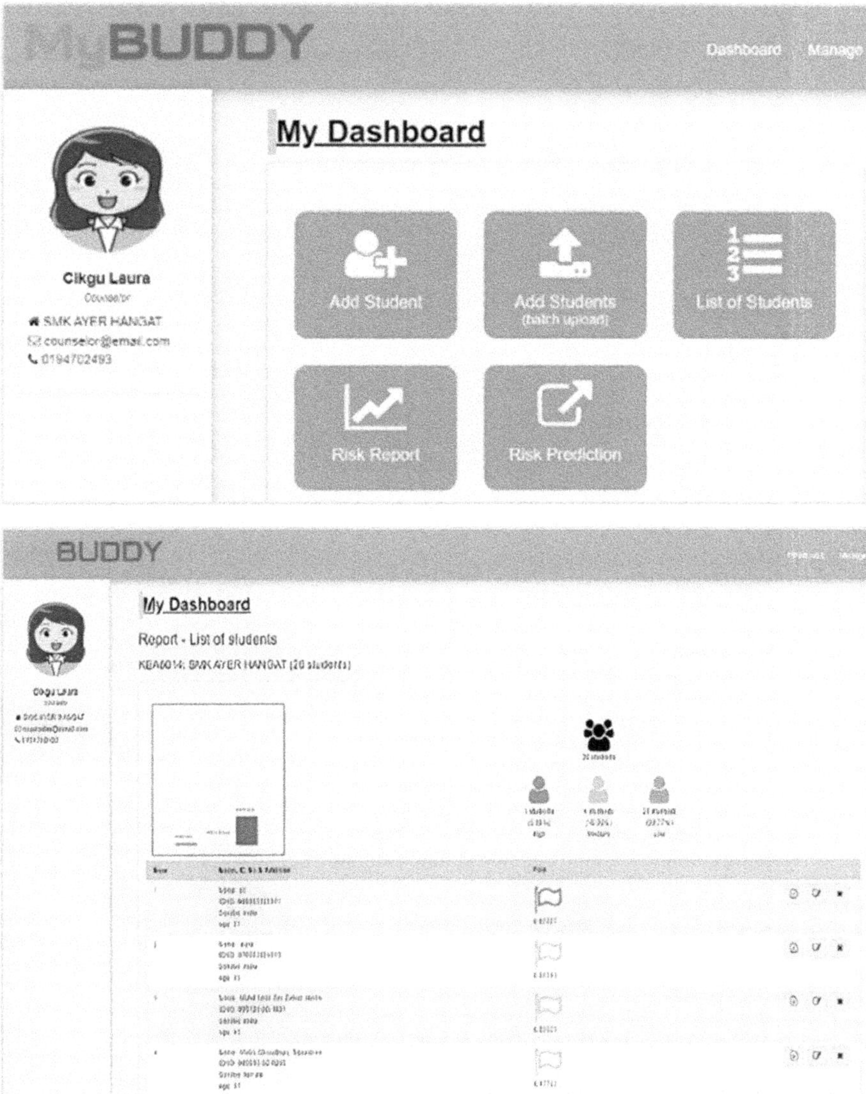

FIGURE 13.1
Interfaces of *MyBuddy* in the web platform.

13.5 Comparing Human Judgement and AI Predictions in Student Risk Assessment

The overall methodology of this study consists of five main phases: development of an intelligent prediction model, translation of the prediction model by developing *MyBuddy*, manual risk assessment, smart risk assessment using *MyBuddy*,

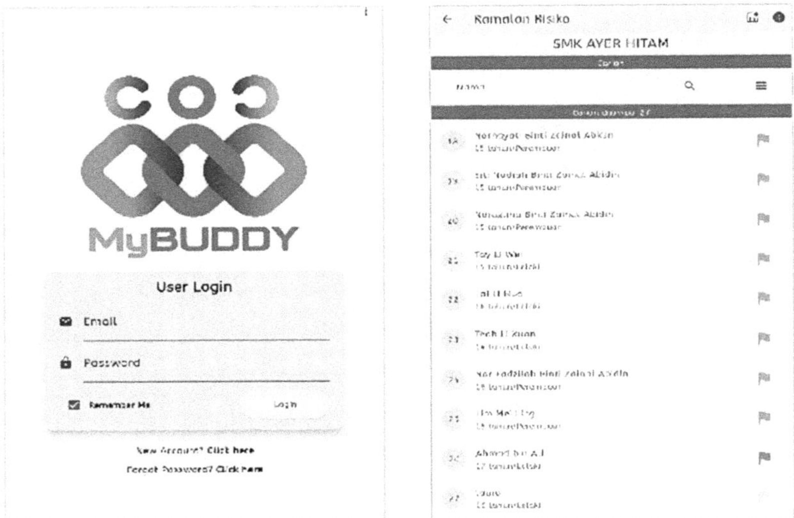

FIGURE 13.2
Interfaces of *MyBuddy* on mobile platform.

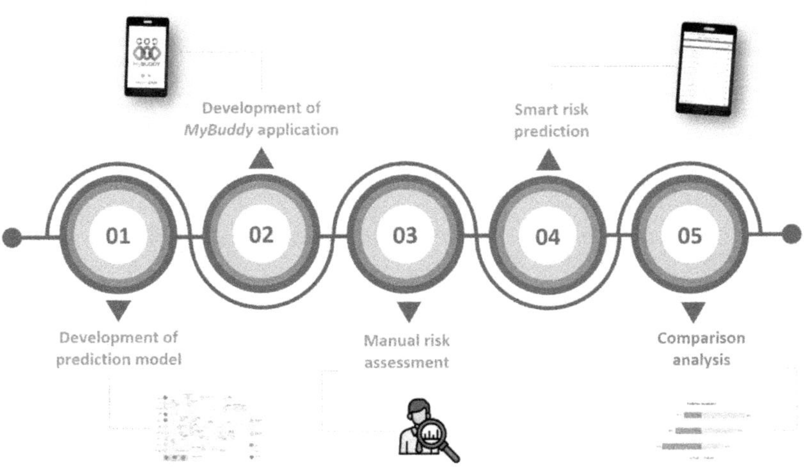

FIGURE 13.3
The overall methodology of the work.

and comparison analysis of risk levels from both approaches. The flow of activities, along with their deliverables, is visually illustrated in Figure 13.3.

13.5.1 Development of a Risk Prediction Model

An intelligent prediction model is designed and developed based on the identified 14 predictors, which belong to five main entities: students, family, school, teachers, and environment. Twenty-six equations have been generated from this model based on the relationships between the predictors. This model serves as the main engine in identifying at-risk students and predicting their risk levels of disengagement.

13.5.2 Development of the MyBuddy Application

The intelligent prediction model that was successfully developed in the previous phase has been translated into a tangible system, namely *MyBuddy*. *MyBuddy* serves as a smart classifier, identifying and predicting at-risk students by assessing their level of disengagement risk. Based on the risk, appropriate actions can be taken by the respective parties to provide early intervention for the students.

13.5.3 Manual Risk Assessment

A manual assessment of students' disengagement risk levels was conducted by school counsellors in two secondary schools in Kubang Pasu, Kedah, Malaysia. A total of 50 students, aged 13–17, from both genders, were evaluated as subjects of this assessment. The risk levels were determined based on the counsellors' expertise, students' historical backgrounds, and professional judgement. The assessment categorised students into three risk levels: low, medium, and high, as depicted in Table 13.1.

13.5.4 Smart Risk Assessment

To calibrate and evaluate the accuracy of the predictive model, a smart risk assessment was conducted using *MyBuddy*, involving the same 50 students previously assessed manually. School counsellors provided data for 14 key predictors, which were then processed through *MyBuddy*'s risk prediction calculator, as illustrated in Figure 13.4.

The predicted risk levels generated by *MyBuddy* will be analysed in the next phase through a comparative study with manual assessments by school counsellors. This evaluation aims to determine the accuracy and reliability of *MyBuddy* in identifying at-risk students. By comparing system predictions with human evaluations, the study will assess the model's effectiveness in supporting early intervention strategies.

13.5.5 Comparison Analysis

The risk levels identified through both manual assessments conducted by school counsellors and the smart predictions generated by *MyBuddy* are systematically compared and analysed using statistical methods. Frequency and percentage are the primary measures employed to evaluate the distribution of risk levels across both approaches. The analysis aims to assess the level of

TABLE 13.1

Risk Assessments Conducted by School Counsellors

Subject	Risk of Disengagement	Subject	Risk of Disengagement	Subject	Risk of Disengagement	Subject	Risk of Disengagement	Subject	Risk of Disengagement
s1	Low	s11	Low	s21	Low	s31	High	s41	Medium
s2	Low	s12	Low	s22	Low	s32	High	s42	Medium
s3	Low	s13	Low	s23	Low	s33	High	s43	Medium
s4	Low	s14	Low	s24	Low	s34	High	s44	High
s5	Low	s15	Low	s25	Low	s35	High	s45	Medium
s6	Low	s16	Low	s26	Low	s36	Medium	s46	Medium
s7	Low	s17	Low	s27	Low	s37	Medium	s47	Medium
s8	Low	s18	Low	s28	Low	s38	Medium	s48	High
s9	Low	s19	Low	s29	Low	s39	Medium	s49	Medium
s10	Low	s20	Low	s30	Low	s40	Medium	s50	Medium

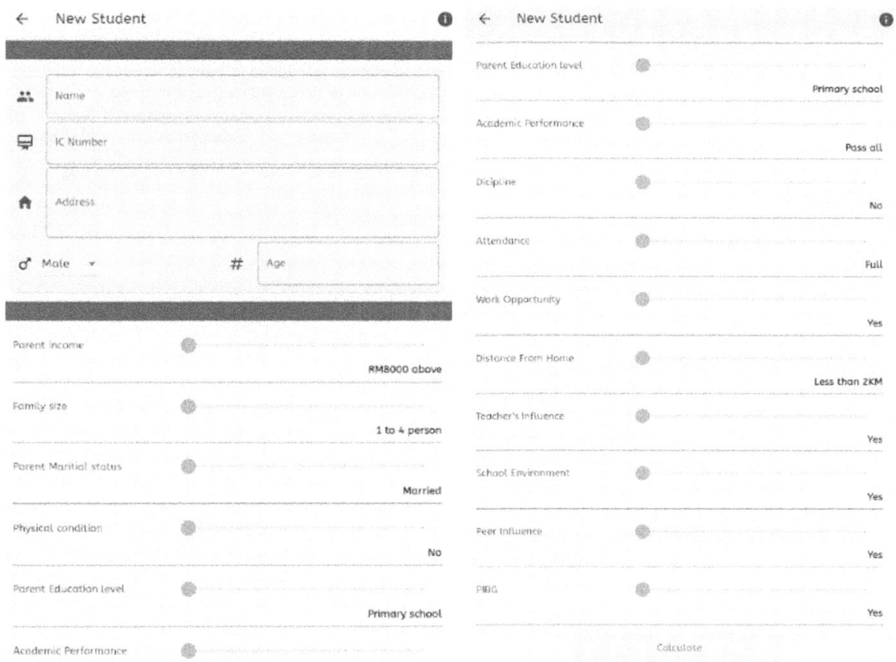

FIGURE 13.4
Risk prediction calculator in *MyBuddy* application.

agreement between human judgement and the predictive model, determining the accuracy and reliability of *MyBuddy* in identifying at-risk students. Additionally, the justification for the findings is derived from a thorough assessment of the raw data provided by school counsellors, ensuring that the analysis is well-supported and grounded in real-world observations. This comparison serves as a critical step in validating the correctness of *MyBuddy* as a predictive tool for early intervention.

13.6 Insights from Human vs AI Prediction of At-Risk Students

A total of 30 students were classified as having a low risk of disengagement based on human judgement conducted by school counsellors, making this the largest group, accounting for 60% of the students. It was followed by the medium-risk category, with 13 students (26%) identified as having a moderate likelihood of disengagement. Meanwhile, only seven students (14%) were classified as high-risk, indicating that, according to counsellors' evaluations, the majority of students were not at immediate risk of dropping out. Detailed distribution of risk levels produced by both methods is presented in Table 13.2.

TABLE 13.2
Distribution of Risk Levels for Human Judgement and Smart Prediction

	Human Judgement			Smart Prediction via *MyBuddy*		
	Low	Medium	High	Low	Medium	High
%	60	26	14	32	34	34
Frequency	30	13	7	16	17	17

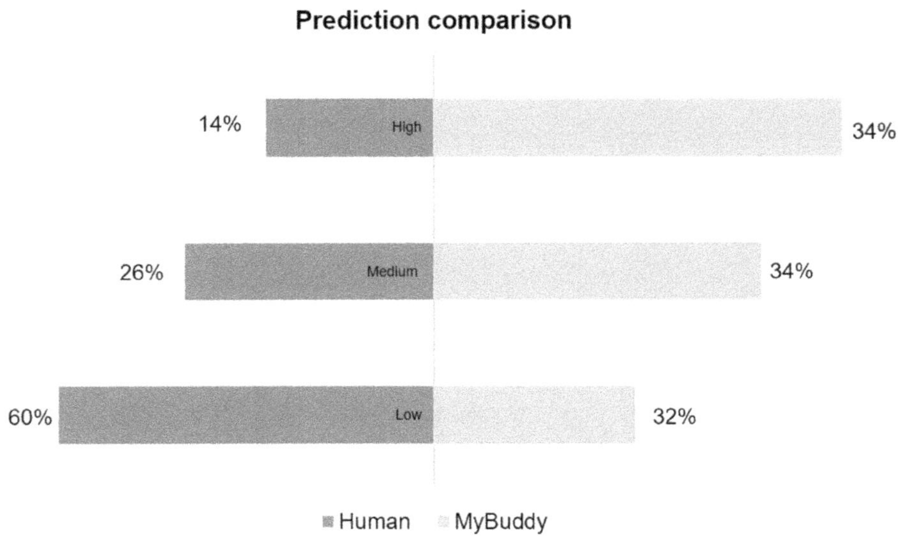

FIGURE 13.5
Prediction comparison between human judgement and smart prediction of *MyBuddy*.

However, the risk levels predicted by *MyBuddy* presented a contrasting trend. *MyBuddy* identified the highest percentage of students as being in the high- and medium-risk categories, with both accounting for 34% of the total students. In contrast, only 32% were categorised as low-risk, suggesting a more evenly distributed assessment of disengagement risk. This disparity between manual assessments and *MyBuddy*'s predictions highlights potential differences in human judgement and data-driven analysis, warranting further investigation into the predictive accuracy of both approaches.

As seen in Figure 13.5, to further analyse the trend, *MyBuddy* identified a significantly higher number of students in the high-risk and medium-risk categories, with increases of 20% and 8%, respectively, compared to manual assessments. It suggests that more students may require intervention than initially determined by human judgement. While school counsellors classified the majority of students (30) as low risk, *MyBuddy*'s prediction reduced this number to 16, indicating that fewer students should be excluded from intervention efforts. These differences highlight the potential of smart prediction in identifying at-risk students more effectively, ensuring that those in need receive timely support and intervention.

13.7 Towards Smarter Education: AI and the Future of Student Support

This study highlights the effectiveness of *MyBuddy* in predicting at-risk students compared to traditional manual assessments conducted by school counsellors. The results demonstrate that while human judgement often categorises the majority of students as low risk, *MyBuddy* identifies a higher number of students in the medium- and high-risk categories, ensuring that more students receive timely intervention. A key weakness of manual assessment is the presence of bias, as counsellors' judgements are influenced by personal perceptions, past experiences, and subjective interpretations of students' behaviour. In contrast, *MyBuddy* applies a standardised, data-driven approach that eliminates bias, offering a more objective and consistent risk classification.

By integrating intelligent prediction models, *MyBuddy* enhances the accuracy of early detection efforts, paving the way for proactive intervention strategies. This study underscores the potential of AI-driven tools in complementing and improving traditional assessment methods in educational settings. Future research could explore refining *MyBuddy*'s predictive capabilities by utilising larger datasets and real-time monitoring to further enhance its impact. Ultimately, leveraging smart prediction systems can significantly improve student support mechanisms, ensuring that no at-risk student is overlooked due to human bias. This study plays an important role in promoting inclusive and equitable quality education by facilitating early intervention strategies that enhance student retention and success, aligning with the United Nations' Sustainable Development Goal 4 (Quality Education).

Acknowledgement

This research is funded by Yayasan Sime Darby (YSD) and Kedah State Government through the Industrial Research Grant Scheme (SO Code 21039 and 14989). The authors fully acknowledge YSD and the Kedah State Government for the approved funds, making this important research viable and effective. We highly appreciate and acknowledge the cooperation and contributions of the Kedah State Education Department, which participated in and assisted with this study.

References

Anderson, R. C., Graham, M., Kennedy, P., Nelson, N., Stoolmiller, M., Baker, S. K., & Fien, H. (2019). Student agency at the crux: Mitigating disengagement in middle and high school. *Contemporary Educational Psychology, 56*, 205–217. https://doi.org/10.1016/j.cedpsych.2018.12.005

Bills, A., & Howard, N. (2021). It's Time to Act: Making the case for a cross sectoral reponse to school disengagement and detachment in South Australia. *Research Report*, Flinders University.

Bjugstad, A., Cardoso, J. B., Chen, T. A., Brabeck, K. M., & Borja, S. (2023). Exploring social and environmental predictors of school engagement among first- and second-generation Latino youth: A multi-dimensional approach. *Psychology in the Schools, 61*(4), 1375–1392. https://doi.org/10.1002/pits.23119

Bóbó, M. L. D. R., Campos, F., Stroele, V., David, J. M. N., Braga, R., & Torrent, T. T. (2022). Using sentiment analysis to identify student emotional state to avoid dropout in e-learning. *International Journal of Distance Education Technologies, 20*(1), 1–24. https://doi.org/10.4018/ijdet.305237

ChePa, N., Ishak, W. H. W., & Shabli, A. H. M. (2023). MyBuddy for Early Detection of School Disengagement: User Assessment of Interaction Elements. *Borneo International Journal, 6*(4), 39–45. ISSN 2636-9826.

Cristea, A. I., Alamri, A., Alshehri, M., Pereira, F. D., Toda, A. M., de Oliveira, E. H. T., & Stewart, C. (2024). The engage taxonomy: SDT-based measurable engagement indicators for MOOCs and their evaluation. *User Modeling and User-Adapted Interaction, 34*(2), 323–374. https://doi.org/10.1007/s11257-023-09374-x

Cui, M., Darling, C. A., Lucier-Greer, M., Fincham, F. D., & May, R. W. (2018). Parental indulgence: Profiles and relations to college students' emotional and behavioral problems. *Journal of Child and Family Studies, 27*(8), 2456–2466. https://doi.org/10.1007/s10826-018-1076-6

Dupéré, V., Dion, E., Cantin, S., Archambault, I., & Lacourse, E. (2021). Social contagion and high school dropout: The role of friends, romantic partners, and siblings. *Journal of Educational Psychology, 113*(3), 572–584. https://doi.org/10.1037/edu0000484

Fredricks, J. A., Ye, F., Wang, M. T., & Brauer, S. (2019). Profiles of school disengagement: Not all disengaged students are alike. In *Handbook of student engagement interventions* (pp. 31–43). Academic Press. https://doi.org/10.1016/B978-0-12-813413-9.00003-6

Garrett-Peters, P. T., Mokrova, I. L., Carr, R. C., Vernon-Feagans, L., Vernon-Feagans, L., Greenberg, M. T., Blair, C. B., Burchinal, M. R., Cox, M., Garrett-Peters, P. T., Frank, J. L., Mills-Koonce, W. R., & Willoughby, M. T. (2019). Early student (dis) engagement: Contributions of household chaos, parenting, and self-regulatory skills. *Developmental Psychology, 55*(7), 1480–1492. https://doi.org/10.1037/dev0000720

González-Rodríguez, D., Vieira, M. J., & Vidal, J. (2019). Factors that influence early school leaving: A comprehensive model. *Educational Research, 61*(2), 214–230. https://doi.org/10.1080/00131881.2019.1596034

Hawkins, R. L., Jaccard, J., & Needle, E. (2013). Nonacademic factors associated with dropping out of high school: Adolescent problem behaviors. *Journal of the Society for Social Work and Research, 4*(2), 58–75. https://doi.org/10.5243/jsswr.2013.5

Helal, S., Li, J., Liu, L., Ebrahimie, E., Dawson, S., Murray, D. J., & Long, Q. (2018). Predicting academic performance by considering student heterogeneity. *Knowledge-Based Systems, 161*, 134–146. https://doi.org/10.1016/j.knosys.2018.07.042

Hoff, N., Olson, A., & Peterson, R. L. (2015). Dropout screening and early warning. Topic brief. University of Nebraska–Lincoln.

Järvinen, T., & Tikkanen, J. (2019). Student disengagement in comprehensive school in Turku, Southwest Finland. In *Resisting education: A cross-national study on systems and school effects* (pp. 81–102). Cham: Springer International Publishing. https://doi.org/10.1007/978-3-030-04227-1_4

Katsantonis, I., Gibbons, R. A., Symonds, J. E., & Costello, N. (2024). To persist or not? Examining the relations between parental education, self-regulation, school engagement and persistence in post-compulsory education. *British Educational Research Journal, 50*(4), 2020–2042. https://doi.org/10.1002/berj.4012

Marlow, S. A., & Rehman, N. (2021). The relationship between family processes and school absenteeism and dropout: A meta-analysis. *Educational and Developmental Psychologist, 38*(1), 3–23. https://doi.org/10.1080/20590776.2020.1834842

Martins, J., Cunha, J., Lopes, S., Moreira, T., & Rosário, P. (2022). School engagement in elementary school: A systematic review of 35 years of research. *Educational Psychology Review, 34*(2), 793–849. https://doi.org/10.1007/s10648-021-09642-5

Mikkay Ei Leen, W., Jalil, N. A., Salleh, N. M., & Idris, I. (2022, July). Dropout early warning system (DEWS) in Malaysia's primary and secondary education: A conceptual paper. In *International Conference on Information Systems and Intelligent Applications* (pp. 427–434). Cham: Springer International Publishing. https://doi.org/10.1007/978-3-031-16865-9_33

Oliva, R. (2003). Model calibration as a testing strategy for system dynamics models. *European Journal of Operational Research, 151*(3), 552–568. https://doi.org/10.1016/S0377-2217(02)00622-7

Peguero, A. A., Merrin, G. J., Hong, J. S., & Johnson, K. R. (2019). School disorder and dropping out: The intersection of gender, race, and ethnicity. *Youth & Society, 51*(2), 193–218. https://doi.org/10.1177/0044118X16668059

Pengpid, S., & Peltzer, K. (2020). High prevalence of school truancy in a national sample of in-school adolescents in Kuwait: Internalizing, externalising and social risk factors. *Journal of Human Behavior in the Social Environment, 30*(6), 687–694. https://doi.org/10.1080/10911359.2020.1736229

Quin, D., Heerde, J. A., & Toumbourou, J. W. (2018). Teacher support within an ecological model of adolescent development: Predictors of school engagement. *Journal of School Psychology, 69*(December 2017), 1–15. https://doi.org/10.1016/j.jsp.2018.04.003

Robison, S., Jaggers, J., Rhodes, J., Blackmon, B. J., & Church, W. (2017). Correlates of educational success: Predictors of school dropout and graduation for urban students in the Deep South. *Children and Youth Services Review, 73*, 37–46. https://doi.org/10.1016/j.childyouth.2016.11.031

Roslan, N., Jamil, J. M., Shaharanee, I., & Alawi, S. J. S. (2025). Prediction of student dropout in Malaysian's private higher education institute using data mining application. *Journal of Advanced Research in Applied Sciences and Engineering Technology, 45*(2), 168–176. https://doi.org/10.37934/araset.45.2.168176

Sagatun, Å., Heyerdahl, S., Wentzel-Larsen, T., & Lien, L. (2014). Mental health problems in the 10th grade and non-completion of upper secondary school: The mediating role of grades in a population-based longitudinal study. *BMC Public Health, 14*(1). https://doi.org/10.1186/1471-2458-14-16

Soland, J., Jensen, N., Keys, T. D., Bi, S. Z., & Wolk, E. (2019). Are test and academic disengagement related? Implications for measurement and practice. *Educational Assessment, 24*(2), 119–134. https://doi.org/10.1080/10627197.2019.1575723

Subramainan, L., Mahmoud, M. A., Ahmad, M. S., & Yusoff, M. Z. M. (2016, August). Evaluating students engagement in classrooms using agent-based social simulation. In *2016 2nd International Symposium on Agent, Multi-Agent Systems and Robotics (ISAMSR)* (pp. 34–39). IEEE. https://doi.org/10.1109/ISAMSR.2016.7809999

Sumardi, N. A., Halif, M. M., Hassan, N., & Dzulkalnine, N. (2023). EDIUSY: The solution of student disengagement. *International Teaching Aid Competition 2023*, 135–141.

Sung, C. L., & Tuo, R. (2024). A review on computer model calibration. *Wiley Interdisciplinary Reviews: Computational Statistics, 16*(1), 1–23. https://doi.org/10.1002/wics.1645

Syaiful, M., Abu, N., Ibrahim, A., Simin, H., & Kamarudin, K. A. (2023). Incidences and causal factors of school dropouts among the indigenous youth in Malaysia. *ISVS E-journal, 10*(9), 343–351. https://isvshome.com/pdf/ISVS_10-9/Old_Files/ISVSej_10.9.24_Ahmed.pdf

Szabó, L., Zsolnai, A., & Fehérvári, A. (2024). The relationship between student engagement and dropout risk in early adolescence. *International Journal of Educational Research Open, 6*(January). https://doi.org/10.1016/j.ijedro.2024.100328

Vázquez-Nava, F., Vázquez-Rodríguez, E. M., Vázquez-Rodríguez, C. F., & Ortega Betancourt, N. V. (2019). High school dropout: Association with family structure, maternal employment, and health-risk habits among female Mexican adolescents. *Journal of Child and Family Studies, 28*(12), 3307–3314. https://doi.org/10.1007/s10826-019-01505-6

Washor, E., & Mojkowski, C. (2014). Student disengagement: It's deeper than you think. *Phi Delta Kappan, 95*(8), 8–10. https://doi.org/10.1177/003172171409500803

14

AI for Inclusion: Sign Language Recognition to Support Hajj Pilgrims

Muhammad Siddik Hasibuan, Yusuf Ramadhan Nasution, Armansyah, Muhammad Ikhsan, Aidil Halim Lubis, and Sriani

14.1 Introduction

Implementing the Hajj pilgrimage is one of the obligations for physically, financially, and mentally capable Muslims. However, the process of carrying out this pilgrimage often presents challenges, especially for pilgrims who have special needs, including those with disabilities. Pilgrims with disabilities, such as those with hearing and speech limitations, often have difficulty communicating, especially when they have to understand complex worship procedures or interact with officers and fellow pilgrims. In line with this, the Ministry of Religion in Indonesia is implementing the theme of 'Elderly and Disability Friendly for the 2025 Hajj pilgrimage; therefore, Hajj officers must possess sign language skills. Arsyad explained that the Ministry of Religion initiated the theme in response to public complaints regarding the lack of attention to elderly and disabled groups.

The ministry received complaints that people with disabilities seemed to be ignored. Therefore, in 2025, this theme will be the primary focus of Hajj services. Sign language is one of the primary means of communication for individuals with hearing impairments (Syamsuddin et al., 2023). However, not all officers or other pilgrims can understand sign language which can cause gaps in information delivery due to this communication limitation. In the context of the Hajj, this can have serious consequences, given the limited time and space of implementation, as well as the need to understand and properly carry out the pillars of worship. In Saudi Arabia itself, the use of sign language in departments related to serving Umrah and Hajj pilgrims requires proficiency in sign language.

The development of artificial intelligence and image processing technology has created opportunities to devise innovative solutions to this problem.

DOI: 10.1201/9781003662433-18

One approach that can be applied is a sign language detection model using machine learning and deep learning (DL)-based algorithms (Caraka et al., 2025). This model can process real-time hand movements and facial expressions, translating them into text or voice to bridge communication between disabled pilgrims and other parties. People with hearing disabilities often need sign language as a means of communication, used in learning and everyday life. This study utilised sign language, specifically BISINDO (Andreas et al., 2024; Sutjiadi, 2023). Several studies on using sign language to assist with daily activities that incorporate information technology continue to grow, such as in India, where there are seven million deaf people and only 250 licensed translators (Fathima et al., 2024). The sign language development system was created to facilitate communication with people with disabilities, recognising the importance of communication accessibility for individuals with hearing or language impairments; many people suffer from hearing impairments, speech disorders, or both. A partial or complete inability to hear in one or both ears is known as hearing loss.

On the other hand, mutism is a disability that interferes with the ability to speak and makes the affected person unable to talk (Adeyanju et al., 2021; Sari, 2023). Mute people can communicate with each other, but generally, normal people need an interpreter to understand the meaning of the mute person's hand gestures. Information technology can help automatically translate hand shapes into alphabet characters A through Z (Indra et al., 2019; Irvanizam et al., 2023). Sign language involves using upper body parts, such as hand gestures, facial expressions, lip reading, head nods, and body postures to convey information. Sign language is a comprehensive means of communication for deaf and mute individuals. Since they cannot speak or hear, they cannot use sound or vocal signals as a means of communication. Instead, they must exchange visual signals to convey their feelings on a daily basis. They use various body language, especially hand gestures, as a form of sign language. The basics of sign language can be broadly divided into two parts, namely digits (numbers) and characters (alphabet) (Das et al., 2023). Arabic Sign Language Recognition (ArSLR) is developed to recognise Arabic letters in the ArSLR System, utilising our image pre-processing method to extract the proper hand position. We propose a Deep Convolutional Neural Network (CNN) architecture that incorporates depth data. The aim is to facilitate easier interaction between deaf people and those who are not deaf (Temel & Vural, 2023). This method will automatically detect and recognise hand gesture letters of the Arabic alphabet based on user input. The proposed model is expected to yield encouraging results in ArSLR, with an accuracy score of 97.07% (Hdioud & Tirari, 2023). DL has significantly helped in recent advancements in artificial intelligence (Chu et al., 2023). DL techniques have outperformed common machine learning approaches in various fields, including computer vision, natural language processing (Lin et al., 2024), robotics science, and human-computer interaction. DL models are ineffective in deciphering their fundamental mechanisms. That is why deep learning models are mainly considered Black-Box (Kothadiya et al., 2023). This process converts sign language into speech to help people who are deaf or hard of hearing understand sign language. The input is obtained from the ROBITA Indian Sign Language Database, and several essential pre-processing steps are performed to eliminate unnecessary artefacts. The proposed model is combined with a multi-layer (ML)-CNN encoder to evaluate the scalability and end-to-end SLR accuracy (Arun Prasath & Annapurani, 2023).

Each language has its signs, and covering them may be very difficult. The objectives of the current study are (i) to present a dataset of 20 Arabic words and (ii) to propose a DL architecture by combining CNN and recurrent neural networks. The proposed architecture reports 98% accuracy on the presented dataset. It also reports 93.4% and 98.8% accuracy for top-1 and top-5 accuracy on the UCF-101 dataset (Balaha et al., 2023). SLR represents a revolutionary technology that aims to establish communication between hearing-impaired and non-hearing-impaired communities, surpassing traditional interpreter-based approaches (Balaha et al., 2023; Miah et al., 2024). As a means of communication, sign language allows individuals to convey messages through hand gestures, body movements, and facial expressions. Those with hearing impairments mainly use sign language to communicate with others. Static SLR primarily relies on CNN and transfer learning approaches to classify hand gesture images. While researchers have been actively working on this problem, few have explored the potential of Vision Transformers (ViT) in addressing the issue of SLR, particularly Arabic signs (Alnabih & Maghari, 2024). This study aims to develop a sign language detection model specifically designed to support the needs of disabled pilgrims. This model is expected to increase inclusivity and comfort in carrying out worship and be one of the strategic steps in realising friendly hajj services for all groups. The following are related studies in Table 14.1.

From the table presented, it can be concluded that various DL approaches, such as machine learning, CNN, ViT, Graph Convolutional Networks (GCNs), and Deep Long Short-Term Memory (DLSTM), have been used effectively in SLR from various types of sign languages (such as BISINDO, Arabic Sign Language, Korean Sign Language (KSL), and baby sign language). Each study shows significant progress in the accuracy of sign language gesture recognition, with some models achieving high accuracy of up to 99.3%. CNN and ViT-based models have proven very effective for sign language character recognition. At the same time, approaches such as GCN and LSTM lead to dynamic and more complex sign recognition, offering solutions to improve communication accessibility for people with disabilities.

Although the approaches used vary, the primary goal of all these studies is to enhance inclusive communication and accessibility for individuals with disabilities, particularly those with hearing impairments. The application of SLR using gesture recognition technology and DL models shows great potential in facilitating more effective nonverbal communication.

TABLE 14.1

Related Research

Title, Researcher, Year	Method/ Algorithm	Result
SLR Using CNN (Gayathri et al., 2024)	CNN	Through webcam input, various sign language movements are captured in real-time and saved as digital images.
Arabic sign language letters recognition using ViT (Alnabih & Maghari, 2024)	CNN approaches	To fine-tune and evaluate our ViT-based model, we utilise the ArSL2018 dataset, which consists of 54,049 images of Arabic sign language letters with 32 classes. Accuracy, F1 score, recall and precision are used for evaluation. The proposed model achieved an accuracy of 99.3% on the ArSL2018 dataset, which outperforms some recent CNN based models. Additionally, we conducted evaluations on real case images to assess the practicality and real-world applicability of our model.
Dynamic Korean SLR Using Pose Estimation-Based and Attention-Based Neural Network (Shin et al., 2023)	GCN to extract graph-based features. These features are meticulously refined through a channel attention module and a general CNN	SLR is crucial for enhancing communication accessibility for the hearing-impaired community and reducing dependence on human interpreters. Notably, while significant research efforts have been devoted to many prevalent languages, KSL remains relatively underexplored, particularly concerning dynamic signs and generalisability.
An optimised automated recognition of infant sign language using an enhanced convolution neural network and deep LSTM (Enireddy et al., 2023)	DLSTM scheme	The optimal characteristics are then selected by a new Life Choice Based Optimiser. Finally, the classification is performed using the DLSTM scheme. The performance of the proposed approach (ECNN-DLSTM) is compared with several deep and machine learning approaches, and it obtains an accuracy of 99% and a kappa of 96%.

Future research can build upon these findings by focusing more on the application of YOLOv8 and YOLOv11 models for Indonesian Sign Language (BISINDO) recognition, utilising larger and more diverse datasets to expand the scope of sign languages that can be automatically recognised. In addition, the development of models for dynamic sign detection in sign languages, such as those used in KSL, can be adopted to improve the accuracy and efficiency of SLR in broader contexts, including Hajj pilgrimage activities for disabled pilgrims. In addition, future research can also explore the application of transformer-based models or a combination of CNN models with attention mechanisms to handle the complexity of more varied sign movements, as has been done in the recognition of Arabic sign language letters. Applying this system will not only enhance the communication experience for people with disabilities but also create opportunities to develop more inclusive technology-based solutions in various sectors, such as education and public services.

14.2 Designing YOLO-Based DL for Inclusive SLR

This type of work is applied research with a DL-based software engineering approach, particularly in object detection using the You Only Look Once (YOLO) algorithm. The goal is to develop a real-time hand sign language detection system to support the inclusion of Hajj pilgrims with communication barriers. Figure 14.1 shows the workflow diagram for the work.

To address the research objectives, this study will use a mixed-methods approach, combining quantitative performance metrics with qualitative feedback from participants to provide a holistic evaluation of the proposed DL-based SLR system. Participants will prioritise individuals with varying levels of sign language proficiency, including native speakers and those learning sign language as a second language, to ensure a comprehensive assessment of the system's usability and effectiveness across skill levels. Qualitative

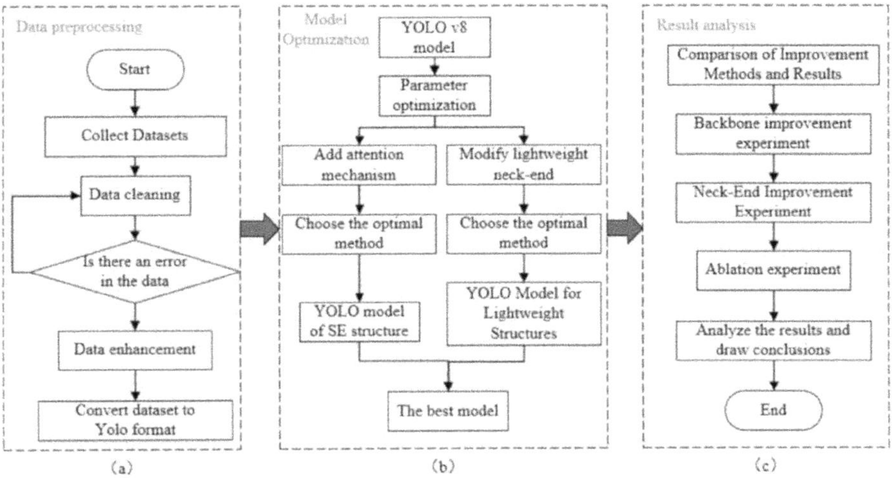

FIGURE 14.1
Workflow diagram. (a) The data processing stage. (b) The model optimisation stage. (c) The result analysis stage (Huangfu & Li, 2023).

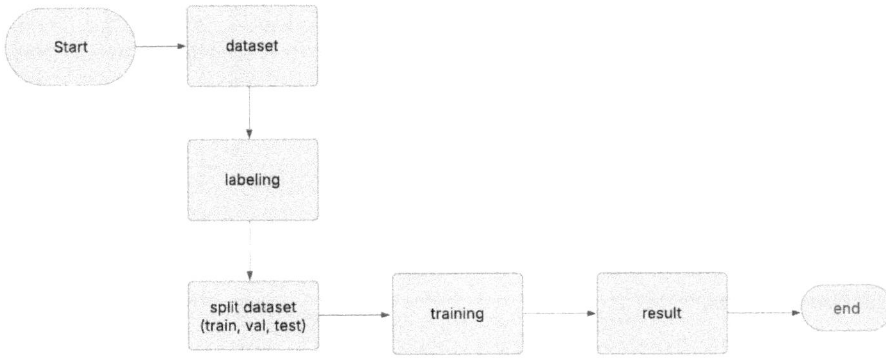

FIGURE 14.2
Research framework.

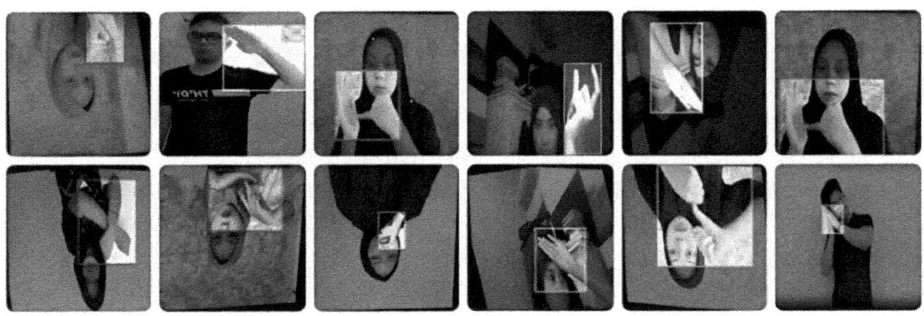

FIGURE 14.3
Images dataset.

data will be collected through structured interviews and focus groups with participants, designed to obtain detailed feedback on their experiences with the system, including its ease of use, perceived accuracy, and overall satisfaction. The quantitative component of the methodology involves rigorous testing of the DL model's accuracy and efficiency in recognising a pre-defined set of sign language signs relevant to the Hajj context. It will entail creating a comprehensive conceptual language video dataset captured in varying lighting conditions and from multiple angles to replicate the real-world challenges of the Hajj environment. To assess the system's performance in realistic situations, the study will incorporate a field testing component, where participants will use the system to navigate a simulated Hajj scenario and complete specific tasks, such as requesting directions or assistance. Next, the data is presented in the form of image data of the Indonesian alphabet and commonly used words in communication. The data is pre-processed in Roboflow, augmented, and resized to a 540 × 540 pixel size. The work framework can be seen in Figure 14.2. On the other hand, Figure 14.3 shows a sample of the dataset used in this work.

14.3 Evaluating YOLO Models for Real-Time SLR

This work aims to develop a BISINDO SLR system using the YOLOv8 method, with a focus on identifying alphabetic symbols and words commonly used in worship services. The dataset used consists of 5983 data points, as shown in Table 14.2. Variations in the dataset include differences in gestures, viewing angles, lighting, backgrounds, and individual variations (Khartheesvar et al., 2024). The YOLOv8 model is trained with a specific configuration, which includes selecting the YOLOv8 version, setting training parameters (learning rate, batch size, and number of epochs), and utilising data augmentation techniques to enhance the model's robustness. The model evaluation uses precision, recall, F1-score, and mAP metrics. An in-depth analysis is conducted to identify classes with the highest and lowest accuracy, as well as potential causes of misclassification, using a confusion matrix. The detection results are visualised by displaying sample images and bounding boxes from YOLOv8 detection results. The discussion focuses on interpreting the research results, identifying factors that affect model performance, comparing the findings with those of other studies, discussing research limitations, and providing suggestions for future research. This research is expected to contribute to the creation of inclusive solutions for pilgrims with disabilities.

Figure 14.4 illustrates a graph displaying the model's performance in the object detection task during training, highlighting key metrics such as mAP (mean Average Precision), box loss, class loss, and object loss across epochs. Explanation of Each Section:

a. Model Performance (Top Section) – This graph shows two key metrics of model performance: mAP and mAP@50–95 (mAP with varying Intersection over Union [IoU] thresholds between 0.5 and 0.95). mAP shows the model's average precision across different categories of detected objects, while mAP@50–95 gives a more detailed picture of the model's performance in detecting objects at different difficulty levels. This graph shows a very rapid increase in performance at the beginning of training (epochs 0–10). Then, the model shows a high level of stability, with mAP approaching 1.0 (the ideal value).

TABLE 14.2

The Category of Dataset

Class	Count
Train	4,986
Val	664
Test	333
Σ	5,983

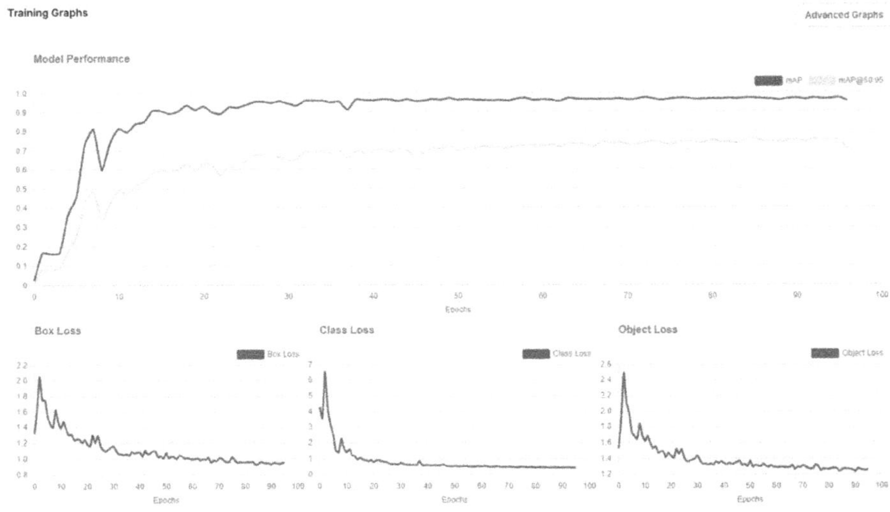

FIGURE 14.4
Training graphs.

b. Box Loss (Bottom Left Section) – Box loss measures the model's ability to predict the bounding box coordinates of detected objects accurately. A lower loss value means the model is more accurate in determining the object's location. This graph shows a sharp decrease in box loss during training, especially at the beginning of training (epochs 0–30). After that, the box loss value decreases gradually, indicating that the model is improving at predicting the bounding boxes of objects.
c. Class Loss (Bottom Middle) – Class loss measures how well the model classifies objects into the correct class. A lower loss value indicates that the model is better at classifying objects. This graph shows that class loss drops sharply at the beginning of training (epochs 0–20) and stabilises at a low value, indicating that the model has learned to recognise object classes well after sufficient training.
d. Object Loss (Bottom Right) – Object loss is a metric that measures the overall error in detecting an object (including its proximity to the correct object and the prediction of whether the object is present). This graph illustrates a steady decline in object loss during training, with the loss decreasing significantly in the early epochs and continuing to decrease gradually thereafter.

Overall, this graph indicates that the model is performing well during training. At the beginning of training, the model quickly decreases the loss (box, class, and object), indicating that the model is starting to learn soon. After a few epochs, the model achieves high stability in object detection, resulting in a significant increase in the mAP metric. This trend indicates that the model has learned to perform object detection accurately on the training data.

These graphs present essential metrics used to monitor the progress and evaluation of a model in tasks such as object detection or classification. In detail, Figure 14.5 consists of several sub-graphs divided into two rows:

a. First Row (Training Metrics)
   i. Train/Box Loss – This graph displays the loss of the bounding box component during training. In general, the loss value decreases with increasing epochs, indicating that the model is getting better at predicting the location of objects.
   ii. Train/cls_loss – This is the graph for the loss of the classification component. Classification indicates the model's ability to recognise object categories. The loss value decreases with training, indicating an improvement in class prediction.
   iii. Train/dfl_loss – This represents the loss for the component in object detection, utilising detection features such as "detection feature loss." Although there are fluctuations, the loss value tends to decrease with higher epochs.
   iv. Metrics/Precision (B) – This graph displays the model's precision value for class B. Precision measures the percentage of optimistic predictions that are correct out of the total positive predictions. Low fluctuation and an increasing trend indicate that the model is more accurate in correctly detecting objects.

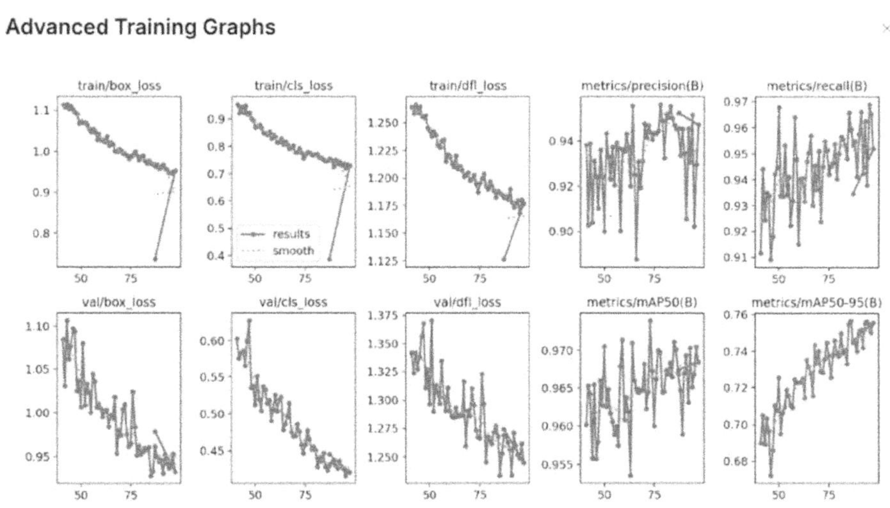

FIGURE 14.5
Training metrics loss.

v. Metrics/Recall(B) – Recall measures how many objects are detected out of the total objects that should have been detected. This graph shows the recall performance for class B, and its fluctuation tends to be more stable.

vi. Metrics/mAP50 – mAP at a threshold of 0.50. This indicates how well the model detects objects across classes, with higher values indicating better detection.

vii. Metrics/mAP50-95(B) – This is the mAP calculated at various IoU thresholds between 0.5 and 0.95. Higher values indicate better model performance at detecting objects at different difficulty levels.

b. Second Row (Validation Metrics)

i. Val/box_loss – This is the validation dataset's bounding box loss. A decreasing value indicates the model can produce more accurate bounding box predictions on previously unseen data.

ii. Val/cls_loss – Classification loss on the validation dataset. Similar to training, a decrease in this loss value indicates that the model is better at classifying objects on validation data.

iii. Val/dfl_loss – Detection loss on validation data. This graph shows the model's performance in minimising false detections on previously unseen data.

iv. Metrics/mAP50 and metrics/mAP50-95(B) – These graphs also display mAP on validation data, which is essential for assessing the model's ability to detect objects with more stable quality on previously unseen data.

Each graph has a dotted line showing a "smoothed" version of the results. It is used to minimise fluctuations and provide a clearer picture of the overall trend during training or evaluation. Overall, this graph provides a comprehensive picture of how the model learned the task and how well it generalised to previously unseen data, as well as showing trends in metrics such as precision, recall, and mAP during training and validation.

A crucial step in the testing phase is to feed the previously trained model into the real-time object detection test. The best pt model, which showed the best results during training, will be loaded into a Python script using YOLOv8. This script will take live video from the camera, process each frame, and infer using this model. The detection results will be displayed by drawing bounding boxes around the detected objects and labelling them. It ensures that the real-time object detection system uses the most optimal model to provide accurate and reliable results when tested with live data. The YOLO model has been trained to perform real-time object detection via webcam. After opening the webcam and loading the model, the programme enters the main loop, where each frame is captured from the webcam. Every

TABLE 14.3
Validation Result

Model	Epoch	mAP
YOLOv8	10	0.814
YOLOv11	10	0.407
YOLOv8	20	0.932
YOLOv11	20	0.905
YOLOv8	30	0.944
YOLOv11	30	0.884
YOLOv8	40	0.960
YOLOv11	40	0.946
YOLOv8	50	0.962
YOLOv11	50	0.954
YOLOv8	60	0.963
YOLOv11	60	0.960

second, the model checks the frame for object detection, generating a bounding box and a corresponding certainty level. If the certainty level exceeds 50%, the programme draws a box around the object and adds a class label and certainty level to the detected object in Table 14.3.

At each epoch, higher mAP values indicate that the model can increasingly accurately detect objects during training. YOLOv8 performs better than YOLOv11 at each epoch listed. The mAP values for YOLOv8 increase consistently, from 0.814 at epoch 10 to 0.963 at epoch 60. On the other hand, YOLOv11 initially performs lower at each epoch. Its map starts at 0.407 at epoch 10 and increases more slowly, reaching a peak of 0.960 at epoch 60. As a notable trend, YOLOv8 exhibits a steady and significant increase in mAP, indicating that the model improves over time and detects objects more accurately. YOLOv11, although also showing improvement in mAP, consistently performs lower than YOLOv8 in each epoch. YOLOv8 outperforms YOLOv11 in mAP across training cycles, indicating that YOLOv8 is more effective in object detection over time. According to the test results, if the goal is to select the best-performing model based on the mAP metric, YOLOv8 is a better choice than YOLOv11.

14.4 Towards Inclusive Digital Pilgrimage: DL for Accessible Communication

Based on the test results and performance analysis of the two models, YOLOv8 and YOLOv11, the following is a comprehensive conclusion regarding the comparison. YOLOv8 shows better performance in terms of mAP in every epoch tested. This model consistently improves, with mAP starting at 0.814 in epoch 10 and continuing to grow to 0.963 in epoch 60. The stable and significant increase in mAP indicates that YOLOv8 can learn better over time, detect objects more accurately, and provide optimal results throughout the training cycle. YOLOv11, although also showing an increase in mAP, starts training with a lower mAP (0.407 in epoch 10).

Despite experiencing slow growth, its peak performance remains below YOLOv8, with a maximum mAP value of 0.960 reached in epoch 60. Despite showing progress, YOLOv11 cannot match the performance of YOLOv8 in terms of speed of improvement and object detection accuracy. YOLOv8 is more effective and efficient in detecting objects throughout training, indicating that the model is superior in accuracy and can handle object detection complexity better compared to YOLOv11. YOLOv11 has progressed, but its performance is slower and more limited than that of YOLOv8.

If the main goal is to get the best performance in object detection accuracy with stable improvement over time, then YOLOv8 is a better choice than YOLOv11. YOLOv8 is more suitable for applications that require faster and more accurate object detection, whereas YOLOv11, although usable, exhibits slower and lower overall performance. Based on the tests conducted, YOLOv8 shows a more significant performance advantage than YOLOv11, both in terms of accuracy (mAP) and the stability of its improvement during training. Therefore, if the model selection is based on mAP metrics and better object detection ability, YOLOv8 is the most recommended choice.

References

Adeyanju, I. A., Bello, O. O., & Adegboye, M. A. (2021). Machine learning methods for sign language recognition: A critical review and analysis. *Intelligent Systems with Applications, 12*, 200056. https://doi.org/10.1016/j.iswa.2021.200056

Alnabih, A. F., & Maghari, A. Y. (2024). Arabic sign language letters recognition using Vision Transformer. *Multimedia Tools and Applications, 83*(34), 81725–81739. https://doi.org/10.1007/s11042-024-18681-3

Andreas, Y., Dwijayanti, S., Hikmarika, H., & Suprapto, B. Y. (2024). Real-time recognition of Indonesian sign language using recurrent neural network. *Sriwijaya Electrical and Computer Engineering Journal, 1*(1), 1–8. https://doi.org/10.62420/selco.v1i1.1

Arun Prasath, G., & Annapurani, K. (2023). Prediction of sign language recognition based on multi layered CNN. *Multimedia Tools and Applications, 82*(19), 29649–29669. https://doi.org/10.1007/s11042-023-14548-1

Balaha, M. M., El-Kady, S., Balaha, H. M., Salama, M., Emad, E., Hassan, M., & Saafan, M. M. (2023). A vision-based deep learning approach for independent-users Arabic sign language interpretation. *Multimedia Tools and Applications, 82*(5), 6807–6826. https://doi.org/10.1007/s11042-022-13423-9

Caraka, R. E., Supardi, K., Kurniawan, R., Kim, Y., Gio, P. U., Yuniarto, B., Mubarok, F. Z., & Pardamean, B. (2025). Empowering deaf communication: A novel LSTM model for recognising Indonesian sign language. *Universal Access in the Information Society, 24*(1), 771–783. https://doi.org/10.1007/s10209-024-01095-1

Chu, H., Jiang, C., Xu, J., Ye, Q., & Jiang, X. (2023). An optimised eight-layer convolutional neural network based on blocks for Chinese fingerspelling sign language recognition. *International Conference on Multimedia Technology and Enhanced Learning,* 11–31. https://doi.org/10.1007/978-3-031-50580-5_2

Das, S., Imtiaz, M. S., Neom, N. H., Siddique, N., & Wang, H. (2023). A hybrid approach for Bangla sign language recognition using deep transfer learning model with random forest classifier. *Expert Systems with Applications, 213,* 118914. https://doi.org/10.1016/j.eswa.2022.118914

Enireddy, V., Anitha, J., Mahendra, N., & Kishore, G. (2023). An optimised automated recognition of infant sign language using enhanced convolution neural network and deep LSTM. *Multimedia Tools and Applications, 82*(18), 28043–28065. https://doi.org/10.1007/s11042-023-14428-8

Fathima, T., Alam, A., Gangwar, A., Khetan, D., & Ramya, K. (2024). Real-time sign language recognition and translation using deep learning techniques. *International Research Journal on Advanced Engineering Hub* (IRJAEH*)*, 2(02), 93–97. https://doi.org/10.47392/irjaeh.2024.0018

Gayathri, D., Ramar, A., Karpagam, S., Sudharsanan, J., Rishwan, S., & Sudalaimani, P. (2024). Sign language recognition using convolutional neural network. *International Journal of Intelligent Systems and Applications in Engineering, 12*(17s), 329–337. https://www.ijisae.org/index.php/IJISAE/article/view/4878

Hdioud, B., & Tirari, M. E. H. (2023). A deep learning based approach for recognition of Arabic sign language letters. *International Journal of Advanced Computer Science and Applications, 14*(4). https://doi.org/10.14569/IJACSA.2023.0140447

Huangfu, Z., & Li, S. (2023). Lightweight You Only Look Once v8: An upgraded You Only Look Once v8 algorithm for small object identification in unmanned aerial vehicle images. *Applied Sciences, 13*(22), 12369. https://doi.org/10.3390/app132212369

Indra, D., Madenda, S., & Wibowo, E. P. (2019). Indonesian sign language recognition based on shape of hand gesture. *Procedia Computer Science, 161,* 74–81. https://doi.org/10.1016/j.procs.2019.11.101

Irvanizam, I., Horatius, I., & Sofyan, H. (2023). Applying artificial neural network based on backpropagation method for Indonesian sign language recognition. *International Journal of Computing and Digital Systems,* 14(1), 975–985. https://hdl.handle.net/20.500.14536/5184

Khartheesvar, G., Kumar, M., Yadav, A. K., & Yadav, D. (2024). Automatic Indian sign language recognition using MediaPipe holistic and LSTM network. *Multimedia Tools and Applications, 83*(20), 58329–58348. https://doi.org/10.1007/s11042-023-17361-y

Kothadiya, D. R., Bhatt, C. M., Rehman, A., Alamri, F. S., & Saba, T. (2023). SignExplainer: An explainable AI-enabled framework for sign language recognition with ensemble learning. *IEEE Access, 11,* 47410–47419. https://doi.org/10.1109/ACCESS.2023.3274851

Lin, C.-S., Tsai, C.-N., Jwo, J.-S., Lee, C.-H., & Wang, X. (2024). Heterogeneous student knowledge distillation from bert using a lightweight ensemble framework. *IEEE Access, 12,* 33079–33088. https://doi.org/10.1109/ACCESS.2024.3372568

Miah, A. S. M., Hasan, M. A. M., Nishimura, S., & Shin, J. (2024). Sign language recognition using graph and general deep neural network based on large scale dataset. *IEEE Access, 12*, 34553–34569. https://doi.org/10.1109/ACCESS.2024.3372425

Sari, I. P. (2023). Closer look at image classification for indonesian sign language with few-shot learning using matching network approach. *International Journal on Informatics Visualization, 7*(3), 638–643. https://doi.org/10.30630/joiv.7.3.1320

Shin, J., Miah, A. S. M., Suzuki, K., Hirooka, K., & Hasan, M. A. M. (2023). Dynamic Korean sign language recognition using pose estimation based and attention-based neural network. *IEEE Access, 11*, 143501–143513. https://doi.org/10.1109/ACCESS.2023.3343404

Sutjiadi, R. (2023). Android-based application for real-time Indonesian sign language recognition using convolutional neural network. *TEM Journal, 12*(3), 1541–1549. https://doi.org/10.18421/TEM123-35

Syamsuddin, S., Pristiwaluyo, T., Saleh, W. A., & Zulfitrah, Z. (2023). Development of Indonesian sign language system (SIBI) dictionary application for students with special needs. *AL-ISHLAH: Jurnal Pendidikan, 15*(3), 3132–3143. https://doi.org/10.35445/alishlah.v15i3.3529

Temel, T., & Vural, R. A. (2023). Turkish sign language recognition using CNN with new alphabet dataset. *Proceedings of the International Joint Conference on Computer Vision, Imaging and Computer Graphics Theory and Applications*, 179–186. https://doi.org/10.5220/0011628700003417

Index

Note: **Bold** page numbers refer to tables and *italic* page numbers refer to figures.

For Product Safety Concerns and Information please contact our EU
representative GPSR@taylorandfrancis.com
Taylor & Francis Verlag GmbH, Kaufingerstraße 24, 80331 München, Germany

www.ingramcontent.com/pod-product-compliance
Ingram Content Group UK Ltd.
Pitfield, Milton Keynes, MK11 3LW, UK
UKHW022130190926
475702UK00013B/1723
* 9 7 8 1 0 4 1 1 1 9 6 5 4 *